J.K. LASSER'S™

REAL ESTATE
INVESTOR'S
TAX EDGE

D0901064

J.K. LASSER'S™

REAL ESTATE INVESTOR'S TAX EDGE

Top Secret Strategies of Millionaires Exposed

Scott M. Estill, Esq.

Stephanie F. Long, Esq.

WILEY

John Wiley & Sons, Inc.

Published by John Wiley & Sons, Inc., Hoboken, New Jersey.
Published simultaneously in Canada.

For general information on our other products and services or for technical support, please contact our Customer Care Department within the United States at (800) 762-2974, outside the United States at (317) 572-3993 or fax (317) 572-4002.

Wiley also publishes its books in a variety of electronic formats. Some content that appears in print may not be available in electronic books. For more information about Wiley products, visit our web site at www.wiley.com.

ISBN 978-0-470-44347-7

Printed in the United States of America.

10 9 8 7 6 5 4 3 2 1

Contents

Warning

This publication is intended to provide accurate and authoritative information in regard to the subject matter covered. However, tax and legal information is constantly changing. Therefore, this book is sold with the understanding that neither the author nor the publisher is engaged in rendering legal, accounting, or other professional services to the reader. Your tax situation is unique, and if specific legal or other professional advice is needed, the services of a competent professional should be sought to assist you.

Introduction

Welcome and thank you for your interest in our real estate investor tax strategy guide. It is our sincere hope that you will find the information contained herein useful and applicable to your specific real estate ventures. We hope that by applying many of the strategies we outline in this book, you will be able to lower your overall tax bill to the legal minimum so that you pay only the correct amount of tax due—no more and no less.

This book is not intended to replace your accountant or other tax professional, since all taxpayers potentially have unique tax situations. Instead, this book is intended to supplement your knowledge of taxes and assist you and your tax professional in formulating appropriate tax strategies to reduce your overall tax bill. In addition, you should be aware that tax laws are constantly changing. This is especially the case today with our many challenges in declining real estate markets and the overall difficult financial environment. We expect President Obama and the Democratic Congress to make many changes to our current tax laws. We have already seen the beginning of these changes with the passage of the American Recovery and Reinvestment Act of 2009 (signed into law on February 17, 2009). Thus it is imperative that you work closely with your tax professional to make sure you are taking advantage of any new tax laws that may affect you and/or your real estate investments.

In each chapter of this book, you will find several examples that use everyday situations to help explain the complex tax rules. In Appendix A we also provide copies of many of the tax forms we discuss in the book. Finally, we strongly recommend that you obtain the IRS publications mentioned in this text. They are available on the Internet at www.irs.gov or in print. You can also contact the

IRS at 1-800-829-3676 to obtain copies. Either way, these publications provide much valuable information and they are free of cost.

Where applicable, we have included references to sections of the Internal Revenue Code, court cases, IRS publications, IRS guidance via rulings, procedures, and letters, and other materials for you to review should you or your current tax professional need any additional information concerning the contents of our materials. We have also included some of our personal forms and checklists in Appendix B for your use.

Best of luck with your real estate ventures!

CHAPTER 1

Understanding Capital Gains

For many real estate investors, the capital gains tax is the single greatest tax obligation on their personal tax returns. Individuals invest in real estate to make money, and many rely on the historical capital appreciation as the sole reason they invested in real estate to begin with. Therefore, limiting capital gains is a major priority when it comes to tax planning for real estate investors. This chapter discusses the major issues concerning capital assets and the tax treatment of any sales.

What Is a Capital Asset?

Gains and losses on the sale of assets must be categorized as either capital or ordinary gain or loss. The gain (or loss) on the sale of a capital asset results in special and sometimes favorable tax treatment. *Capital assets* are generally assets or property used for investment purposes or other property not specifically excepted from capital asset treatment. *Investment property* is property held for the production of income or anticipated appreciation in value, other than property used in your trade or business. Thus, rental property and any type of real estate that is held for investment purposes will be subject to capital treatment upon its sale or disposition. Dealer property, discussed in Chapter 5, is not investment property and does not receive capital treatment upon its sale or disposition.

For purposes of our discussion, a capital asset is *not:*

- Inventory or stock in trade.
- Property held by the taxpayer for sale to customers in the ordinary course of the taxpayer's business (i.e., "dealer property").
- Depreciable property used in a trade or business.
- Real property used in a trade or business.
- Copyrights and certain property created by the taxpayer's own efforts.
- Accounts receivable or notes receivable.[1]

Instead, a capital asset *is:*

- Property held for personal use, such as your home, auto, or furniture.
- Property held for investment or production of income, such as a rental property, a piece of raw land, or general real estate not held in the ordinary course of your trade or business.[2]

The tax rates are much more favorable on the sale of profitable capital assets as opposed to other types of assets. On the other hand, losses on the sale of capital assets receive unfavorable tax treatment because the deduction on these capital losses is limited per year. At the current time, capital losses can only be deducted up to the total capital gains reported for any particular tax year, and any excess losses are limited to $3,000 per year or the actual capital loss, whichever is less. Married taxpayers filing separate income tax returns are limited to a maximum capital loss deduction of $1,500 per year on each separate tax return. Any excess capital loss not fully utilized in the year of sale can be carried forward indefinitely and can be used in the future to offset other capital gains or to utilize the $3,000 capital loss deduction per year.[3]

Example

Sara sells real estate and stocks during 2009. She has long-term capital gains and losses for the year. After she adds up her basis in each, she realizes that she made $50,000 in profit from her real estate ventures, whereas her stock sales lost $75,000. Here is what her Schedule D (tax form to report gain or loss on sale of capital assets) looks like in numerical terms:

Stock losses:	$75,000
Real estate gains:	$50,000
Total net losses:	$25,000
Loss to deduct in 2009:	$ 3,000
Amount carried over to 2010:	$22,000

In 2010, Sara sold real estate again for a $50,000 net profit and had no stock sales. Here is what her 2010 Schedule D looks like in numerical terms:

Real estate gains:	$50,000
Loss carried forward from 2009:	$22,000
Taxable gains in 2010:	$28,000

Tax Tip

If you are carrying forward large capital losses that will take you several years to recover due to the $3,000 capital loss limitation per year, you might want to consider selling your investment property (or invest in an investment property) to utilize these losses. For example, you can sell a piece of rental property you own or purchase a piece of real estate for resale. Any capital gains you earn on the sale will be tax free up to the amount of the capital losses you are carrying forward. Also, you might want to consider selling your highly appreciated personal residence or vacation home where the Section 121 exclusion is not available or when your overall gains exceed the $250,000 or $500,000 maximum exclusion on the sale of your personal residence (as discussed in Chapter 2).

Capital Gains Tax Rates

If you sell a capital asset that you held for more than 12 months, the holding period is considered long term, and you will receive favorable tax treatment on the sale. Long-term capital gains tax rates were recently reduced by the 2003 Tax Act, implemented on May 5, 2003. The current rates are as follows and depend on your current income tax bracket.

If you're in the 10 or 15 percent income tax bracket (this would apply to married taxpayers filing jointly with a taxable income of less than $65,100 for 2008 and single taxpayers earning up to $32,550 in 2008):

- For sales and exchanges of capital assets sold after May 5, 2003, and through December 31, 2007, your long-term capital gains tax rate is 5 percent.

- For sales and exchanges in 2008, your long-term capital gains tax rate is 0 percent.

- Beginning in 2009, your long-term capital gains tax rate will again be 5 percent for capital assets that you owned for more than 12 months.

If you're in an income tax bracket higher than 15 percent (this would include most real estate investors):

- For sales and exchanges of capital assets sold after May 5, 2003, your long-term capital gains tax rate is 15 percent.

The tax rate for short-term capital gains is subject to the same tax bracket as your ordinary income tax bracket (currently between 10 and 35 percent). For C corporations, the tax rate for all capital gains is the same as the corporation's tax rate for ordinary income (currently taxed between 15 and 39 percent).

Will the Capital Gains Tax Be Repealed in 2009 and Future Years?

We are frequently questioned as to whether it is wise to engage in tax planning methods now with the expectation that the capital gains tax for those in the lowest tax bracket will be repealed in 2009 (as it was in 2008), as stated previously. For those of you in lower tax brackets, it might look as though you will be able to sell your appreciated capital assets and pay no tax if you sell the assets in 2009.

However, do not get too excited. These tax provisions applied only to 2008. It is extremely doubtful that these changes will be made permanent for any tax years after 2008, especially due to the current large federal budget deficits. This is certainly the case for 2009, for which the 5 percent rate for those in the lowest tax brackets will apply. Furthermore, the tax laws will likely revert to the way they were before the passage of the 2003 Tax Act or that new provisions will be implemented. Therefore, we would not count on the 0 percent rate to remain the law for any years after 2008, especially if the large federal budget deficits continue.

Holding Periods for Capital Assets

To determine whether your capital asset will receive the preferential long-term capital gains tax treatment upon its sale, you first need to determine its holding period. Long-term capital gains, as stated previously, are taxed at a much more favorable rate than the sale of noncapital assets or short-term capital assets.

The following six steps will assist you in determining the overall holding period:

1. Determine how the property was acquired. If it was acquired as a regular purchase, follow the formula stated in Step 2. If the property was acquired as a gift, inheritance, or exchange, special holding periods will apply, as explained in Steps 4 and 5.

2. Count the time you have held the property. Start counting on the day after acquisition and stop counting on the date of the disposition. For real estate, the closing day of the purchase does not count, but the closing day of the sale does count.[4]

3. Determine whether the holding period is short term or long term based on the preceding counting method and the explanation that follows:

    a. *Long term.* You must hold the property for at least one year and one day.[5] Be careful here, because if you hold the property for only one year, you will be taxed at your ordinary income tax rate (currently up to 35 percent). If you keep the property for one year and one day, you will receive the much more favorable long-term capital gains rate (maximum of 15 percent).

b. *Short term.* Property held less than one year and one day, as calculated in the previous step.

Example

Jake buys a house on December 1, 2009, and sells it on December 1, 2010. He cannot count December 1, 2009, as the date of acquisition, so his holding period is only one year. Thus he will be taxed at his regular income tax rate because he did not hold the property for at least one year and one day.

4. *Inheritances.* Taxpayers get a break here because the gain is categorized as long term no matter how long the capital asset was held by the deceased.[6]

5. *Gifts.* If you receive your capital asset as a gift, the holding period is transferred from the donor (the person giving you the gift) to the donee (you).[7] This means that your holding period is added to the donor's holding period to determine whether it is long term or short term.

Example

If your mom gifts you a piece of property and she has held the property for 10 years, your holding period on receipt of the property is 10 years. If you sell the property one day after receiving it, it is taxed as a long-term capital gain.

6. *Transfers.* If the property was acquired via an exchange or transfer (for our purposes, a like-kind exchange), it has the holding period of the property transferred.[8]

Example

Michael owns a rental property and has held it for five years. It has also been rented for each of these years. Michael decides to use a 1031 exchange (a like-kind exchange) and exchange this property for a new rental property. His holding period in the newly acquired property is now five years, with one exception: This holding period only applies up to and including the transferred property's basis!

What does this mean? *See the next example.*

Example

This scenario involves the same facts as the previous example except that Michael's old property has a basis of $200,000. The newly acquired property is purchased for $300,000. Because the new property has a higher basis than the old property, the long-term holding period will only apply to the $200,000 of basis. The other $100,000 of new basis will start a new holding period beginning on the date of closing.

Tax Tip

Make sure you are including *all* your expenses related to the sale of your property. See the discussion later in this chapter for a list of expenses to include as part of your cost basis to help you offset your gain. If you miss some expenses, you will overpay your taxes, which we do not recommend!

Example

John owns a piece of real estate that he purchased and has rented since August 1, 2009. John decides to sell the property on August 2, 2010, for $250,000. His adjusted basis in the property (or his cost plus improvements) is $210,000. John has also taken $4,000 of depreciation over the past year on his tax return. John's gain and tax are calculated as follows:

Sale price:	$250,000
Less:	
Adjusted basis (includes):	$210,000
Purchase price:	($180,000)
Improvements:	($ 10,000)
Selling expenses:	($ 10,000)
Purchase expenses:	($ 10,000)
Plus depreciation:	$ 4,000
Equals gain:	$ 44,000
	($250,000 − $210,000 + $4,000)
Long-term capital gains tax rate:	$ 6,000 (15% of $40,000)
Depreciation recapture (discussed later):	$ 1,000 (25% of $4,000)
Total tax:	$ 7,000

If John had made the mistake of selling his property on August 1, 2010, he would have ended up paying tax at his ordinary income tax rate. If John's tax rate is 35 percent, he would have ended up paying taxes of $15,400 on the sale, instead of the much lower $7,000. As you can see, this would have caused John to pay an additional $8,400 in tax simply because he failed to hold onto the property for a few more months before selling!

Multiple Holding Periods

Real estate can sometimes have more than one holding period. This often applies to real estate developers who acquire land and then construct a building. In this case, there are two holding periods: one for the land and one for the building. The building may also have multiple holding periods if multiple portions are completed (Revenue Ruling 75-342).

Tax Tip

C corporations do not receive the favorable long-term capital gains rates on the sale of capital assets held one year or more. Thus we do not advise our real estate investor clients who are holding property on a long-term basis (for investment purposes) to hold such property in a C corporation. However, C corporations may be a beneficial business entity for dealer property, which is discussed in Chapter 5.

What Is "Basis"?

Understanding the rules concerning *basis* is important to help you determine your overall gain or loss on the disposition of property, including capital property. The higher your basis in relation to the sales price of the property, the less tax that will be calculated on the sale. Thus it is important to make sure that all your expenses are properly captured. The following are some important terms and concepts regarding basis issues:

- *Adjusted basis.* Adjusted basis is the original cost or basis of the property, plus any improvements, less any depreciation already taken on the property. Your basis will differ depending on how you acquired the property.
- *Purchased property.* The adjusted basis is your cost in the property (generally the purchase price plus expenses), plus improvements, less depreciation already taken.

Example

Jake purchased residential real estate for $350,000. He has also put an additional $50,000 in improvements into the property over the years. He has taken $25,000 in depreciation on his previous tax returns. Jake's adjusted basis is $375,000 ($350,000 + $50,000 − $25,000 = $375,000).

- *Inherited property.* The basis of property acquired by inheritance is the fair market value on the date of death.[9] This is commonly referred to as a *step up* in basis.

Example

Jake inherits a house from his mother. On the date of her death, Jake's mother's adjusted basis was $25,000. The fair market value on the date of death is $350,000. Jake's adjusted basis is now $350,000.

Compliance Tip

Capital gains and losses are reported on Schedule D (and attached to Forms 1040, 1041, 1065, 1120, and 1120S). A copy of Schedule D can be found in Appendix A.

For inherited property, it will be necessary to determine the fair market value at the time of death to receive the step up in basis. *Fair market value* is defined as the price that property would sell for on the open market. It is the price that would be agreed on between a willing buyer and a willing seller, with neither being required to act and both having reasonable knowledge of the relevant facts.[10] For a taxpayer selling the property immediately after receiving it from an estate, the fair market value will usually be the sales price. However, if you do not sell the property immediately after you inherit it, it will generally be necessary to have an appraisal of the property done at the time of death. You can use a person other than an appraiser, such as a real estate agent, but we recommend that you pay for a formal appraisal, since this will provide you with much better ammunition in the event of a tax audit.

Certain appraisal guidelines must be followed to determine the fair market value of a property.[11] Note that appraisals can vary significantly depending on the appraiser you use. You will want to seek out the most aggressive appraisal you can, since this will save you significant tax dollars when you sell the property.

Note that in certain cases, it might not be advantageous to seek out a higher fair market value of the property. This can happen when the higher fair market value will increase any estate taxes that may be due. See your tax advisor for assistance with this issue, since it can get very complicated if you have competing tax goals.

The basis of property acquired by gift is its basis in the hands of the donor (the person making the gift) right before its transfer to the donee (the person receiving the gift), plus any gift tax paid on the gift.[12] This is commonly referred to as *carryover basis*. Property received as a result of divorce or marriage is also considered a gift under the Tax Code.[13] You do not get a step up in basis when you receive property via a gift.

Tax Tip

The future of the step up in basis for inherited property is in jeopardy if the federal estate tax is repealed. This development will need to be monitored as any estate tax legislation is considered in the near future.

Example

Jake's mother gives him a house worth $350,000. Jake's mother's adjusted basis right before the gift is $25,000. Jake's adjusted basis is $25,000.

For transferred property/1031 exchange property, the basis of the newly acquired property is the same as the relinquished property, decreased by the "boot" received (usually money or other property) and increased by the amount of gain the taxpayer recognizes. The concepts of boot and other 1031 exchange issues[14] are discussed in detail in Chapter 4.

Example

Jake exchanges, via a 1031 exchange, a rental building for another rental building. He has received no boot and he does not realize any gain on the exchange. His adjusted basis in the relinquished property is $100,000. The fair market value of the replacement property is $110,000. Jake's basis in the replacement property is $100,000, the same as his basis in the relinquished property. There is no step-up basis when a 1031 exchange is done.

Again, your basis in the property ultimately determines how much tax you will (or will not) have to pay upon its disposition. You also must know the property basis for determining how much depreciation you can take for any given year on a rental property. The higher the basis, the more of a depreciation deduction you will receive on your tax return for the year and the less in taxes you will be obligated to pay.

You can use the following formulas to determine your adjusted basis for real estate. For your convenience, we have included these formulas in Appendix B for you to make copies and utilize each time you need to determine your basis.

Adjusted basis (short formula)

Original purchase price: $_____

Plus purchase expenses (see long formula below): $_____

Plus improvements: $_____

Less depreciation allowed: $_____

Equals adjusted basis: $_____

Adjusted basis (long formula)

Original purchase price: $_____

Plus purchase expenses: $_____

   Cash paid

   Mortgages created

   Settlement or HUD costs (see below)

   Mortgage interest not taken as expense

   Real estate taxes not taken as expense

   Legal fees (not related to HUD)

   Broker fees (not related to HUD)

   Travel expenses

   Meals and entertainment expenses

   Auto expenses

   Supplies

   Advertising

   Construction costs

   Repairs

   Any expenses related to the purchase not noted above!

Plus improvements: $_____

Less depreciation allowed: $_____

Equals adjusted basis: $_____

Settlement, Closing, or Housing and Urban Development (HUD) Costs

Closing costs (commonly referred to as *settlement costs* or *HUD costs*) are certain costs incurred due to the acquisition of real estate. The tax treatment of closing costs depends on the type of cost involved. Certain costs will be entirely deductible; others will not be deductible at all. Some closing costs will get rolled into your basis in the property, but others will be depreciated or amortized. It is important to know which costs are deductible so that none are missed, since missed expenses typically mean a higher overall tax bill than is necessary. Generally, the costs listed here will be deducted on either Schedule E (rental property income and expenses) or on Form 4562 (depreciation and amortization). Both of these forms are supplied in Appendix A. If the purchase involves your personal residence, the only expenses that are currently deductible (on Schedule A) are mortgage interest and real estate taxes. The following is a list of common items you will see on your closing statement and the tax treatment of each.

Item	Buyer Closing Costs	Where to Deduct Buyer Closing Costs	Seller Closing Costs	Where to Deduct Seller Closing Costs
Commissions	Added to basis	Form 4562	Sales expense	Schedule D or Form 4797

Items Payable in Connection with the Loan

Loan origination (points)	Amortized	Form 4562	Sales expense	Schedule D or Form 4797
Loan origination (points)	Amortized	Form 4562	Sales expense	Schedule D or Form 4797
Appraisal fee	Amortized	Form 4562	Sales expense	Schedule D or Form 4797
Other loan costs	Amortized	Form 4562	Sales expense	Schedule D or Form 4797

Items Required by the Lender to be Paid in Advance

Interest	Deductible	Schedule E or Form 8825	Deductible	Schedule E or Form 8825
Mortgage insurance (PMI)	Amortized	Form 4562	Sales expense	Schedule D or Form 4797
Hazard Insurance	Deductible	Schedule E or Form 8825	Deductible	Schedule E or Form 8825

Reserves Deposited with Lender

Reserves	Not deductible	—	Not deductible	—

Title Charges

Title charges	Added to basis	Form 4562	Sales expense	Schedule D or Form 4797

Government Recording and Transfer Items

Recording fee: deed	Added to basis	Form 4562	Sales expense	Schedule D or Form 4797
Recording fee: mortgage release		Form 4562	Sales expense	Schedule D or Form 4797
Tax stamps/transfer tax	Added to basis	Form 4562	Sales expense	Schedule D or Form 4797

Additional Charges

	Added to basis	Form 4562	Sales expense	Schedule D or Form 4797
Pest inspection	Added to basis	Form 4562	Sales expense	Schedule D or Form 4797
Closing fee	Added to basis	Form 4562	Sales expense	Schedule D or Form 4797

Tax Tip

If you see "POC" on your closing statement, this means you have paid items outside the closing. These items may or may not be deductible, but you should check with your tax professional to determine the tax status of such items.

Note that real estate dealers treat their costs from buying and selling real estate, as shown on the closing statement, as ordinary expenses incurred from the sale and purchase of real estate.

In the table, we have used certain terms in the buyer and seller columns. For purposes of this chart, "Added to basis" means that the item will be added into the overall cost of the property. For rental real estate, these costs will be included in the depreciable basis. The current depreciable rate for residential rental real estate is 27.5 years, whereas commercial rental real estate is depreciated over 39 years. For residential real estate held for resale, these costs will be added to basis to offset any capital gain on the disposition of the property.

"Sales expense" means that the seller will include these costs as part of the costs to sell the property, and these costs will offset any gain the seller receives on the disposition of the property.

"Deductible" means that these costs are fully deductible for a rental property on the appropriate line item on Schedule E, or on Form 8825 for an entity holding title to the real estate. Copies of these forms are included in Appendix A. Otherwise, these costs are added to the basis of the property.

"Not deductible" means that these costs are neither added to basis nor deductible at the current time for rental property. These items (such as real estate taxes or insurance) are usually held in escrow and are held for the benefit of the owner. When these items are actually paid, they become fully deductible items.

Compliance Tip

Depreciation for rental real estate is calculated on Form 4562, which is then transferred to Schedule E (for rental real estate held in your personal name or in a single-member LLC) or to Form 8825 (for rental real estate held in an entity such as a partnership).

"Amortized" means that these costs are taken over the life of the loan. Make sure that you indicate to your tax return preparer the term of your loan, or the professional could wrongly assume that you have a 30-year mortgage term when you actually have a 15-year term or less. This error is common and results in a lower overall tax deduction every year. Amortized expenses are calculated on Form 4562 and then transferred to the applicable Schedule E or Form 8825. For amortizable costs with respect to any startup expenses incurred prior to October 22, 2004, you are allowed to deduct these costs over a five-year period. For amortizable costs incurred after October 22, 2004, you can deduct $5,000 in the first year and the remaining amount over the next 15 years.[15]

Tax Tip

Acquisition points and other loan costs are amortized over the life of a loan. However, when the loan is paid off (as is commonly done through a refinance or when the property is sold), the points and other loan costs that have not yet been deducted can be claimed in full in the year paid. Only amortized loan costs and points (and not costs added to your basis or otherwise not deductible) are eligible to be fully written off in the year of refinance. Note that you must refinance with a different lender to take advantage of this deduction.[16]

Example

Emma placed a piece of rental property in service in 2007. She paid $2,000 of points to obtain the loan. In 2007, 2008, and 2009, she deducted as amortization $75 per year for a total of $225. In 2010, she refinanced the loan with a different lender. The remaining $1,775 of points would be fully deductible in 2010, the year the loan is paid off through the refinance. If she paid any points on the new loan, a new amortization period would begin.

Acquisition points and other loan costs are amortized over the life of a loan. However, when the loan is paid off (as is commonly done through a refinance or when the property is sold), the points and other loan costs that have not yet been deducted can be claimed in full in the year paid. Only amortized loan costs and points (and not costs added to basis or not deductible) are eligible to be fully written off in the year of refinance. Note that you must refinance with a different lender to take advantage of this deduction. Delete this? Same as above.

Gain or Loss Calculation

Now that you understand what is or is not a capital asset as well as comprehending the basis and holding periods, let's look at how you determine the calculation of the gain or loss on the sale of property, including capital property. A quick and simple formula for calculating gain or loss on the disposition of property is as follows:

Sales price: $_____
Less sales expense: $_____
Less adjusted basis: $_____
   Original purchase price: $_____
   Plus purchase expenses: $_____
   Plus improvements: $_____
   Less depreciation allowed: $_____
Equals net gain or loss: $_____

Let's look at an example to illustrate the formula.

Example

John purchases a piece of rental real property on December 15, 2002, for $150,000. His closing costs on the purchase were $2,000. He has put $15,000 of improvements into the property over the years. He has taken $5,000 in depreciation during this time as well. John sells the property for $275,000 on June 17, 2009. His closing costs on the sale are $4,000. His gain is calculated as follows:

Sales price:	$275,000
Less sales expense:	$ 4,000
Less adjusted basis:	$162,000
Original purchase price:	$150,000
Plus purchase expenses:	$ 2,000
Plus improvements:	$ 15,000
Less depreciation allowed:	$ 5,000
Equals net gain or loss:	$109,000

John's net gain is $109,000. He has held the property for longer than one year, and therefore he will pay tax at the long-term capital gains rate of 15 percent. He will also pay tax on the depreciation recapture at a rate of 25 percent. (Depreciation recapture is discussed in the next section.) His overall tax bill will be $16,850, an amount that is calculated by taking 15 percent of his gain of $104,000 (without the depreciation) and 25 percent of the $5,000 of depreciation claimed.

Sales and Exchanges Between Related Parties

If you sell or exchange property with a related party such as your child or parent, special rules may apply to the tax treatment of your sale. For instance, if you sell a capital asset to a related party, the gain may not be taxed as capital gain but rather as ordinary income. Losses on the sale of a capital asset sold to a related party may also not be deductible.

If you sell or exchange depreciable property (such as a rental property) to a related party and it results in a gain, the gain is ordinary income if the sale is either directly or indirectly between the following:

- A person and the person's business entity in which there is a controlling interest.
- A taxpayer and any trust in which the taxpayer is a beneficiary.
- An executor and a beneficiary of an estate, unless the sale is in satisfaction of a pecuniary bequest (a specific bequest in the will).

A loss on the sale or exchange (either directly or indirectly) of property between related parties is not tax deductible. The following are considered related parties for purposes of these rules:

- Family members such as brothers, sisters, spouse, lineal descendants, and ancestors.
- An individual and a corporation if the individual owns 50 percent or more of the stock in the corporation.
- Two business entities that are members of the same controlled group or in which the same persons own 50 percent or more of the value of the stock or interest of the business entity.

If you receive property from a related party who had a loss (either through a purchase or exchange) and you later sell the property, you will recognize gain only up to the amount that the gain exceeds the original loss to the related party.

Example

Your mother sold a rental property to you for $150,000. Your mother's adjusted basis was $200,000. Her loss of $50,000 is not deductible for her due to the related-party rules. You later sell the property for $250,000. Your realized gain is $100,000 ($250,000 sale price less adjusted basis of $150,000). Your recognized gain, however, is only $50,000 ($100,000 – $50,000) because you would get the tax benefit of your mother's $50,000 loss.

Sales of Business Property (Noncapital Property)

As discussed, you must classify the property you sell as either capital property or ordinary business property, and you must also classify your gains and losses as either capital or ordinary (and your capital gains as either short term or long term). We have discussed the sale of capital property; now let's discuss the sale of business property.

In general, business property fits into one of three possible categories: Section 1231 property, Section 1245 property, or Section 1250 property. We discuss each of these types of property in the following sections.

Section 1231 Property

Property used in a trade or business is called *Section 1231 property*. Like a capital asset, 1231 property is entitled to favorable capital gains treatment upon its sale or disposition. Section 1231 property receives long-term capital gains tax rates if there is a gain (with the exception of any depreciation that must be recaptured), but it receives ordinary loss tax rates if there is a loss.

The following common property types qualify as 1231 property (not exclusive):

- Rental real estate.
- Business real estate.
- Depreciable personal property used in a real estate activity.
- Any property used in your business.
- Leaseholds.

Note that dealer property and inventory used in the ordinary course of your business are not considered 1231 property.[17] Also, be aware that the portion of the gain from the sale of 1231 property that is subject to depreciation recapture, as discussed in a moment, is taxed at a higher tax rate of 25 percent.

Example

John sells the following property used in his rental real estate business and that he held for at least one year and one day:

Rental building and land:	$20,000 (gain)
Washer and dryer:	$ 100 (gain)
Computer:	$ 300 (gain)
Refrigerator:	($ 1,000) (loss)
Total gains:	$20,400
Total losses:	($ 1,000)

Because the overall gains exceed the overall losses, each gain and each loss is treated as a long-term capital gain and a long-term capital loss. If the losses had exceeded the gains, the entire loss would be treated as an ordinary loss and would be deductible in full and not subject to the $3,000 limitation per year on capital losses.

DEPRECIATION RECAPTURE

If you sell depreciable or amortizable property and have a net gain, your gain might be subject to ordinary income tax rates. *Depreciation recapture* is subject to a separate tax calculation and does not receive the more favorable long-term capital gains rates. Any gain attributable to depreciation recapture is subject to a top tax rate of 25 percent. Section 1245 and 1250 (in some cases) property is subject to depreciation recapture as well, since these types of property, discussed next, are depreciable or amortizable property.

Example

John sells rental property he held for at least one year and one day at a gain of $20,000. Of this $20,000 gain, $5,000 was previously taken as depreciation. The taxes are calculated as follows:

	Net Gain	Tax Rate	Tax
Total gain:	$20,000		
Gain attributable to prior depreciation:	$ 5,000	25%	$1,250
Remaining 1231 property gain:	$15,000	15%	$2,250
Total taxes due:	$ 3,500		

Section 1245 Property

Any gain on the sale of 1245 property is treated as ordinary income to the extent of the depreciation allowed or allowable on the property. *Section 1245 property*, for our purposes, is property that is depreciable or amortizable and is tangible or intangible personal property (such as a car or a computer). Section 1245 property does not include any buildings or their structural components. The gain on the sale of 1245 property is the lesser of the following:

- The depreciation and amortization taken or allowable on the property.
- The gain realized on the disposition.

The following types of depreciable and amortizable property are subject to depreciation recapture[18]:

- Ordinary depreciation deductions.
- The 30 percent special depreciation allowance for property acquired after September 10, 2001.

- The 50 percent special depreciation allowance for property acquired after May 5, 2003.
- Property for which a Section 179 expense deduction was elected.
- Amortization for:
  - Lease acquisitions.
  - Lessee improvements.
  - Pollution control facilities.
  - Section 179 intangibles.

Example

In 2005, you purchased a vehicle that cost $25,000 for your real estate business. You took $10,000 of depreciation over the years. You sold the vehicle in 2009 for $22,000. You figure your gain and depreciation recapture as follows:

Amount realized:	$22,000 (sale price)
Basis:	$25,000 (cost)
Depreciation taken or allowable:	$10,000
Adjusted basis (original basis less depreciation):	$15,000
Gain realized (adjusted basis less amount realized):	$ 7,000
Gain taxed as ordinary income (lesser of depreciation taken or gain realized):	$ 7,000

You should be aware that the depreciation actually taken or allowable is subject to depreciation recapture. If you failed to take any depreciation on the property, you still must figure the depreciation in your calculation. Thus we recommend amending your prior returns, if possible, to capture the depreciation deductions that should have been taken in earlier years. If you are going to be taxed on the depreciation either way, you might as well get the tax benefits!

Section 1250 Property

If you sell *Section 1250 property*, the gain is taxed as ordinary income to the extent of additional depreciation allowed or allowable on the property sold. Section 1250 property includes the following:

- All real property subject to depreciation and that is not 1245 property.
- Leaseholds of land.

ADDITIONAL DEPRECIATION

If Section 1250 property is held longer than one year, the additional depreciation is the actual depreciation adjustments that are more than the depreciation figured using the straight-line method. If the property is held one year or less, all the depreciation is additional depreciation. This is not as confusing as it sounds, as we will hopefully demonstrate.

There will not be additional depreciation if the following rules apply to the property you sold:

- You used the straight-line method on the property, you held it longer than one year, and you did not take the special 30 percent or 50 percent depreciation deductions on Qualified Liberty Zone property.

- The property was residential rental property placed in service after 1986, you held it longer than one year, and you did not take the special 30 percent or 50 percent depreciation deductions on Qualified Liberty Zone property.

Example

Tom purchased a residential rental building for $25,000 in 2000. He takes depreciation of $2,500 over the years using the straight-line method of depreciation. Because Tom has held the property longer than one year, because he has used the straight-line method of depreciation, and because the property is residential rental property, Tom has no additional depreciation to report.

Example

Tom gives his daughter a residential rental building for which Tom's adjusted basis is $50,000; over the years Tom has taken $15,000 for depreciation. Of this amount, $1,000 is additional depreciation. After the gift, his daughter takes a carryover basis, including the additional depreciation. She then sells the property. Her additional depreciation is $1,000 and taxes are unfortunately due on this amount.

There are many other unusual instances for which your basis may need to be computed differently than in any of the examples we have provided in this chapter. We strongly suggest that you obtain IRS Publications 554 and 551 prior to any sales so that you can compute the overall tax ramifications with respect to any potential sale. This way, you will not receive any unplanned tax liabilities come April 15.

If you fail to make payments you owe on a loan or mortgage on a property you own, the lender may foreclose on the property or repossess it. The foreclosure or repossession is treated as a sale or exchange for which you may realize gain or loss. You may also realize ordinary income, which may be taxable from cancellation of debt if the loan balance is more than the fair market value of the property.

The gain or loss on a foreclosed property is the difference between your adjusted basis and the amount realized. If you are not personally liable for repaying the loan (a "nonrecourse" loan), the amount you realize as income includes the full canceled debt, even if the fair market value of the property is less than the canceled debt amount. If you are personally liable for the loan (a "recourse" loan), the amount realized on the foreclosure or repossession does not include the canceled debt. However, if the fair market value of the transferred property is less than the canceled debt, the amount realized includes the canceled debt up to the fair market value of the property. You must realize ordinary income from the canceled debt for the part of the debt that is more than the fair market value.

Cancellation of Debt

If property is repossessed or foreclosed on and there is a loan secured on it for which you are personally liable, you generally must report as ordinary income the amount by which the canceled debt is more than the fair market value of the property. Report this income on Line 21 of your Form 1040. Businesses report this income as "other income" on their tax return. The lender should send you a 1099-C showing the canceled debt amount. If the lender does not send you a 1099-C, be advised that this usually means the lender has reserved its right to sue you personally on the deficiency (this will usually happen when the lender has sent you a 1099-A instead of a 1099-C).

Please be aware that recent legislation has removed most debt cancellation income if it originated from debt secured by your personal residence and was incurred in the acquisition, construction or substantial improvement of your personal residence. In this case, the first $2 Million ($1 Million for married filing separate taxpayers) of debt cancellation is tax free. This will certainly assist taxpayers who have lost their main home to foreclosure. We expect to see many more tax changes in this area due to current economic conditions and, as such, we highly recommend that you consult with your tax advisor to determine if any changes have been made to this area of the tax law.

Tax Tip

There is an exception to the rule of claiming cancellation of debt as income. This rule applies if you are bankrupt or insolvent, if the debt is qualified personal residence debt, or if the debt is qualified real property business or farm debt. IRS Form 982 will need to be filed and attached to your tax return to claim this exception. Please also note that some states do not allow this exception. Consult your tax advisor for details.

Conclusion

A thorough understanding of capital gains is essential for all real estate investors. It is counterproductive to spend much time and energy maximizing your overall profits, only to give too much of the profits back to the IRS and state taxing agencies. Although some of the concepts discussed in this chapter can get complicated, it is important for you to understand how you can compute your overall cost basis, along with how you treat expenses at the closings and while you own the property. An accurate estimation of these numbers will also help you avoid any unpleasant surprises come tax time.

Finally, proper tax planning concerning capital gains has helped many of our clients reduce their overall tax bills to the absolute legal minimum, a goal that all of us consider especially worthwhile.

CHAPTER 2

Your Personal Residence

For many Americans, a personal residence represents the single greatest tax shelter available today. Congress has always been aware of the importance of home ownership for the average U.S. family. For this reason, the current Tax Code permits homeowners to claim as an itemized deduction (on Schedule A) most mortgage interest and real estate taxes paid during any given year. However, better than these current expense deductions is the way you are taxed when you are ready to sell your home. In this chapter we discuss all the important issues concerning your personal residence.

Home Mortgage Interest Tax Rules

For most taxpayers, the interest paid on first and second homes is completely tax deductible. This differs from most other personal interest, such as interest on credit card debt and many bank loans, for which the interest is not deductible. As long as the loan is secured by your real property (first or second home), it will typically be deductible. To be deductible, the loan does not necessarily need to relate to a home.

Example

Caitlin buys a car for $25,000 and secures the loan with the vehicle. The interest on this loan is not tax deductible unless the vehicle is used for a business purpose (and then only the business portion of the interest based on

(Continued)

the business use percentage is deductible). However, if Caitlin instead buys the car with money obtained as the result of a home equity line of credit, this interest could be fully deductible, even if the vehicle is solely used for personal reasons.

As explained in a moment, the amount of interest that can be deducted is limited to a grand total of $1 million of acquisition indebtedness. *Acquisition indebtedness* is the amount used to purchase, construct, or substantially improve your primary residence or second home and is secured by the primary or secondary residence. In addition, it also includes up to $100,000 of home equity indebtedness.[1] These amounts are reduced for taxpayers who are married and who file as separate taxpayers and not jointly (thus $500,000 and $50,000, respectively). You are entitled to deduct the interest if you are the legal or equitable owner of the property and you have a legal obligation to pay the interest on the mortgage.[2] Thus, under these rules, the maximum amount of debt that a married taxpayer can claim for purposes of deducting the interest as a personal itemized deduction is $1.1 million.[3]

Example

Caitlin and Buddy are married and file joint tax returns. They purchase their primary residence and obtain a loan for $300,000. They also take out a loan for $50,000 to renovate their basement. Both of these loans are secured by their primary residence. All the interest paid on both loans is tax deductible.

Example

The scenario is the same as the previous example except that the initial loan on Caitlin and Buddy's personal residence is $1.5 million. They are limited in their tax deductions to only the interest on the first $1 million of this loan. (The interest on the other $500,000 would not be tax deductible.) They could, however, deduct the interest associated with their $50,000 home renovation loan as long as it was secured by their primary residence.

For purposes of the two homes for which interest can be legally deducted, the taxpayer, not the IRS, chooses which two will qualify, in the event that the taxpayer owns more than two homes.[4] A second home is one you occupy more than 14 days per year or more than 10 percent of the days it is rented for fair market value.[5] If you do not rent the property at all, there are no minimum time amounts that must be spent in the second home for it to qualify as a second home for tax purposes. This can provide some nice planning opportunities if you own more than two homes, since you might be able to pick the homes with the greatest amount of interest, to maximize your overall itemized deductions.

Example

Emma owns three homes and has mortgages on two, with the third owned free and clear. She can thus choose the homes with the mortgages so that she can maximize her tax deductions concerning the overall interest she pays every year.

Timeshares

Interest and/or taxes can be deducted on a timeshare as a second home as long as the taxpayer does not lease out the timeshare. (It would then become a potential rental property, depending on the number of days the timeshare is used as a rental.[6])

Deductibility of Points

Many real estate loans have "points" associated with the financing of the loan. For purposes of our discussion, *points* are considered charges paid to obtain a mortgage. These are often called *loan origination fees* or *discount charges* on the final settlement statement and are most often a percentage of the overall loan amount (often 1–2 percent).

The deductibility of points depends on when the points were paid. If they were paid with the closing of your principal residence, they are deductible in full in the year that they were paid. However, points that were paid in connection with a refinance are never deductible in the year paid. (This is true for a personal residence or a rental/investment property.) Instead, these are deducted on a monthly basis over the life of the loan.[7] This is called *amortization*.

Example

Matthew pays $3,600 in points for a refinance of his personal residence. The loan is a 30-year loan. Matthew is permitted to deduct $10 per month in points paid ($3,600 divided by 360 months = $10 per month).

If the loan is paid off in full prior to the end of the loan (often due to a new refinance of the loan or the sale of the property), the remaining points can be deducted in full in the year the loan is officially eliminated (the new refinance must be done through a different lender). This permits the borrower to be able to effectively accelerate the full deductibility of the points that were paid.

Example

The scenario is the same as the previous example except that in Year 2, Matthew refinanced his loan. If we assume that he had his loan for 10 months in the previous year and thus deducted $100 on his tax return ($10/month × 10 months), he would be permitted to deduct the remaining $3,500 in points paid in the year he again refinanced his loan. In addition, any points paid with his new refinance would also be deductible using the same amortization rules.

Real Estate Taxes

You are permitted to deduct the real estate taxes paid on your personal residence and any other real property that you currently own. These taxes are deducted in the year they were actually paid and not for the tax year involved with the taxes.

Example

Megan pays $2,000 in property taxes on December 1, 2009, for her real estate taxes for 2008 (the assessor's office works on a one-year lag period). Megan can claim a tax deduction for the $2,000 paid on her 2009 tax return.

Private Mortgage Insurance

If you paid any qualified mortgage insurance in 2007 or later, you may be able to claim a tax deduction for this payment as an itemized deduction on Schedule A. This deduction is subject to income phase-outs if your income was more than $100,000 (married filing jointly) or $50,000 (single or married filing separately). To qualify, you must have mortgage insurance issued by the Veterans Administration, the Federal Housing Administration, the Rural Housing Administration, or a qualified private lender.

The Sale of Your Personal Residence

Prior to the Taxpayer Relief Act of 1997, homeowners had to move into another, more expensive home or be taxed on built-up capital gains on the sale of a personal residence. There was a one-time exception to this rule for taxpayers who were at least 55 years of age. These rules have been eliminated and replaced by the following current law:

You can exclude up to $250,000 (if single or married filing separately) or $500,000 (if married filing a joint tax return with your spouse) of capital gains on the sale of your personal residence. This rule, like most other rules found in our Tax Code, has several components and exceptions; these are the focus of this section.

The $250,000 exclusion is available if you meet both of the following conditions:

- You owned the home for at least two years of the five years before the date of the sale (called the *ownership test*).

- You lived in the home for at least two years of the five years before the date of the sale (called the *use test*).

For purposes of each of these tests, the time period does not need to be continuous, and the two-year periods do not need to be met at the same time for you to qualify.

Example

Jordan, a single taxpayer, lived in and owned her home in Chicago for two years. She is transferred to Phoenix as the result of her employment. She then rents out her Chicago home to tenants for two years while she rents an apartment in Phoenix. If she wanted to sell her home in Chicago, she could do so and exclude up to $250,000 of the gains because she lived there and owned it for at least two of the five years prior to the sale.

Example

Assume the same facts as in the prior example except that Jordan rented the home first in Chicago as a tenant and did not actually buy the home until after she moved to Phoenix. Her two years of use and ownership thus occurred at different times, without any overlap. The same result would be obtained in that she could exclude up to $250,000 of capital gains from this sale.

The $500,000 exclusion is permitted if you meet all the following conditions:

- You are married and file a joint tax return for the year of the sale.
- Either you or your spouse meets the ownership test.
- Both you and your spouse meet the use test.
- During the two-year period before the sale, neither spouse used the capital gains exclusion for another personal residence sale.

If any of these requirements are not met, you will not be eligible for the maximum $500,000 exclusion and must therefore settle for the $250,000 exclusion (assuming that you satisfy the requirements for the $250,000 exclusion).

Like-Kind Exchanges

If you acquired your personal residence as the result of a like-kind exchange (discussed in Chapter 3), you are required to hold the property for at least five years to be able to fully utilize the capital gains exclusion. This rule applies to all sales after October 22, 2005.

Example

Caitlin has a rental property she acquired in a like-kind exchange on December 1, 2005. She rented the property for two years and then decided to move in and live there. To maximize her capital gains exclusion, she cannot sell the home before December 2, 2010.[8]

Temporary Absences

In computing the amount of time you actually lived in any given home for purposes of the two-year rule, temporary absences are not taken into consideration. For instance, a two-week vacation trip every year would not be excluded time, so you could include this time in your two-year computations, even though you were not physically present in your home during these short vacations. In addition, you can rent out your home while you are away on vacation and the time will still count for purposes of the two-year use test.

Example

Michael owns his main home in Detroit and decides to take a two-month vacation in Jamaica. Because this absence is temporary, the two months he spends in Jamaica would count toward his two-year ownership and use test calculations.

Military Members

Members of the military have special options available for computing their overall time period calculations. If you are a member of the military or foreign service and are on *qualified official extended duty* (defined as being located at a station more than 50 miles from your main home or while you live in government quarters under governmental orders), you can choose to have the five-year period suspended while you are away from home. This gives members of our military an extra method of excluding the gain on the sale of their personal residences. The period of suspension cannot last more than 10 years and you cannot use the five-year exclusion for more than one property at a time. This favorable provision works for members of the U.S. Army, Navy, Marines, Coast Guard, and

Air Force, along with members of the commissioned corps of the Public Health Service and the National Oceanic and Atmospheric Administration.

Example

Jackson lives in his home with his wife for three years. He is called to the Middle East for his military service and stays there four years. When he returns he decides to sell his home. For most taxpayers, the exclusion of gains could not be satisfied because the taxpayer did not live in the home for at least two years prior to the sale (even though the ownership test was met). However, because Jackson was in the military, he can elect to disregard the four years spent in the Middle East and can thus exclude up to $500,000 of capital gains (if he files jointly with his wife).

Ownership and Use Tests Met at Different Times

It is also possible to satisfy the ownership and use tests at different periods of time during the five-year period preceding a sale.

Example

Morgan lived in her home in Miami for one year beginning in January 2004 under the terms of a lease option. She decided to exercise the option and purchased this home in January 2005. In February 2006 she was transferred to Atlanta for her job. She continued to own the Miami home and rent it out to tenants. She did this for two years, and in February 2008 she sold the property. Morgan would be able to exclude up to $250,000 of the gain as a single taxpayer because she lived in the home for two years and also owned it for at least two years before the sale, even though these periods of time were not overlapping.

Which Is Your Main Home?

The first requirement in deciding whether you can take advantage of this favorable tax shelter is that the capital gain can be excluded only on your main home or personal residence. If you own only one home, this requirement is easy to satisfy. However, if you own two or more homes, you may have some nice tax planning opportunities to be able to exclude more than one gain from your home sales. Fortunately, the IRS and Tax Court have provided guidance in this area. Factors to consider in determining which residence is your main home include the following[9]:

- Your place of employment.
- The location of your family members' main home.

- Your mailing address for bills and correspondences.
- The location of the banks you use.
- The location of religious organizations to which you belong.
- The location of any recreational clubs to which you belong.
- The address used on your federal and state tax returns, voter registration cards, driver's licenses, and/or vehicle registrations.

You must physically occupy the home on more than a token basis for the home to qualify. For instance, merely moving furniture into a home isn't sufficient.[10]

It is also possible that your home might not be a typical single-family residence. Instead, it could be an apartment, mobile home, boat, or condominium.[11] As long as you live in and occupy it as your primary (main) residence, it will qualify.

If you live in two homes about the same period of time and perhaps cannot determine from the above-referenced factors which home qualifies, the IRS permits you to use the home where you spend the most time based on the number of days actually spent at each residence. The determination for all taxpayers is made on a "facts and circumstances" test.[12] You are not permitted to have more than one principal residence at any given time.[13]

Example

Sara lives in Denver, Colorado, but also owns a winter beach house in Miami, Florida. She spends approximately 50 percent of her time at each place. She files her tax returns using her Denver address and owns a business in Denver. She also has a Colorado driver's license. Based on these facts, it would be appropriate to use the Denver home as her main home, even though she might have spent only 50 percent of her time there.[14]

Example

You live in New York but your job now requires you to be in Washington, D.C., eight months per year. You decide to keep your New York home and also purchase a home in Washington. You would be permitted to claim the Washington residence as your main home based on the number of months per year that you now spend in Washington.[15]

Exceptions to the Two-Year Rule

It might be possible to claim at least some exclusion from capital gains taxes if you live in your main home less than two years. For taxpayers who can satisfy various exception tests, you could qualify for a reduced exclusion from the $250,000/$500,000 capital gains exclusions under the Tax Code. Currently, the IRS permits a reduced exclusion if you can show that the sale of your primary residence was due to a change in your place of employment or health or for unforeseen circumstances. The following factors will assist you in making the determination of whether one of the exceptions applies to your situation[16]:

- If the sale of the home and the health, employment, or unforeseen circumstances were close in time with each other, you then may qualify for a reduced exclusion.

- If your financial ability to pay for the home materially changed (such as losing your job so that you can no longer afford to live there), you then may qualify for a reduced exclusion.

- If the suitability of your main home changed, you could be entitled to a reduced exclusion.

- If the circumstances causing the sale of your main home were not reasonably foreseeable, you then may be entitled to a reduced exclusion.

We discuss each of these potential exceptions in the next few pages to assist with this analysis. It is important to remember that to use the reduced exclusion for tax purposes, the *primary reason* for the sale of the home must be related to one of the following exceptions.

Change of Place of Employment

The first exception is for a change of place of employment. This is one of the most commonly used exceptions. It is invoked when you move due to a change in your place of employment (for yourself, a spouse, a co-owner of the home, or a person whose main home is also your main home). For purposes of this exception, employment is considered to be the start of work with a new employer, a transfer with your current employer, or the start or continuation of your self-employed business. There is also a 50-mile distance test that is used to determine whether the sale of your personal residence was work related. This is considered a "safe harbor" in that if the new job or business is more than 50 miles away from your old home or at least 50 miles farther from your home than was your prior place of employment, you can "safely" consider the move to be based on a change in your place of employment. If you do not satisfy this 50-mile test, it does not mean that you cannot use this exception to the rule. Instead, you must satisfy a "facts and circumstances" test and be able to prove that the move was work related.

Furthermore, the change of place of employment can be voluntary and not the result of a transfer or some other event beyond your control. For instance, there is no reason that you could not make a move because you wanted to live and work in another locale or simply because you could make more money in another city.

Change in Health

The next exception is for taxpayers who must move due to a health-related issue. The IRS defines a health-related move as one being "to obtain, provide, or facilitate the diagnosis, cure, mitigation, or treatment of a disease, illness, or injury for a qualified individual."[17] A qualified individual is one of the following, for purposes of the health exception:

- You, your spouse, and any children living at your home.
- A co-owner of the home.
- A person whose main home is the same one as yours.
- A parent, grandparent, stepmother, or stepfather.
- A child, grandchild, or stepchild.
- A brother, sister, stepsister, or stepbrother.
- A mother-in-law, father-in-law, brother-in-law, sister-in-law, son-in-law, or daughter-in-law.
- An uncle, aunt, nephew, niece, or cousin.

To support this exception, in the event of an audit, it is very advisable that you obtain a written statement from your physician outlining the medical condition and the reason that a change of residence would be medically advantageous. The more written evidence you have, the more likely this exception will survive scrutiny in the event of an IRS audit of your tax return.

Example

Cam lives in New York City and suffers from a medical condition complicated by high humidity. His physician advises him to move to a dry climate to alleviate his medical condition. If Cam follows his doctor's advice and moves to Phoenix, he can utilize the health exception and obtain a reduced exclusion. He should, however, get his doctor's advice in writing in case he faces a tax audit in the future.

There is another exception available if a taxpayer is forced to reside in a nursing home due to physical or mental incapacity. In these instances, as long as the taxpayer owned and used the residence as his or her personal residence for at least one year (not the full two years) and then becomes mentally or physically disabled and needs to live in a state-licensed nursing facility, the full exclusion is available.[18]

Unforeseen Circumstances

The next exception is when a move is due to unforeseen circumstances. The IRS has provided some guidance on what constitutes such circumstances. Basically, if your home sale was due to some event that could not have been anticipated before purchasing and occupying the residence, you may qualify.[19] Unfortunately, it is difficult to predict with absolute certainty whether or not you will qualify for an exclusion based on unforeseen circumstances. However, some events are automatically considered to be unforeseen circumstances. These include:

- A natural or manmade disaster.
- An act of war or terrorism.
- An involuntary conversion of your home.
- Death, unemployment, or change in employment for yourself, your spouse, a co-owner of the home, or another person whose main home is the same as yours.
- Divorce or legal separation from your spouse.
- Multiple births from the same pregnancy.
- Events specifically determined by the IRS Commissioner in published guidance (such as the September 11, 2001, terrorist attacks on the United States).

Here are a few situations in which the taxpayer has been granted this type of relief:

- The taxpayer's son was released from a rehabilitation facility and the neighbors did not want him to live in the neighborhood, forcing the taxpayers to move shortly after they had moved into a new residence.[20]
- The taxpayer, a police officer, received a promotion to the K-9 unit and had to move because his current townhouse did not permit any dogs.[21]
- The taxpayers bought a two-bedroom home that they used as their personal residence. They later gave birth to twins and needed to move to a bigger home.[22] The IRS has also privately ruled that an adoption of twins (and the subsequent need for additional space) also qualifies as an unforeseen circumstance.
- The taxpayers lived in California and their main home suffered significant damage as the result of an earthquake. They were forced to move to a new location.[23]
- The taxpayer is engaged to be married. He and his fiancée purchased their primary residence but later split up without getting married. Neither of them can afford the home without the other person's income.[24]

- The taxpayer's mother-in-law suffered a paralyzing injury and she was forced to move into her child's home. The home could not accommodate her disability and they had to sell the house and move. This was an acceptable medical reason for the sale.

To utilize the unforeseen circumstances exception, the events that were unforeseen must be negative. If they are positive—for instance, that a larger, more expensive home can now be afforded—the exception cannot be invoked.

More Than One Home Sold in Any Two-Year Period

The tax law provides that only one home may be sold and the gain excluded for every two-year period. Therefore, you can use this gain exclusion only once every two years. However, there is an exception that could apply to this rule: If the reason you sold the second main home within the two-year period was because of a change of employment, health, or unforeseen circumstances, you may be entitled to claim a reduced exclusion.

Example

Matthew bought his primary residence on July 1, 2006, and sold it on August 1, 2008. He was able to exclude all of the gain ($250,000 or less). On August 2, 2008, he purchased a new main home. On August 2, 2009, he sold his new main home due to a job transfer. Matthew can exclude up to $125,000 of any gain based on the reduced gain exclusion amount ($250,000 / 2 for one year of use as a personal residence). If the reason Matthew moved was because he wanted a different house, all the gain on the second main home would be taxable because he failed to satisfy the two-year use and ownership tests, and no exception would apply.

How to Compute Reduced Capital Gain Exclusion

The following formula is used to compute the reduced exclusion:

$$\frac{\text{Maximum capital gains exclusion}}{\text{Either } \$250,000 \text{ or } \$500,000} \times \frac{\text{Number of days}}{730 \text{ days}}$$

For the number of days, you should use the shortest of the following periods:

- The period of time that you owned the residence as your main home.
- The period of time that you used the residence as your main home.
- The period of time between the date of a prior sale that you used the capital gains exclusion and the date of the current sale.

Example

Reese is single and lived in her home for 200 days before she received a job transfer that forced her to sell her house. She moved immediately, and it took another 100 days to sell her house (thus giving her a 300-day period of actual ownership). She uses the following formula to calculate her reduced exclusion:

$$(\$250,000 \times 200)/730 = \$68,493$$

She must use 200 days because the period of time she lived in the home was shorter than her actual ownership period. However, as long as her overall gain on the sale was less than $68,493, she would not be required to pay any capital gains on the sale of her personal residence.

Vacant Land

Ordinarily, vacant land cannot be considered your main home for purposes of the capital gains exclusion. However, as expected, there are exceptions to this rule as well. Here they are:

- The vacant land is adjacent to your main home.
- You owned and used the vacant land as a part of your main home.
- The sale of your home satisfies the exclusion requirements and occurs within two years (either before or after) the date of the sale of the vacant land.
- The other requirements for the exclusion of gains have been satisfied.

The Tax Court has been forced to make the determination of whether or not adjacent vacant land qualifies as part of a personal residence for exclusion of capital gains purposes. These cases are decided on a "facts and circumstances" basis, meaning that no hard and fast rules exist with respect to whether the land portion of the gain can be excluded. Here are a few of the results:

- In one case, 43.5 farm acres out of 51 total acres were considered part of a personal residence.[25]
- Homesite + 28.6 acres of dry pastureland constituted a personal residence.[26]
- Homesite + vacant land in which the homesite was owned by the taxpayers (gain excluded) and vacant land owned by a family limited partnership (gain taxable; *Farah v. Commissioner*, TC Memo 2007-369).

Converting Rental Property to Your Personal Residence

One of the nice ways to avoid paying capital gains taxes on a rental property is to convert the rental property to your primary residence and ultimately be able to satisfy the two-year ownership and use tests to exclude the gain. However, even if all the gain may be excludible, if any depreciation was claimed after May 6, 1997, this amount cannot be excluded from the gain and must be "recaptured" (or included in income). The amount of the depreciation recaptured is taxed at a flat 25 percent for federal income tax purposes.

Example

Sara bought a rental property on June 1, 2006, and rented it out for one year. The property appreciated in value by $100,000, and she would pay taxes on any capital gains if she sold it. Instead of selling the property, she moved into the property on June 1, 2007, and lived there until July 1, 2009. She would be able to exclude up to $250,000 on this sale because she owned the property for a period of three years and one month (June 1, 2006, to July 1, 2009) and used it as her personal residence for two years and one month (June 1, 2007, to July 1, 2009). She would pay taxes, at a flat rate of 25 percent, on any depreciation claimed for the one year that it was a rental property.

The Home Office and Exclusion of Capital Gains

If you claim a home office deduction and later sell the property, you may need to pay some taxes on this sale. Although the capital gains can be excluded if you satisfy the use and ownership tests, you may need to recapture any depreciation claimed on the office portion of your home. If the home office was not attached to your main home but was a separate structure, there are different rules that apply. This would be the case if you had a farm in which part was worked as a farm and the house was your residence or if your home office was located in a completely separate structure from your main home. In these cases, you must allocate the price for the main home and the business portion because the parcels are treated differently for tax purposes. In the instance in which you must make this allocation, you need to report the business portion of the sale on Form 4797 (copy included in Appendix A).

Example

You owned your home for 10 years and used it as your personal residence for each of those years. You thus qualify for the full capital gains exclusion. However, you also used a room in your home as an office for 2004 and 2005 and claimed $400 of depreciation for each of these years. Although the entire capital gain would be excluded from your income, the $800 of total depreciation you claimed would be subject to taxation (depreciation recapture).

Example

This scenario involves the same facts as the previous example except that the home consisted of a residence and a horse stable, which was leased to local residents for their horses. Even though you satisfied the use and ownership tests, you must pay capital gains taxes on the portion of the sale price that was allocated to the horse stable. The taxable gain attributed to recaptured depreciation must be reported on Form 4797 and Schedule D (copies included in Appendix A).

Sale of a Home in the Year of Divorce

If you get divorced and sell your main home, you are considered to have used it as your main home during any timeframe in which you still actually owned the property and your spouse was permitted to occupy the property pursuant to a divorce or legal separation agreement (and actually used it as his or her main home).

If your home is transferred to your ex-spouse as the result of a court order from a divorce, no sale is deemed to have occurred and the transfer is not taxable to either spouse.[27] However, this transfer could have the effect of transferring the tax liabilities to the spouse who ultimately receives the property. This is the case because the spouse will be able to exclude only $250,000, not $500,000, of the gain unless the spouse remarries and the new spouse can satisfy the two-year ownership and use tests. If the couple sells the home prior to the divorce, a $500,000 exclusion may be available to them (if they satisfy the use and ownership tests and file a joint tax return).

Unmarried Couples and the Exclusion

If you and a significant other, friend, or family member own a home together as a personal residence and later sell the home, both homeowners are permitted to utilize a $250,000 exclusion on their own tax returns. Although they will not get to utilize the $500,000 exclusion unless they are legally married filing a joint tax return, the net effect is the same if each gets a $250,000 exclusion.

Sale of a Home in the Year of Death of One Homeowner/Spouse

If your spouse dies and you do not remarry before the sale of your home, you are considered to have owned and lived in the home as your primary residence during any period of time in which your deceased spouse also owned and lived in the home as a main home. If you sell the home during the year of the spouse's death, you are eligible to file jointly with your deceased spouse and can then take advantage of the full $500,000 exclusion of gain. If the sale does not occur until a future year, this exclusion is reduced to $250,000 if you are single in the year of the sale.

Example

Joe and Selma are married and have owned and lived in their home for 10 years. On February 1, 2008, Selma dies. If Joe sells the home during 2008, he can claim the full $500,000 exclusion, since he is permitted to file jointly with Selma in the year of her death. If he waits until 2009 to sell and he remains single, his exclusion will be capped at $250,000.

Incapacity

If you become physically or mentally incapacitated, you are still considered to be using your home for purposes of the use test, even during the period of time you lived in or are living in a licensed assisted-care facility (for example, a nursing home). If this rule applies to you, you must be able to demonstrate that you owned the home and lived there for at least one year of the five years prior to the sale.[28]

First-Time Homebuyer Credit

If you are making your first personal residence purchase, you may qualify for a one-time tax credit of up to $7,500. The first year this option was available was 2008, and it applies to any first-time personal residences purchased between April 8, 2008, and December 31, 2008. The American Recovery and Reinvestment Act of 2009 extended these provisions and made them a bit more attractive by changing the maximum credit to $8,000 for any first-time home purchases made before November 30, 2009. A key point to remember is that the applicable date is the date of the closing and not the date of the executed contract. You can use this credit as long as your income is less than $150,000 (married filing jointly) or $75,000 (single or married filing separately). Any amounts earned in excess of these income limitations will result in a partial or complete phase-out of the credit. Although this credit is certainly worthwhile, keep in mind that for homes purchased in 2008 the credit will need to be repaid beginning in 2010 (and over a 15-year period). Thus, if you claimed the full $7,500 credit on your 2008 tax return, you would need to pay an extra $500 in taxes beginning in 2009 (and for 15 years). If your purchase occurred in 2009 (under the new Tax Act), you can eliminate any repayment requirements if you live in your new home for at least 36 months.

Loss on the Sale of a Personal Residence

The Tax Code requires taxpayers to report a gain on the sale of a personal residence if the exclusion amounts cannot be utilized (that is, if there is no exception to the two-year rule that could apply) or if the exclusion amounts were exceeded (for example, a single taxpayer has a capital gain of $300,000 on a sale and can exclude only $250,000, thus making $50,000 of the sale proceeds subject to capital gains taxes). The Tax Code is not, however, a two-way street when it comes to losses on the sales of personal residences. Any sale of a personal residence that results in a loss is not tax deductible.

Tax-Free Rental Income

You also have an opportunity to obtain tax-free rental income using your personal residence or other real property to rent on a short-term basis. Under Section 280A of the Internal Revenue Code, if you rent out your home for 14 days per year or less, you are not required to report this income and it thus becomes tax-free income. However, you are also not permitted to claim any deductions, other than for mortgage interest or real estate taxes, during this time.

Example

Jordan owns a ski condo near Park City, Utah. She rents this unit out during the last week of December for $2,000. Assuming that she does not rent out the property for more than 14 days during the year, the $2,000 is tax-free income and does not need to be reported as income.

Foreclosure of Primary Residence

In the unfortunate situation that you lose your primary residence to a foreclosure, some tax benefits are now associated to the debt that was forgiven. Previously, in most circumstances the debt forgiveness would be taxable to you as additional income. Now, however, debt forgiveness on a personal residence up to $2 million ($1 million if married filing separately) is no longer taxable if the debt secured by your personal residence was incurred in the acquisition, construction or substantial improvement of your personal residence. To take advantage of this relatively new law, you must file IRS Form 982 with your tax return in the year the debt was forgiven (foreclosed). You may also find IRS Publication 4681 helpful in this area.

Conclusion

For many taxpayers, their personal residences are the single most valuable assets they own. Therefore, it is important to understand the primary tax rules associated with this asset. We have seen far too many taxpayers fall into a tax trap when they sell their homes simply because they were unaware of the current tax laws concerning capital gains exclusions. Unfortunately, some sold before the two years elapsed, and they could not satisfy any exclusion. With a bit of planning and understanding, these tax traps could have been avoided. We certainly hope that you now understand the tax rules concerning your personal residence so that you do not become a victim of overpaying your taxes on the sale of your personal residence.

CHAPTER 3

Deductions for Rental Property

Rental property owners are aware that many tax deductions are available such that it might be possible for the owner to experience a positive cash flow on a monthly basis (the rental income exceeds all expenses for the property) and obtain an overall tax loss ("paper loss") come April 15. This chapter covers the major tax issues for rental property owners today, including how to report income and what expenses are legally deductible.

What Is Rental Income?

Income received as rent must be reported in the year you actually receive the funds, if you use the cash basis of accounting (nearly all taxpayers with rental income use the cash method). However, if you use the accrual method of accounting, you would report the rental income when you earn it as opposed to when it is actually received.

Example

Your tenant has rent that is due on December 1, 2008. However, he does not actually pay this rent until January 3, 2009. If you use the cash basis, you would report this payment as rental income for the 2009 tax year. An accrual basis taxpayer would report this income in 2008 (when it was earned), even though it was not actually received until the following year.

In addition, the following are other examples of rental income (or income associated with a rental property):

- *Advance rent payments.* Advance rental payments include any funds you receive for a period of time in the future. This needs to be included as income in the year you receive it, no matter what accounting method you utilize.[1]

- *Security deposits.* Normally, security deposits are not included as income. However, if you keep part or all of the security deposit to satisfy missed rent payments or to cover damages to your property, the amount you keep is included as income in the year it is received. In addition, if you earn interest on any security deposit accounts and local law does not require these amounts to be credited to the tenant, the interest earned also must be taxed to you for income tax purposes.

- *Tenant paid expenses.* If your tenant pays for any of your expenses, the amount paid is income to you. However, you are permitted to deduct the amount of the expense, so in effect it is a tax wash. For instance, if your tenant makes a minor plumbing repair and pays $25 for parts, you are taxed on this $25 as rental income, but you can claim an extra $25 of deductions for repairs and maintenance.

- *Garage or other parking charges.* Parking charges are very common in urban areas where optional parking spaces are available with the rental of a residential or commercial unit. Any extra amounts you receive for parking or garage charges are considered additional taxable rental income.

- *Laundry or other coin-operated machine income.* If you receive income from these sources, including soda and candy machines in a larger residential or commercial unit, these funds must be accounted for as income. You are permitted, however, to claim any expenses and/or depreciation relating to the machines themselves.

- *Lease cancellation fees.* At times a tenant will find it desirable to pay you to cancel a lease, often the result of falling local rents or the need for more or less space. This is considered income to you in the year it is received.

- *Barter for rent.* If you trade your property for other property or services, you are required to include the fair market value of the trade ("barter") as income in the year the trade took place. For instance, if your tenant offers to renovate the kitchen in his unit in exchange for three free months of rent and you agree, the fair market value of the three free months of rent must be calculated and included in your rental income for the year. This may also be the case if you provide a "free" apartment for your property manager. The fair market rental value of the "free" apartment is included in your income, although it may also be possible to claim a management expense for this amount as well.

- *Personal use of rental property*. If your rental property is used by a friend or family member and they do not pay you any rent, the fair market value of the rental must also be included as income.

In determining rent for any rental property, the market will normally determine how much can be charged. However, if you rent your property to a friend or relative, the IRS will require a fair market rental rate. If you fail to do so and this issue is raised during an audit, the IRS may assert that you had additional income (the difference between what was a fair rental rate and what you charged). The following list of factors should be considered to determine how much rent should be charged:

- *Location*. The more desirable the location, the higher the rent.
- *Size*. The larger the rental unit, the higher the rent.
- *Purpose of rental*. Commercial rent is usually higher than residential rent.
- *Condition*. The better the condition, the higher the rent.
- *Furnishings and amenities*. A fully furnished unit with excellent building amenities (such as a pool, workout rooms, commercial facilities, etc.) will command a higher rent than a building unit without these amenities.

Common Rental Property Tax Deductions

In general, you are permitted to deduct the expenses associated with your rental property in the year that the expenses are paid. This is for cash-basis landlords, which includes nearly all rental-property taxpayers. However, if you are on the accrual method of accounting, this will vary slightly in that the expenses become deductible in the year they are incurred rather than paid (this applies to a small minority of property owners). The following list shows expenses that are the most common tax deductions associated with your rental property. You might also want to obtain a copy of IRS Fact Sheet 2007-21 (available at www.irs.gov), which lists some rules associated with rental properties. Keep in mind that any expense that is both "ordinary and necessary" with respect to your rental property is allowed as a tax deduction. In addition, the amount of the expense must be "reasonable." An expense is generally considered to be ordinary and necessary if it is common, helpful, and appropriate for your rental activity.[2] An expense is considered to be reasonable if it is a prudent and economical way to handle the expense. If it is excessive or extravagant, the IRS will not permit the deduction.

Example

Michael owns a residential rental property complex and pays his 12-year-old son $40 per hour for snow removal and lawn maintenance. Even though the expense might have actually been paid, it would not be "reasonable" based on the age of the worker and the hourly rate other, unrelated parties would likely charge for the same type of work.

- *Mortgage interest.* Mortgage interest paid on a rental property is deductible in full during the year paid. Remember that any amounts paid toward the principal each year are not tax deductible. These amounts must be deducted via depreciation based on your basis in the property. For this reason, you must utilize an amortization schedule for your loan if your lender does not provide a mortgage interest statement (Form 1098) to you on an annual basis.

- *Mortgage expenses and points.* Any expenses that you incur to get a mortgage, including title, legal, closing, and other fees, are not currently deductible but must be added to your basis and depreciated. If you pay any "points" in connection with your mortgage (see Chapter 4), these must be amortized over the life of the loan and are not deductible in full in the year of the loan. For rental properties, this is the case whether the points were for the original purchase or a refinance of an existing mortgage.

- *Credit card interest.* Any amounts paid for credit card interest used to purchase goods or services for your rental property are deductible in full in the year paid. This is a major exception from the normal rule that credit card interest is not tax deductible. With respect to your rental property, as long as the purchase is related to the property, such as buying a new refrigerator using a credit card, the interest will be deductible because it relates to a trade or business. For this reason, we recommend using a separate credit card for your rental activities so that the interest will not be confused with personal purchases for which any interest would not be tax deductible.

- *Mortgage insurance.* Any amounts paid for private mortgage insurance for your rental property are deductible in full each year. This is somewhat common for properties in which a minimal down payment was utilized with the lender.

- *Real estate taxes.* All real estate taxes paid to any governmental agencies (state or local) for a rental property are deductible in full during the year paid. These taxes are usually based on the property's assessed value for tax purposes, although some jurisdictions use the actual fair market value to compute these taxes.

- *Repairs and maintenance.* Any current-year expenses to keep the property in good working order (as opposed to prolonging the useful life of the property) are deductible in full during the year they are incurred and paid. Maintenance expenses are deductible in the year incurred and do not need to be depreciated. Maintenance differs from repairs in that maintenance expenses are incurred before a problem occurs, whereas a repair occurs after a problem has surfaced. Thus, if you spend money to have an annual checkup of your air conditioning or heating units, that is maintenance. If you call an air conditioning repairperson because the air conditioner broke (probably during a nasty heat wave in August, when you needed it most!), that is a repair. Either way, the expense is deductible in full during the year the expense was incurred and paid. However, for tax reporting purposes, the two types are treated differently and deducted on different lines of the tax return. These expenses often must be considered with improvements, which are depreciated rather than expensed. We have devoted an entire section to the repairs issue later in this chapter.

- *Improvements.* The tax treatment of improvements is discussed in detail in the following section.

- *Advertising.* Any amounts spent on newspaper, Internet, or other advertising means are deductible if the intent is to find new tenants for any of your rental properties.

- *Gifts.* If during the course of your rental activity you provide any gifts, such as a welcome gift for a new tenant, these are deductible up to $25 per person per year. Any amounts over this amount are not tax deductible.

- *Commissions.* If you pay any real estate agents or other professionals a fee to find a tenant for your rental property, this amount is deductible as a rental expense. If this amount is over $600 and paid to an individual (not a corporation), you also will need to issue a Form 1099-MISC to the agent after the close of the year.

- *Travel expenses.* If your rental property is located away from your main home, it may be necessary to travel to the property so that you can perform repairs or maintenance or check on the condition of the property or if you otherwise need to collect rent or handle other matters associated with the property. As long as the primary purpose of your trip was related to the rental property (and not a personal vacation or some other nonrental property reason), all travel expenses are tax deductible. If you travel partially for rental purposes and partially for nonrental purposes, an allocation of expenses must be made. Travel expenses, though a broad term, include transportation, hotel, meals, and entertainment (subject to a 50 percent limitation), local transportation costs (including car rentals), and other travel expenses. You can deduct these expenses as long as they are "ordinary and necessary," which basically means that the travel was helpful to your rental activity. The expenses also must be reasonable in nature to claim a valid tax deduction. For each trip in which you are claiming a travel deduction, you must be able to show why the trip was necessary. A wider discussion of travel expense deductions appears later in this chapter.

- *Automobile used for rental activities.* For most local travel, the use of your personal automobile is a tax-deductible rental expense. You are permitted to use either the actual expense method or the standard mileage rate. The actual expense method permits you to deduct the total of the business (rental) portion of your automobile expenses, including gasoline, oil changes, repairs, maintenance, insurance, taxes, license fees, car washes, lease payments (if not owned), interest, parking, tolls, and depreciation (if owned). You must add up all expenses incurred during the year and multiple the total by your business rental use percentage. Thus a mileage log is necessary so that you can prove how much use of your vehicle was personal or business. An easier method is to use the standard mileage method, which unfortunately still requires a mileage log. The standard method allows 55¢ per business mile (in 2009). These amounts include all costs associated with the vehicle except parking, tolls, interest, and taxes (which are added to the overall amount computed using the 55¢-per-mile rate).

- *Points paid for mortgage.* The rules here vary from rules for a personal residence. Basically, *points* are the amounts paid by a borrower to obtain a mortgage. These amounts are also referred to as *loan origination fees* or *discount charges.* These fees are usually based on a percentage of the loan value, such as 1 percent of the total amount borrowed. These amounts can be deducted on a straight-line basis (amortized) over the life of the loan or claimed as a deduction in full in the year the loan matures. For most taxpayers, the use of amortization will result in a more favorable tax treatment and is the way to best maximize tax deductions rather than claiming as a deduction in the year the loan matures.

- *Tax return preparation fees.* The fees that your accountant or tax attorney charges to prepare your rental property tax return are legally deductible. If you own a separate business entity for your rental property (such as a limited liability company, a limited partnership, or a corporation), this fee will generally be easy to compute. However, if you file Schedule E for your rental property along with your Form 1040 personal tax return, you should make sure that your tax professional breaks out the specific fees for preparing your rental property returns. This would also include any forms for depreciation, sales, passive activity rules, home office, and so on. This will be easier to claim on your rental property return than on Schedule A (copy included in Appendix A), since the itemized deductions require a 2 percent limitation for tax return preparation fees that the Schedule E does not have. In other words, you will get more of a tax "bang for your buck" if you report the fees on Schedule E rather than on Schedule A in most cases, since many taxpayers face limitations on the amounts they can claim on Schedule A.

- *Equipment rental.* If you need to rent equipment for your rental property, such as special tools, machinery, or the like, you are permitted to claim a tax deduction for this expense.

- *Office rental.* If you use an outside office for your rental activities (common if you own several units and need a management office), the rents paid are deductible, assuming that they are reasonable in nature. You also might be able to qualify for the home office deduction if you have an office inside your home. To use this deduction, you must use your home office regularly and exclusively for your rental activity. This means that the home office cannot be used as a spare bedroom or playroom. Instead, the only activity that can be conducted in the office must be business related. The home office deduction is discussed in greater detail later in the chapter.

- *Insurance.* Any liability or other insurance, including hazard insurance, is deducted based on the number of months in the year for which the insurance premium was paid.[3] This insurance would cover you (the owner) in the event that a tenant, guest, or other individual is injured on your property. You are not permitted to claim a full deduction in the year paid. For example, if you pay the 2009 insurance bill in December 2008, you can only claim $\frac{1}{12}$ of this amount on your 2008 tax return (even though it was paid in full in 2008) and $\frac{11}{12}$ on your 2009 tax return. The net effect is that only the first and last years of the lease will actually be affected as far as your tax deductions are concerned. For instance, in the previous example, even though the entire insurance bill was paid in 2008, only $\frac{1}{12}$ would actually be deductible. You will get a full tax deduction for insurance premiums paid in all full 12-month periods for all other rental years. You are not permitted to deduct title insurance costs as an expense but instead must include them in the basis of the property and depreciate them over the property's useful life.

- *Cleaning.* If you need to pay someone to clean common areas or to clean a vacant unit in anticipation of the next tenant, these amounts are currently deductible as an expense. If you incur cleaning expenses in connection with any improvements being made to the property, be sure to get separate invoices. Without these, the cleaning expenses may need to be depreciated with the improvements as opposed to getting a current-year tax deduction.

- *Legal and professional fees.* Funds spent to evict a noncompliant tenant, review leases, or handle any other professional matter associated with your rental property are deductible expenses. In addition, if the IRS or any other taxing agency decides to audit the rental portion of your tax return, the professional fees associated with defending your rental property return are also tax deductible. Any legal expenses incurred to start up your business entity (such as an LLC or corporation) must be claimed on Form 4562 (copy in Appendix A) and need to be amortized over a period of years rather than currently expensed (see the following discussion of startup expenses).

- *Management fees.* If you pay another individual or business entity a fee for managing your rental properties, such as to provide legal, accounting, or other day-to-day management services, this fee is also deductible. This is a common expense for taxpayers who own several rental property units.

- *Utilities.* If you, and not your tenant, pay for any utilities, these are fully deductible. Common utility deductions for landlords include electricity, gas, water, sewer, Internet, and cable.

- *Dues, publications, and subscriptions.* Expenses used to purchase books, seminar materials, and other educational materials so that you can properly manage the financial, tax, and other matters concerning your rental properties are also deductible. You also may claim deductions for expenses related to joining any real estate boards, chambers of commerce (if related to your rental activity), and any other groups as long as the focus of the group is not to provide entertainment facilities (such as a country club).

- *Startup expenses.* Expenses such as legal fees for setting up a limited liability company, corporation, or other business entity; license fees; or research and other expenses can be claimed as tax deductions. These costs also include hiring and training employees, including building managers, for your rental activities. Such expenses incurred after October 22, 2004, can be expensed in full for the first year, assuming that these expenses do not exceed $5,000.[4] If they are over $5,000, the excess must be amortized over 15 years.[5] For all startup expenses incurred prior to October 22, 2004, these expenses must be amortized over the first five years (no immediate expense deduction is permitted). To use this special rule concerning amortization, you must make an election on your tax return. For this reason (along with making your first depreciation deduction calculations), the first tax return you file for your rental activity will usually be the most important, the most complex, and the one you should scrutinize the closest. Make sure that you obtain competent and experienced tax advice prior to filing this tax return.

- *Homeowners association dues.* If you pay any fees to a homeowners association or other community association to handle upkeep of common areas (especially prevalent in condominium and townhouse developments), these can be claimed as a current-year tax deduction.

- *Supplies.* Supplies, such as office, cleaning, and hardware supplies that are used in connection with your rental property or properties, are also currently deductible.

- *Salaries and wages.* Any amounts you pay to any employees, such as office personnel, maintenance workers, or other service personnel, are also tax deductible in the year paid. Remember that any salaries or wages paid will require you, as the employer, to withhold taxes and file Forms 940, 941, W-2, and W-3 as well as any necessary state forms.

- *Meals and entertainment.* Any amounts that you spend on entertaining or meals are deductible if done in connection with your rental property. These include any entertainment (including tickets to a sporting event, concert, outdoor activities such as golf or skiing, or meals) to potential tenants, investors, real estate agents, property managers, property owners, professional advisors, suppliers, or employees. You can claim an expense deduction equal to 50 percent of the total costs for you and your guest. This is available as long as you discuss business either before, during, or after the entertainment and as long as the amount spent was reasonable in nature. To claim a legitimate tax deduction, you must also show the business purpose of the entertaining (that is, why were you taking this person out to dinner or a show?). If your return is audited, you must be able to show the "who, what, where, when, and why" of the entertaining (who did you entertain, what was the entertainment, where did the entertainment take place, when did it occur, and why did you decide to entertain this particular person?). If you cannot prove the business purpose, you cannot claim a tax deduction. Given the potential personal nature of this expense, documenting the business purpose is critical here.

- *Depreciation.* We cover this expense in detail in Chapter 10. In brief, you are permitted to claim depreciation beginning with the first month that the property was available for rent. It does not matter when it was actually rented as long as it was available for rent. For any personal property, you can begin to claim a deduction when the property (such as a refrigerator) is placed into service.

We frequently see many missed rental expenses when we review prior-year returns for our clients. Thus, we have included a checklist of rental expenses that you should review (or give to your current tax preparer) before your return is completed. The checklist is provided in Appendix B for you to copy and utilize for your benefit.

Repairs vs. Improvements

This is often one of the most confusing issues facing landlords and other property owners today. The general rule is fairly straightforward: If the work you do to the property keeps the property in good working order and does not add any real significance to the overall life or value of the property, the expense can be treated as a repair and can be deducted in full in the year paid. However, if the work done to the property adds to the overall value or the expected life of the property, the expense must be depreciated and cannot be expensed in the year it is incurred.[6] This area produces a great deal of disagreement between taxpayers and the IRS, since a taxpayer would nearly always want an expense to be a repair rather than an improvement, whereas the IRS desires the exact opposite result. A repair returns the property to the same condition it was in before it stopped working properly (such analysis will often be quite helpful in this area).

Tax Tip

If you are fixing something that is broken, make sure that you use similar parts and materials in terms of quality as were used in the unit before the repair. If you upgrade the parts and materials, you will be making an improvement, which will be subject to the depreciation rules, and you will not be able to claim a current-year expense deduction. It is also helpful for you to have photographs of the "before and after" situations so that visual documentation is present. This is especially helpful for larger jobs or ones in which the IRS may challenge the immediate-year repair deduction and insist on the expense being depreciated.

You need to keep track of all expenses relating to repairs or improvements. This includes materials, supplies, and labor costs. Unfortunately, you cannot include the value of your time spent in personally making the repairs. You must actually pay the money out to be able to claim it as part of the overall cost of the project. If the job includes both repairs and improvements, such as hiring a contractor to patch a hole in some drywall (a repair) and replacing an old wooden floor (an improvement), you should be sure to get an itemized invoice for the jobs so that you can differentiate between the two types of costs for tax purposes. The following is a list of improvements (which must be depreciated) courtesy of the IRS and Publication 527, which we strongly recommend all rental property owners obtain:

- Room additions such as bedrooms, bathrooms, decks, patios, garages, and porches.
- Heating and air conditioning.
- Interior improvements.

- Insulation.
- Lawn and grounds.
- Plumbing.

Tax Tip

Make sure that you get a detailed invoice for all work done on your property so that you can support your tax deductions in the event of an audit. This issue comes up at nearly every audit when rental properties are part of the tax return. The better your documentation, the more likely the IRS will permit you to treat your expense as a repair because they will know specifically what the money was spent on.

In most cases, a repair will cost less than an improvement. For instance, if you patch a leaking roof, this may be a repair, but if you replace the entire roof, this will be an improvement (because it materially adds to the value of the building and greatly prolongs its useful life). However, you cannot use cost as the sole determining factor, because courts have permitted large expenses to be currently deducted as a repair rather than needing to be depreciated as an improvement.[7] The Tax Court has previously stated the rule succinctly as follows: "to repair is to restore to a sound state or to mend, while a replacement connotes a substitution."[8] Here are a few differences from various courts concerning the "repairs versus improvements" issue and how it has been interpreted in the past:

Carpeting

- Replacing worn sections of carpeting is a repair and currently deductible in full.[9]
- Installing new carpeting throughout an apartment was an improvement.[10]

Tax Tip

Preventive maintenance expenses are currently deductible and do not need to be depreciated. If you try to keep your property in good working order, your tenants will be satisfied and your tax situation will be much better due to the permitted current-year expense deductions.

Roof

- Replacing an entire roof must be depreciated over its useful life.[11]
- Replacing some sections of a roof but not the entire roof constituted a repair and could be deducted during the year the expense was incurred.[12]

- Replacing major section of a roof (which cost $50,000) but not an entire roof was a repair because it was done to fix a leaking problem and the entire roof was not replaced.[13]

- The cases for roofing repairs versus improvements are often very difficult to reconcile. The IRS issued new regulations on March 10, 2008, which discussed roof repairs or improvements and provided several examples of how to claim deductions for your expenses. The IRS looked at roof replacements and basically concluded that as long as the roof was not a "betterment," the costs could be expensed rather than depreciated. For instance, if you replace the roof with the same or similar materials, you can claim a repair expense rather than the less favorable depreciation deduction. If you substantially change the roofing materials and thus add to the roof's useful life, you will need to claim a depreciation deduction. We strongly recommend that you work with your tax professional whenever you are replacing a roof, to make sure you have all documentation necessary to support your tax deduction should you claim the roof costs as an expense rather than deprecation.

Flooring

- Pouring concrete over an existing floor in a leased facility did not add to the material value of a building and was properly deducted as a repair.[14]

- Replacing an entire floor was a capital improvement.[15]

Walls

- An amount spent to tear out a front wall of a building and erect a replacement wall was a capital improvement.[16]

- Costs associated with tuck pointing and cleaning of exterior walls are repairs and not improvements.[17]

Driveways/parking lots

- A gravel driveway that was replaced with an asphalt driveway is an improvement and must be depreciated.[18]

- A resurfacing of a parking lot can be an expense if it was done to restore the parking lot to its original condition.[19]

Building

- Structural changes to a building, such as installing new telephone or electrical wiring, are improvements that must be depreciated.[20]

- Flood damage to a building and the necessary repairs to put the building back in the same condition as it was in pre-flood are deductible expenses.[21]

Home Office Deduction

If you maintain a home office for your rental property business, you may be able to claim the home office deduction on your tax return.[22] The Tax Court has permitted this deduction if the taxpayer can demonstrate that he or she used the office regularly and exclusively for bookkeeping and general management functions relating to the rental property business.[23] Here are the requirements to be able to claim this deduction:

- *Business activity.* To claim the home office deduction, your rental activity must be a business and not an investment activity. As long as you regularly spend time on your rental properties and are actively involved in the management decisions (lease reviews, tenant issues, collecting rent, making repairs, and so on), you should have no problem qualifying your rental activity as a business for purposes of the home office rules.

- *Regular office use.* The "regular use" requirement simply means that you use the office on a continuing basis and not on a sporadic or irregular basis. This requirement is relatively easy to satisfy; if you use the office consistently throughout the course of the year, you will satisfy this rule.[24]

- *Exclusive business use.* You must use the office space exclusively for business to qualify for the tax deduction. Unfortunately, this means exactly what it says. You are not permitted to use a room as a spare bedroom and office and be able to claim the home office deduction. You must use the space as a dedicated office space and not for a nonbusiness purpose. This rule is strictly enforced, and you must be able to support your exclusive use if your return is selected for an examination.

Tax Tip

You should take photographs of your office and have some drawings available to demonstrate how you computed your overall office size. We have seen situations in which taxpayers change residences and later have a prior tax return selected for audit. Without this documentation and given that they no longer reside in the residence where the home office was located, they are at the mercy of the IRS examiner (not a good situation to be in!).

Exhibit 3.1 shows a helpful flowchart, courtesy of IRS Publication 587, to see whether you can qualify for this tax deduction.

If you determine that you qualify for this deduction, the next step is to determine how much space is used for your home office. This is simply done as follows:

1. Square footage of home office.
2. Square footage of entire home.

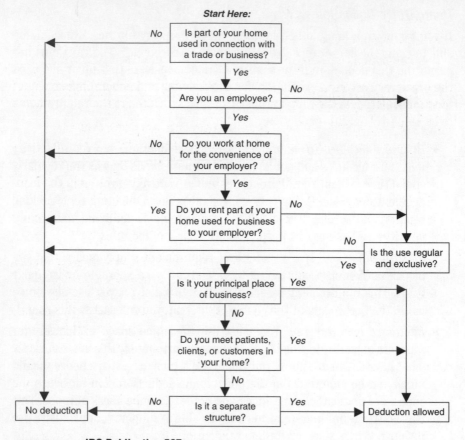

EXHIBIT 3.1 IRS Publication 587

3. Percentage of home used for business (divide Line 1 by Line 2 and enter the result as a percentage).

Once your office percentage is computed, you are then permitted to multiply your household expenses by the office percentage to determine your overall tax deduction. Common expenses to consider are as follows:

- Insurance payments (homeowners or renters).
- Utilities (including electricity, gas, water, sewer, trash removal, and the like).
- General repairs.
- Mortgage interest.
- Real estate taxes.
- Homeowners association dues.
- Cleaning expenses.

- Rent (if you do not own your home).
- Security system expenses.
- Depreciation (but this must be recaptured when you sell your home).

Tax Tip

You can use a portion of a room, such as a basement, as an office and still qualify for the deduction. You simply measure the actual office space (some type of partitioning is helpful to delineate the actual office space) and use these measurements for the computations involving the office percentage. In this case, you will need to use all the basement space when you calculate your home's overall square footage.

You are permitted to deduct your home office only if you have an overall net profit from your rental business. If you have a net loss, you cannot claim the deduction in the current year and must carry these disallowed amounts to a future year when they can be fully utilized. However, Form 8829 (copy in Appendix A) is used for sole proprietorship businesses (Schedule C) and is not necessary if you use Schedule E to report your rental expenses. Instead, if you have net income from your rental activity, the home office deduction can be claimed on Line 18 of Schedule E. You can write "home office expenses" or "business use of home" on this line to indicate what the amount is for. The amount to claim is calculated as follows:

Home office percentage of home: _____
Home expenses
Insurance: $_____
Utilities: $_____
Rent: $_____
Mortgage interest: $_____
Real estate taxes: $_____
HOA dues: $_____
Cleaning: $_____
Repairs: $_____
Security system: $_____
Other: $_____
Total expenses: $_____

You simply multiply the total expenses by the office percentage to determine how much can be claimed as a home office tax deduction. Be aware that any taxes or interest you deduct for your home office must be reduced on your Schedule A itemized tax deductions.

Tax Tip

If you do not qualify for a home office deduction or otherwise do not want to claim this deduction, you still are permitted to deduct some of the expenses. For example, the costs associated with your business telephone, furniture and computer equipment, office supplies, and any other ordinary and necessary expenses for your business can still be deducted as business expenses.

Example

You paid $15,000 of mortgage interest and $3,000 of taxes on your principal residence. If your office space represented 10 percent of your home, you would deduct $1,500 of interest and $300 of taxes for your home office. You must reduce your itemized deductions by these amounts and thus can now claim $13,500 and $2,700 as itemized deductions. Make sure you perform this calculation so that you do not "double dip" on the deductions.

Unpaid Rent

If a tenant defaults on his or her lease, you are generally not permitted to claim a loss for the rent not received.[25] This is the case because most rental property activities are conducted using the cash method of accounting, which generally means that income is recognized when received and expenses are deducted when paid. If you do not recognize the receipt of rental income because your tenant failed to pay, you do not get a corresponding deduction for this failure. The only time that you can claim a deduction for the unpaid rent is if you are using the accrual method of accounting, which means that you report the income and expenses when they are incurred, not when the funds are actually received or paid.

Expenses Due to Governmental Agencies

If a federal, state, or local governmental agency requires you to expend funds on your property, the same analysis we discussed earlier must be made concerning repairs versus improvements. Simply because you are required to change your building in some way does not alter this analysis. For instance, if the government requires you to put a new roof on the property, this must be depreciated even though you were forced to make this improvement. Likewise, the IRS considers most environmental cleanups, such as asbestos or lead paint removal, to be an improvement and subject to depreciation rather than expensing.[26]

There is some relief, however, if the expenses relate to changes made on behalf of the disabled or elderly. This rule allows up to $15,000 of expenses to be deducted as a repair for making changes that will make your building more accessible to the disabled or the elderly.[27] Without this provision, the typical changes to roads, walkways (such as widening a hallway to accommodate a wheelchair), and stairways or entranceways (such as installing a wheelchair ramp to permit access to a building) would need to be depreciated. If your costs exceed the $15,000 cap with this issue, you are permitted to depreciate the excess over its useful life per the IRS depreciation tables. If you are planning to use this special provision, you must make sure that your renovations comply with the Americans with Disabilities Act standards. These standards can be found on the Internet at www.access-board.gov.

Vacant Rental Property

If your property is available for rent but is vacant while awaiting the next tenant, you are permitted to continue deducting any expenses associated with the property. This includes depreciation and any management or maintenance fees associated with the property. In addition, any interest, insurance, utilities, or other expenses are also deductible during this time. As long as the property is available for rent, these are fully deductible expenses. However, you are not permitted to deduct any lost rental income as an expense.

Property Not Rented for Profit

If you do not rent your property for a profit (perhaps because it is a second home or other investment property in which the primary purpose is not to make a profit), you are permitted to deduct all rental expenses up to your overall rental income. You are not permitted to claim a rental property tax loss for a property that is not rented for a profit.

Part-Year Rental Property

For many taxpayers, the rental property will not be available for use during an entire 12-month year. This may be due to purchasing the property in the middle of the year or converting a personal residence or other structure to a rental property during the year. In these instances, only those expenses incurred while the property was available as a rental property are tax deductible.

Example

Jack buys a property on June 1, 2009, and makes it available for rent on July 1, 2009. He is permitted to claim rental property deductions for all expenses from July to December of 2009. Thus, he can claim six months of deductions for utilities, insurance, and any other expenses incurred.

Tenant Repair Issues

In many instances, you will need to decide whether you as the landlord or your tenant is responsible for any repairs. Absent an agreement with your tenant to the contrary, if the tenant caused the damage, the tenant is legally liable for making the repair. If the damage was caused by normal wear and tear or by outside forces (such as weather), the landlord is responsible for the repairs. This will make a difference with respect to the use of security deposits. Thus, carpeting that has faded over time or suffers noticeable wear in commonly used areas would be considered normal wear and tear. The landlord in such a case would be ultimately responsible for cleaning or making any repairs. However, if the carpet problems occurred as the result of cigarette burns or some other damage that was not normal wear and tear, it is perfectly acceptable to charge to the tenant costs associated with this type of repair.

If your tenant makes a repair and you reimburse him or her, you are permitted to claim a tax deduction for the costs of the repair. However, if you do not reimburse your tenant, you are not permitted to claim a tax deduction for the cost, even if the repair would normally be tax deductible if you had made the payment.

Rental Property Arrangements with Related Parties

If you decide to rent your property to relatives (including parents, brothers, sisters, children, grandchildren, and the like), you must charge them a fair market rent (and report this as income). Otherwise, the rental days will count as time you and your family spent at the rental property for personal use. This could make a difference in how much you can deduct as expenses if your rental property receives a large amount of personal use. It can also affect your ability to claim a tax loss for the rental property on your tax return.

Home Used as a Partial Rental Property

If you use your property partly as a second home for yourself and partly as a rental property, the tax treatment will depend on how many days you personally use the property for personal use. This information must be disclosed on your tax return (see copy of Schedule E in Appendix A).

RENTED FEWER THAN FIFTEEN DAYS PER YEAR

If you rent your property for fewer than 15 days per year, you do not need to report any of the rental income as taxable income during the year it is received.[28] This is one of the few instances where income that is earned is not taxed. This gives you an opportunity to legally avoid paying taxes on income earned. However, you are not permitted to deduct any expenses associated with this property, except for any mortgage interest or taxes that may otherwise be deductible on your Schedule A (Itemized Deductions).

Example

Caitlin has a ski condominium in Vail, Colorado. She decides to rent the condo during the 2016 Winter Olympics for $500 per day for two weeks. She receives $7,000 in rental income. Under current tax laws, none of this $7,000 is taxable to her (assuming she does not rent the condominium for any more days in that year).

Example

Joe owns a rental property in Las Vegas. He periodically leases this property to his corporation to hold meetings for the company's nine board members. Assuming that the rent he charges is fair and the total number of days is fewer than 15 for the year, none of this income is taxable to him. The corporation also gets a tax deduction as an ordinary and necessary business expense, again assuming that the amount it pays is reasonable.

RENTED FIFTEEN DAYS OR MORE PER YEAR

If you rent your property for at least 15 days per year and also use the property as a second home for yourself or your family, all income received as rents is included as income. The way your expenses are treated depends on how often you and your family use the property for personal use.

- *Limited personal use.* If you and your family use the property for 14 days or fewer per year or less than 10 percent of the number of actual rental days, you receive favorable tax treatment in that you simply report all your rental income and expenses. Unfortunately, all rental income is taxable to you (you do not get the favorable provisions of not needing to report all income, as in the situation when you rent the property fewer than 15 days per year). You also get a tax deduction for all ordinary and necessary rental expenses incurred.

- *Greater personal use.* If you and your family use the property for personal use 15 days or more per year or 10 percent or more of the total number of actual rental days, there are special provisions applicable to the deductibility of expenses. If you received more rents than expenses (and thus had a net profit for the year), all your expenses are tax deductible. However, if you had a net loss for the year, you are permitted to claim deductions only up to the amount of rental income (you cannot have a deductible tax loss in this instance). Any excess loss can be carried forward and used in a future year in which you have a net profit. If you are in this situation, the expenses that are deductible up to your rental income must be claimed in this order:

1. Mortgage interest.
2. Real estate taxes.
3. Direct rental expenses (such as management fees, advertising, etc.).
4. Operating expenses (such as utilities, cleaning, insurance, etc.).
5. Depreciation (if you still have income left to offset with deductions).

- To determine how many days a property is used for personal-use reasons, you must include one of the following:

  - Any days that you or any other person with an interest in the property uses it for personal reasons.

  - Any days that a family member uses the property, unless the family member pays a fair market rental rate. For purposes of this rule, a "family member" includes a brother or sister, half-brother or sister, spouse, parents, grandparents, children, and grandchildren.

  - Any days that the property is used by a charitable organization as the result of your donation of the use of the property to the charity—for instance, the charity resells or auctions off the property at a fundraising event and the buyer at the fundraising event uses the property.

  - Anyone who rents the property for less than a fair market value.

The following days do not count as personal use for purposes of making this calculation:

- Days utilized to make repairs or perform maintenance on the property.
- Days spent searching for new tenants.
- Days spent dealing with realtors or property managers.

Travel Expenses with Rental Property Activities

If you travel for a rental property you currently own, such as to check on the tenants or make repairs or modifications to the property, you will generally be able to deduct these expenses. However, many taxpayers engaged in real estate activities often travel to view potential new rental properties. These expenses may be deductible, but they often depend on whether you actually purchased the property or not.

- *Travel expenses incurred for property you ultimately purchase.* If you actually buy the property you were traveling to see, you can add these travel expenses to your basis in the property and depreciate these expenses over 27.5 years (residential rental) or 39 years (commercial rental).[29]

• *Travel expenses incurred for property you do not ultimately purchase.* If you look but do not buy, you cannot claim a tax deduction for these expenses unless you were looking in an area in which you were already engaged in business. It is unclear how large the geographic area would be with respect to this potential deduction. For instance, if you currently own a rental property in Chicago, Illinois, would Milwaukee, Wisconsin, or Gary, Indiana, be considered the same geographic area? Given that this issue is based on a "facts and circumstances" test and is often unclear, be sure to have excellent records for any amounts you are claiming as a tax deduction. It is also unclear about deducting travel expenses in this "look but do not buy" situation if you have a business entity, such as an LLC or corporation, set up specifically for business. If you use this business entity on a full-time basis and it is your primary means of support, it is likely that this deduction would be allowed. Again, this would assume that the expenses are reasonable and not extravagant in nature. In general, your argument would be that you are in business with respect to your rental properties and are not simply an investor. However, given that this issue is a tax gray area, it is not guaranteed that these expenses would be permitted in an audit situation.

Lease Options

If you have a lease option arrangement with your tenant in which the tenant has the right to purchase the property at a certain time in the future, the option payments you receive under this arrangement are not considered payments of rent and are not reported as rental income.[30] Any rental payments received by the seller/optionor are ordinary income, but all normal operating expenses paid by the seller/optionor are also deductible as rental expenses. If the tenant eventually exercises his or her option (or it lapses) and purchases the property, the payments received after the date of the sale are considered payments relating to the option and are included as income. Be advised that there have been many cases where the IRS has made the argument that the lease option was really a disguised installment sale. In such cases, the tax consequences have been detrimental to the seller as the seller then forfeits depreciation and other deductions and the option deposit is taxable income. See your tax advisor to make sure your transaction is indeed a lease option and not a disguised installment sale.

Passive Activity Rules for Rental Properties

In general, rental properties are considered passive activities, and there are very specific rules concerning whether or not any net losses can be deducted. For purposes of these rules, a rental property is considered one for which you receive rental income for use of the property as opposed to services that you provide.

The rules concerning passive activity losses are among the most complicated in the Internal Revenue Code.

Rental Property Losses and Deductibility

There are specific income limitations associated with deducting rental property losses. For all taxpayers, income can be divided into three broad categories:

- *Active.* Active includes any income or losses from a business, wages, and Social Security or other retirement plan benefits.
- *Passive.* Passive includes income or losses from any business activity in which you do not materially participate or from rental property activities.
- *Investment.* Investment includes income from stocks, bonds, and mutual funds, along with interest earned on investments or accounts at banks or credit unions.

In general, the income or expenses that are allocated to each of these three categories must stay in that particular category. With some limited exceptions, you are not permitted to offset income in one category with losses from another category. Many taxpayers are aware, especially after the recent stock market bubbles and losses, that they cannot deduct their total stock market losses against income earned from their wages/businesses. Instead, there is a special rule that permits only $3,000 of capital losses per year to be deducted against other income.

The same is true with respect to passive activity losses as the result of rental real estate, except that the losses are not capped at this $3,000 amount. When rental real estate is concerned, many taxpayers are permitted to claim a loss of up to $25,000 per year to be used against other nonpassive income.[31] Of course, there are three specific requirements to be able to use this tax loss:

1. You must actively participate in your rental activity.
2. You must meet the income requirements.
3. You must own at least 10 percent of the rental activity.

Given the overall complexity of these rules, we have devoted Chapter 7 to discussing the passive activity loss rules. However, we wanted to mention this issue in our rental property chapter because it must be considered and understood by nearly all rental property owners.

The Real Estate Professional and Rental Property Losses

A real estate professional is not bound by the rules concerning the $25,000 loss limitations per year.[32] This is the case because these individuals are engaged in real estate activities as their primary business, and this business should be treated like most other businesses that don't concern real estate. A real estate professional is any individual who meets each of the following conditions:

- More than 50 percent of all time spent on trades or businesses during the year was spent on real estate activities.
- The total amount of time spent on real estate activities was more than 750 hours.
- He or she materially participates in the rental activity.

There are specific rules associated with each of these parts of this test; each of these rules is discussed in detail in this chapter and in Chapter 7. For nearly all taxpayers, qualifying as a real estate professional will be beneficial from a tax perspective. However, if you qualify as a real estate professional, you must treat yourself this way on your tax return. It is not optional nor can it be opted out of.

The One-Half-Time Requirement

This rule requires you to spend at least one-half of your total time spent in working at all business activities in your rental property activity. The total time is computed by adding all time you spend on nonreal estate businesses, including time for working as an employee. You then add all time spent on your real estate activities. For purposes of this particular calculation, time spent on real estate activities includes the following:

- Real estate rental activities.
- Real estate broker activities.
- Real estate management services.
- Real estate construction services (often as a contractor but can be as a builder).

It becomes very difficult to satisfy this test if you have a full-time job as an employee of another type of business. If this is the case and you work 40 hours per week, you must work at least another 41 hours per week in real estate activities. This would be difficult to prove, since you would have at least 81 hours per week of actual work time. To prove whatever time is spent on real estate or other activities, it is imperative that some type of time log is accurately maintained. It is up to you, not the IRS, to prove how much time you spent on any given activities during the year in question. One benefit for married taxpayers is that either spouse may satisfy this test, so if the wife works 40 hours per week as an employee, the husband could satisfy this test on his own and both of them would benefit if they filed a joint tax return.

The 750-Hour Requirement

This rule sets up an additional hurdle to the one-half-time rule in that you must also work more than 750 hours per year on your real estate activities to qualify as a real estate professional. This rule is set up to prevent someone from working a minimal amount of time every year and calling herself a real estate professional. Again, it is up to you to prove how many hours you worked on your real estate activities during the year, so a time log is indispensable when it comes to this proof.

Example

Reese is involved with a real estate brokerage firm and she works 500 hours per year selling real estate. She also owns 10 rental units, on which she spends another 350 hours per year. Even though each of these activities did not meet the 750-hour rule, together they add up to 850 hours, so she would thus satisfy the real estate professionals test (assuming she made an election to aggregate her time for purposes of the 750-hour rule).

The Material Participation Test

The final requirement for real estate professional status is the material participation test. You need to satisfy only one of the following tests to pass this particular requirement. For most taxpayers, if you satisfy the 750-hour and one-half-time tests, you will also satisfy the material participation test. In general, you materially participate in an activity if at least one of the following is true:

- You did substantially all the work of the activity.
- You worked more than 500 hours per year at the activity.
- You participated for more than 100 hours and you participated more than anyone else at the business activity.
- You spent between 100 and 500 hours on two or more real estate activities and the total for both was more than 500 hours.
- You satisfy any of these tests for at least 5 of the previous 10 years.
- The overall facts and circumstances demonstrate that you materially participated.

Again, these requirements are discussed in full in Chapter 7 on passive activity rules. Fortunately, you are able to aggregate all time spent during the year on all rental activities to meet the material participation requirements. You also must make an election on your tax return to treat all rental properties as one activity.

Given the overall complexity of this issue, it is strongly recommended that you seek professional tax guidance during the year to review your unique circumstances. Do not wait until April 15 to get this help.

How to Calculate Your Time

For purposes of the rule concerning the one-half-time requirement, the following are considered *days* for purposes of these calculations:

- Spend more than four hours in one day on your rental activities.
- Spend more than four hours traveling for your rental activity (calculated from the time you leave your home until you arrive at your destination, or vice versa if on a return trip).
- Spend more than four hours in one day traveling and working on your rental property (in combination).
- Drive at least 300 miles for your rental activity. (This can be averaged so that if you are gone three days and drive 900 miles total, you have satisfied this rule, even if some days were shorter in terms of number of miles driven.)
- Spend weekends at your destination to prevent needing to come home and travel again the following week. This rule works well if you have appointments on Friday and Monday and do not want to return home over the weekend (often due to the high costs of doing so and the fact that it would be cheaper to stay rather than to return home over the weekend).

Using these rules, it is often very easy to limit your rental activities to the minimum requirements and still take advantage of the travel expenses.

Example

Morgan owns 10 residential rental properties in Las Vegas. She lives in San Diego, California, and decides she must travel to Las Vegas to check on these properties because she is having some problems in a few of the units. If she travels on Wednesday and the trip takes more than four hours, this is considered a day spent on her rental activities, and all expenses that are ordinary and necessary are tax deductible. If she works from 9:00 a.m. to 2:00 p.m. on Thursday and Friday, these days are also business related. If she decides to stay for the weekend and then work on Monday, again working a minimum of four hours on Monday, her weekend expenses would also be deductible, even if she did not actually work at her properties on the weekend. In addition, the weekend days would also qualify as "days" for purposes of calculating her time spent in real estate activities.

It is your burden to calculate the amount of time you spend on your rental activities. Thus a time log is imperative. You should get into the habit of writing down all time you spend on rental property activities, including telephone calls, physical visits to your properties, shopping for supplies, making repairs or improvements or interacting with contractors hired to make these repairs, evicting tenants or interacting with professionals, travel, attending meetings, attending seminars on your rental property, advertising activities, and so on.

Tax Credits for Rental Properties

Until this point in this chapter, we have discussed all expenses for purposes of claiming a tax deduction. However, some tax credits are available for rental property owners as well. These can make a big difference, since a tax deduction permits the taxpayer to claim an expense against income, so its value depends on the tax bracket of the taxpayer/landlord (current personal income tax brackets range from 10 to 35 percent). A tax credit, on the other hand, permits a taxpayer to claim a dollar-for-dollar credit against any taxes owed for the year at issue. Thus a $1 tax deduction is worth anywhere from 10¢ to 35¢, whereas a $1 tax credit is worth $1 against any other taxes owed for the year. For residential rental property owners, there are generally two primary credits available: the low-income housing credit and the rehabilitation tax credit.

- *The low-income housing credit.* This credit is available to landlords who make their residential rental properties available to low-income individuals. This credit was established to encourage the building or renovation of properties in lower-income residential areas. To use this credit, the property must be certified by the IRS or other federal or state agencies. There are limitations on the amounts that can be claimed as a low-income housing credit. For new construction costs that are not federally subsidized, these are limited to 70 percent of the total costs spread out over a 10-year period (or 7 percent per year).[33] For existing buildings or federally subsidized new buildings, the credit amount dips to 30 percent of the total costs, again spread out over a 10-year period (or 3 percent per year).[34]

- *The rehabilitation tax credit.* This credit is typically available for owners of designated historic properties. This credit applies to properties listed on the National Register of Historic Places or locations in a specifically designated and registered historical district. Furthermore, the property must be "significant" to the historic district before the credit can be utilized. A landlord must receive a certification from the U.S. Department of the Interior and/or the National Park Service before this credit can be claimed. This certification is not easy to obtain, but the value of the credit itself can make the application process worthwhile. There are limitations on the amount of the credit that is permissible; currently only 20 percent of the costs for capital improvements for certified historic buildings can be claimed.[35] If the building is not certified, it may be possible to obtain a credit for 10 percent of the total costs.[36]

Recordkeeping Requirements for Rental Properties

To fully maximize all rental property deductions, it is important that you have an excellent recordkeeping system in place. This can involve the use of commercial software programs such as QuickBooks or the use of simple ledger sheets. It does not matter which system you choose as long as you are consistent and fully understand exactly what you are doing. In addition to being able to use these records to maximize your tax deductions, you may also need these documents in the event of an IRS or state tax audit. While the number of audits is still relatively low (1 to 2 percent of all tax returns), it is increasing. During audits, the IRS will often review a rental property to check the following:

- Was all rental income reported?
- Were all claimed rental expenses actually incurred?
- Were all claimed expenses actually used for the rental property, or were they personal in nature and thus not deductible?
- Was the proper depreciation method and period utilized for the rental property?
- Was the taxpayer permitted to deduct any rental property losses?

No matter what system you use to keep track of your rental property income and expenses, the following records should be maintained:

- Copies of all receipts for your rental properties, such as the invoice from a plumber or the sales receipt for purchase of a new microwave oven for your rental unit.
- Copies of credit card statements for purchases used in connection with your rental property. Again, we recommend using a separate credit card dedicated to your rental activity to distinguish charges from any personal expenses.
- Copies of cancelled checks used to pay for any rental property expenses.
- Copies of the closing statements used when you purchased the property.
- Copies of the closing statements used when you sell the property.
- Copies of any loan documents for your original mortgage, along with any equity loans or refinanced mortgages.
- A ledger to show rental income receipts.
- Copies of bank statements relating to the income and expenses associated with your rental property.

- A calendar or time log to show all time spent in connection with your rental property, along with any information on entertainment used with your rental activity (the "who, what, where, when, and why" information we previously discussed).

- An automobile log if you use your vehicle for local transportation related to your rental property.

- Asset records, including purchase and sale information, if applicable.

It is recommended that all records be kept at least six years, since the IRS has a minimum of three years to audit any tax return (six years in some limited circumstances). With respect to any assets you purchase for your rental activity, including the property itself or any personal property used in connection with the activity, these records should be kept for at least six years after you dispose of the asset. (These records are needed in the year the property is sold.)

Tax Forms for Rental Property Activities

Most rental property activities are reported on Schedule E (a copy of which is included in Appendix A). This is the case for property that you own by yourself (or with a spouse on a joint tax return). However, some rental property activities are reported in a different manner. If you own your property in a business entity, the rental property income and expenses are typically reported on Form 8825 (again, a copy is included in Appendix A). This form is used for multimember limited liability companies (a single-member LLC will usually use Schedule E), partnerships, or S corporations. If you are considered a dealer, you will need to use Schedule C to report your rental property income and expenses (copy provided in Appendix A). Finally, if you rent out your property for fewer than 15 days per year, you are in the best situation of all in that no schedule is required because the income is tax free!

Conclusion

We have found that most landlords correctly report all rental income received, since it is usually a consistent amount (e.g., $1,000 per month equals $12,000 per year). However, they often miss some deductible rental expenses, thus resulting in more instances of overpaying their ultimate tax liabilities. We hope that this chapter assists you in avoiding this problem and correctly claiming all tax deductions for your rental properties that the Tax Code currently permits.

CHAPTER 4

Like-Kind Exchanges and Section 1031

A *like-kind exchange* (also known as a *1031 exchange*) is one of the most powerful tax savings techniques available for real estate investors. Any capital gain from a like-kind exchange of real property is not taxable until you sell or otherwise dispose of the property you receive (unless you do a like-kind exchange on that property as well).[1] The benefits of a like-kind exchange can be tremendous and can save you thousands of dollars in taxes at both the federal and state levels. Like-kind exchanges should be utilized as often as possible, since they are an extremely beneficial tax savings tool.

Some of the benefits of a like-kind exchange are:

- Deferral of taxes.
- Increase of appreciation on properties exchanged.
- Increase of cash flow.
- Ability to move up into bigger and better properties.
- Ability to help build your real estate portfolio.
- Ability to reduce or eliminate the alternative minimum tax (one of the biggest triggers for capital gains).

Example

Tom sells a rental property for $300,000 that he has held longer than one year. His original purchase price was $100,000. The property has $100,000 of debt

(*Continued*)

on it, and the property has been fully depreciated. (We have not assigned a value to the land for purposes of this example.) The capital gain on the sale is $300,000 ($300,000 sales price less adjusted basis of $0). The federal tax due is as follows, assuming that no alternative minimum tax is due on the sale:

$100,000 (depreciation recapture) × 25% = $25,000

$200,000 (gain on sale) × 15% (capital gains rate) = $30,000

Total tax due: $55,000

The total tax due does not include any state taxes that might be owing, and state taxes would need to be added to the preceding figure, if applicable. For example, in Colorado, an additional 5 percent tax would need to be paid:

$300,000 × 5% CO state tax = $15,000

Total taxes (federal and state): $70,000

If Tom had instead exchanged the property via a like-kind exchange, he could have deferred the entire $70,000 in taxes and paid no tax on the immediate sale.

Many requirements must be met for an exchange to qualify for deferral of taxes under IRC Section 1031. First, the property relinquished and the property acquired must be both of the following:

- Qualifying property.
- Like-kind property.

Qualifying property means that the property relinquished and the property acquired must be held for investment purposes or for productive use in your trade or business.

Examples of qualifying property (used in your trade or business or as investment property) are:

- Machinery.
- Buildings.
- Land.
- Autos and trucks.
- Rental property.[2]

Personal property, such as your home or car, is not qualifying property. The following are also not qualifying property:

- Stock in trade or other property held primarily for sale to customers, such as inventories, raw materials, and real estate dealer property.
- Stocks, bonds, notes, or other securities or evidence of indebtedness, such as accounts receivable.

- Partnership interests.
- Certificates of trust or beneficial interest.
- Choses in action.[3]

Like-kind property means that the exchanged properties are properties of the same nature or character (even if they differ in grade or quality). Exchanging any type of real estate for any other type of real estate qualifies as a like-kind exchange.

Tax Tip

Report the exchange of like-kind property on Form 8824 and attach it to your tax return in the year you close on the relinquished property (not in the year you acquire the replacement property). This reporting form is not optional; you *must* attach the form to your tax return to show the exchange. The form can be complicated to prepare, so make sure that you engage a competent tax advisor to assist you with its completion.

Here are some examples of qualifying like-kind property for real estate purposes:

- Land for land.
- Rental building for rental building.
- Land for rental building.
- Improved real estate for unimproved real estate.
- Thirty-year or more leasehold for land.
- Tenant-in-common interest in real estate for rental building.
- Apartment building for retail store.
- Condo for office building.
- Hotel for trailer park.

There are generally three types of like-kind exchanges: simultaneous exchanges, deferred exchanges, and reverse exchanges. These three types of exchanges and the requirements to properly complete each are discussed in detail next.

Simultaneous Exchanges

We rarely see *simultaneous exchanges*, where the relinquished property and the received property are exchanged at the same time. Instead, *deferred exchanges* are more common. It is unlikely that the timing will be right to relinquish your property and replace your property at the same time. However, on occasion, we do see simultaneous exchanges; therefore you should be aware of the requirements to properly complete such an exchange.

As stated earlier, the relinquished property and the received property must be qualifying property and like-kind property. Many of you are also aware that certain timing requirements are imposed within which the exchange must be completed (the 45-day and 180-day rules, discussed later in this chapter). However, with a simultaneous exchange, no such timing requirements exist, since the properties are exchanged at the same time.

Example

Jake is interested in selling his rental property that he has owned for 20 years. Jake is aware that he may have to pay thousands of dollars of taxes on the sale; therefore, he is looking at other options to help him avoid capital gains taxes. He is also interested in moving into a much larger property to help him build his real estate portfolio.

Jake's friend Emma is also interested in avoiding taxes on the sale of her apartment building. Emma is tired of the hassles of being a landlord, and she wants a smaller property to manage. Jake and Emma decide to exchange their properties via a like-kind exchange. They exchange the properties at the same time (assuming all other requirements are met), and Jake is able to defer all taxes on the relinquishment of his rental property.

Deferred (Nonsimultaneous) Exchanges

A deferred exchange (often called a *delayed exchange*) occurs where the relinquished property and the replacement property are exchanged at different times. Most like-kind exchanges fall into this category.

The Tax Code states that to be eligible for nonrecognition of capital gains treatment, the properties need not be exchanged simultaneously. Instead, the exchange must meet two separate timing requirements.[4] If neither of the requirements is met, the property received in the exchange is treated as nonlike-kind property, and the exception to the general rule allowing deferral of taxes does not apply. The two requirements relate to the timing of the identification of replacement properties and the receipt of the property to be received in the exchange.

The requirements in timing involving both the identification and receipt of replacement property were enacted in 1984 after a 1979 decision by the United States Court of Appeals. In *Starker v. U.S.*,[5] the Court decided the issue of whether a delayed exchange of property was allowed as a like-kind exchange. In *Starker*, A transferred property to B under a contract in which B agreed to acquire other property in the future and convey title back to A. The IRS argued that the exchange did not qualify as a like-kind exchange because the exchange of properties was not simultaneous and in fact the transfers occurred more than one year apart. The Court, however, held that A and B did not need to exchange the properties simultaneously and that the transaction between A and B was legitimate as a like-kind exchange.

There was significant controversy and confusion after the *Starker* case, and in 1984 the Tax Reform Act addressed some of the uncertainties of the timing requirements to properly complete a like-kind exchange. As a result of the Tax Reform Act, the following time requirements were implemented to help clear the confusion:

- The property to be received must be identified within 45 days after the date of transfer of the property given up in the exchange. No extensions are available.[6]

- The closing of the replacement property must take place within 180 days after the date the relinquished property is transferred or the due date, including extensions, for the tax return for the tax year in which the transfer of the relinquished property occurs, whichever is earlier. No extensions are available.[7]

Note that these time requirements are strictly interpreted. Failure to follow these time limits will result in the disqualification of your exchange.

The Identification Period

Any property actually received during the identification period will be considered to have been identified. You must identify the acquired property in a signed written document and deliver it to the owner of the acquired property or the qualified intermediary involved in the exchange, as discussed later. Only you, as purchaser, must sign the document. This written document must include the address of the acquisition property (that is, the legal description or street address). This document does not have to be a formal document drafted by an attorney, but it must be in writing and signed by the purchaser. We also recommend proof of mailing (either through certified mail or some other trackable method) if you will be mailing the identification document. The letter can be sent via facsimile or mail, but make sure that it is postmarked by the 45th day.

Tax Tip

A sample identification form is given in Appendix B for you to copy and use for your purposes.

Example

Becky decides to exchange her rental property via a like-kind exchange. She relinquishes her property on June 1, 2008, and receives and closes on the replacement property on June 30, 2008. Becky is considered to have properly identified the replacement property, even if she did not provide written notice of identification to the owner of the replacement property within 45 days of the date of transfer of the relinquished property. This is the case because she actually closed on the replacement property within 45 days of the relinquishment of her other property.

You can identify more than one replacement property. We strongly recommend that you do this in the case that you are unable to close on one (or all) of the properties you have identified. Having one or two backup properties will help prevent having to find another replacement property on short notice or risk disqualifying your exchange.

Example

Paul wants to exchange his rental property for another rental property. He relinquishes his property on June 1. On June 30, he identifies the replacement property in a signed written document delivered to the other party. On July 10, the owner of the replacement property tells Paul that due to unforeseen circumstances, she will no longer be able to sell her property to Paul as part of the exchange. Paul now has only five days to find an acquisition property to complete his exchange.

Tax Tip

A like-kind exchange is an extremely powerful tool for deferring taxes on the gain from the transfer of real estate. We emphasize *deferring* here because that is what a 1031 exchange does: It defers the taxes, it does not eliminate them. At some point, when the final property is sold, the gain will be recognized and you will have to pay tax on it.

The maximum number of replacement properties that you can identify is the larger of the following:

- Three properties.
- Any number of properties for which the total fair market value at the end of the identification period is not more than double the total fair market value, on the date of transfer, of all the properties relinquished.[8]

If at the end of the identification period you have exceeded the number of identified properties, the only property that will be considered to be identified is:

- Any replacement property you received before the end of the identification period (that is, any replacement property on which you closed within the 45 days). If this is the case, the identification period is automatically met, even if no written identification was provided.

- Any replacement property identified before the end of the identification period and received before the end of the receipt period, but only if the fair market value of the property is at least 95 percent of the total fair market value of all the identified acquisition properties. Fair market value is determined based on the earlier of the following: the date you received the property or the last day of the receipt period.[9]

Note that you can also revoke any identified property within the same 45-day period. This must be done in writing in a letter to the qualified intermediary before the 45 days expire.

The 180-Day Period

To be eligible to defer all gains and taxes on a like-kind exchange, the identified replacement property must actually be received before the end of the exchange period.[10] The exchange period begins on the date that the relinquished property is transferred and ends on the date that is the earlier of 180 days after the date of the transfer or the due date (including any extensions) of the income tax return for the taxable year in which the relinquished property was transferred. If more than one property is relinquished as a part of the exchange, the 180-day period within which the replacement property must actually be received begins as of the date of transfer of the first of such properties.[11] The timing requirements must be strictly observed. Courts have disqualified exchanges in which the replacement property was received within 180 days of the transfer of the relinquished property but after the due date of the tax return of the party relinquishing the property. The following example was an actual Tax Court case in which the timing requirements were not followed and the court disqualified the taxpayer's exchange.

Example

The taxpayers filed their tax returns on April 15 and later performed a like-kind exchange of properties. The replacement property closing was within 180 days of the closing on the relinquished property but after the taxpayers had already filed their tax returns. The Tax Court ruled that there was not a valid exchange because the taxpayers had not completed their exchange by the due date of the return.[12]

Tax Tip

The taxpayers in the preceding case could have avoided the disqualification of their exchange by requesting an automatic extension of the due date for their tax return. This could have been done by filing Form 4868 with the IRS on or before the due date of their tax return. An extension of time to file their return would have had the effect of extending the time within which the replacement property had to be received and the tax return filed.

Reverse (Starker) Exchanges

The last type of exchange is called a *reverse exchange* or *reverse Starker exchange* (named for the court case). A situation may occur in which you have already found the replacement property and closed on it before the property to be relinquished is sold.

Example

Tom has listed his rental building for sale with the intention of exchanging the rental building for a much larger property. While Tom is waiting for a buyer for his rental property, his broker informs him that an apartment building just went on the market at a great price. After Tom looks at the apartment building, he realizes that the price is a deal he cannot pass up. The seller of the building must also sell the property immediately. Tom understands that the apartment building will not last long on the market at its current price, and thus he decides to buy the property. Tom will need to perform a reverse exchange in this situation.

Before 2000, tax professionals frequently avoided reverse exchanges because there was no guidance from the IRS that explained how they worked. However, in 2000, the IRS adopted safe harbor rules for reverse exchanges. The IRS issued specific advice for properly accomplishing a reverse exchange.[13]

These rules specify that an *exchange accommodation titleholder* (EAT) must acquire the replacement property and hold it for up to 180 days. The owner can then sell the relinquished property. If the safe harbor provisions are met, the IRS will not challenge the exchange. The safe harbor rules are as follows:

- The EAT must hold title and this person cannot be the taxpayer or a disqualified person.
- The exchanger must have a bona fide intent to exchange.

- No later than five days after acquisition of the replacement property, the EAT and the exchanger must enter into a qualified exchange accommodation agreement (QEAA). The EAT must agree for tax purposes that he will be the beneficial owner of the property.

- No later than 45 days after transfer of property to the EAT, the exchanger must identify the relinquished property.

- The property held by the EAT must be transferred to the exchanger no later than 180 days after acquisition by the EAT.

- The combined time period the relinquished property and the replacement property are held under the QEAA cannot be longer than 180 days.[14]

If you are considering a reverse exchange, make sure to find a professional to assist you before you enter into any agreements to buy or sell property. We have had many clients try to accomplish a reverse exchange after making the decision to buy the replacement property and after they took title to the property. Once title was taken, the client was disqualified from making a reverse exchange. Reverse exchanges can also result in additional accommodation fees. Thus, if the gain on the sale of the relinquished property is low, it might be better to simply sell the property.

Reverse exchanges outside the safe harbor provisions are allowed, but special care must be taken to ensure that the like-kind requirements for reverse exchanges are met. Consult a qualified tax advisor regarding these complex provisions.

Additional Requirements to Properly Complete a Like-Kind Exchange

In addition to the previously described timing requirements, contractual requirements between the owner of the replacement property and the owner of the relinquished property must also be met. A *qualified intermediary*, or QI, discussed shortly, can assist you with these requirements.

Both the purchase and sale agreements between the owner of the replacement property and the owner of the relinquished property should be assignable. Your exchange contract should state that you are not prohibited from assigning the contract as either buyer or seller. When a QI is used, the QI is usually listed as the seller on the settlement sheet instead of the taxpayer.

In addition to the assignment rule, the exchange agreement must also specifically state all of the following:

- The seller of the relinquished property has the intent to perform a like-kind exchange.

- The contract releases the buyer of the relinquished property from any liabilities and expenses from the exchange.

- The contract notifies the buyer in writing of the assignment.

The agreement stating these requirements should be executed prior to the closing of the relinquished property.

To illustrate these requirements and the problems that occur if they are not met, let's examine a few court cases:

- In one case, the taxpayers did not properly identify the replacement property as an exchange property within 45 days of the transfer of the relinquished property. The court held that since the taxpayers never specifically named the replacement property as the exchange property, the transaction was disqualified as a like-kind exchange.[15]

- In another case, the taxpayers purchased their replacement property after the 180 days had already expired. The taxpayers argued that they had made a "good faith" effort to meet the time requirements, but the Tax Court ruled that the exchange was not valid because the time requirements were not met.[16] The court noted that there were no exceptions to the 180-day rule.

- In our final case, the taxpayer backdated the identification document so that it showed that the 45-day rule was met. The IRS discovered this intentional alteration of the document. The Tax Court later ruled in favor of the IRS, and the taxpayers were assessed $2.2 million in capital gains taxes and a $1.6 million fraud penalty.[17]

As these cases show, the timeframes are absolute and must be met. In addition, they show the problems with creating false or fraudulent documents with the IRS. This should never be done.

Qualified Intermediaries

You must hire a qualified intermediary (commonly referred to as an *accommodator* or *qualified intermediary*) to assist you with your like-kind exchange, whether simultaneous, reverse, or deferred. This is required[18] and can greatly simplify your like-kind exchange; it can also protect your like-kind exchange from being disqualified by the IRS. A QI is a person with whom you enter into a written agreement to acquire and transfer the relinquished property and to acquire the replacement property and transfer it to you. A QI should be contacted as soon as you have started to consider that you might want to complete a like-kind exchange on your property. You will need enough time to interview a QI if you do not already have one lined up. The QI will also assist you with the exchange, to make sure that it meets IRS requirements so that it is not disqualified.

The contract between you and the QI must expressly limit your rights to receive, pledge, borrow or otherwise obtain the benefits of money or other property held by the QI.[19] Note that at no time are you allowed to take possession of the sale proceeds of your relinquished property. These proceeds must be held by the QI. The sale proceeds will be held in a qualified escrow account for your benefit. To qualify the exchange, the QI must do the following:

- Acquire and transfer legal title to the property.
- Enter into an agreement to transfer the relinquished property to another person and actually transfer that property to that person.
- Enter into an agreement with the owner of the replacement property to transfer that property to you and then follow through on the transfer of the property.

A QI must be an independent third party. A QI cannot be one of the following:

- Your attorney.
- Your employee.
- Your accountant.
- Your agent.
- Your investment banker.
- Your real estate broker or agent within the two years prior to the transfer of the relinquished property.
- Your relative.
- An entity in which you have more than 10 percent ownership.

A QI charges for services, but these fees vary by company. Fees can range anywhere from $1,000 to $3,000 or more, depending on the type of exchange you are doing (residential versus commercial or amount and type of service). It is a good idea to shop around for a QI and/or ask for references before hiring one. Referrals are often the best way to make sure that your QI is competent and reasonably priced.

The Boot

If you receive money or unlike property (called *boot*) in addition to the like-kind property received during your exchange, you may have a taxable event. Part of your like-kind exchange will be tax free (the like-kind portion); however, the boot portion will be taxed. You will be taxed on the gain you realize from the receipt of boot. In addition, if the other party to your exchange assumes any of your liabilities, you may also have what is referred to as *mortgage boot,* and you will be taxed on the transaction as though you had received cash in the amount of the liability.[20]

Furthermore, if you transfer unlike property as part of the exchange, you must recognize gain or loss on the unlike property you relinquish. The gain or loss is the difference between the fair market value of the unlike property and the adjusted basis of the unlike property.

Example

Tom exchanges a piece of rental property for a piece of land. Tom's adjusted basis in the relinquished property is $100,000. The fair market value of the replacement property is $150,000. As part of the exchange, Tom receives $10,000 in cash (cash boot). His exchange expenses are $1,500. The total gain realized on the exchange is $60,000 ($50,000 gain plus $10,000 cash), but only $8,500 will be taxed as boot ($10,000 cash received less $1,500 in exchange expenses).

Example

The facts of this scenario are the same as in the prior example except that the property relinquished is subject to a $30,000 mortgage. The other party to the exchange has agreed to assume the mortgage (assumption of liability). The total realized gain is $88,500 (fair market value of property received of $150,000, plus cash received of $10,000, plus assumption of mortgage of $30,000, less exchange expenses of $1,500, less the adjusted basis of property relinquished of $100,000). The portion of the gain that will be taxed as boot is $38,500 (cash received of $10,000 less exchange expenses of $1,500 plus the mortgage assumption of $30,000).

Example

Tom exchanges a piece of rental real estate with a fair market value of $150,000 and an adjusted basis of $100,000 for another piece of rental real estate with a fair market value of $175,000. He also exchanges a computer he uses in his business with a fair market value of $3,000 and a basis of $2,000 as part of the exchange (an example of relinquished unlike property). He does not recognize gain on the exchange of real estate. However, he must recognize a $1,000 gain on the exchange of the computer because it is unlike property (the difference between the fair market value of the unlike property and the adjusted basis of the unlike property).

To defer all capital gains, the replacement property must have a fair market value equal to or higher than the relinquished property. To accomplish this goal, you can relinquish one property and acquire more than one property to make sure that the price is equal to or more than that of the relinquished property.

Example

Tom relinquishes property with a fair market value of $300,000. To defer all taxes, he must acquire one or more properties with a minimum fair market value of $300,000. Otherwise, he will have boot and will have to pay tax on any deficiency. Acquisition expenses such as closing/settlement costs are included in the fair market value of the replacement property.

Example

This scenario is the same as the prior example except that Tom's replacement property is worth $250,000. Tom will be taxed on the difference in values between the two properties, or $50,000.

Formula for calculating boot:

1. Amount of liabilities assumed: _____
2. Amount of liabilities surrendered: _____
3. Cash given as part of the exchange: _____
Minus:
4. Fair market value of other property (boot) given up: _____
5. Boot received (Line 1 less Lines 2, 3, and 4; not less than 0): _____
6. Fair market value of other property (boot) received: _____
7. Cash received as part of exchange: _____
Equals:
8. Boot received (total of Lines 5 through line 7): _____

Example

Jake like-kind exchanges a rental property for an apartment building. The fair market value of the rental property is $200,000. The fair market value of the apartment building is $210,000. The mortgage on Jake's rental property that he will relinquish is $150,000. The mortgage on the apartment building that Jake will assume is $200,000. Jake puts $10,000 cash down on the apartment building. Jake determines whether he has boot as follows:

1. Amount of liabilities assumed: $200,000
Minus:
2. Amount of liabilities surrendered: $150,000

(*Continued*)

3. Cash given as part of the exchange:	$10,000
4. Fair market value of other property (boot) given up:	$ 0
5. Boot received (Line 1 less Lines 2, 3, and 4; not less than zero):	$40,000
6. Fair market value of other property (boot) received:	$ 0
7. Cash received as part of exchange:	$ 0
Equals:	
8. Boot received (totals of Lines 5 through 7):	$40,000

Here is a quick analysis to determine whether your entire gain will be tax deferred:

1. Are you receiving as much property as you are relinquishing (that is, are you trading up)?
2. Will you have used all the proceeds from the exchange (that is, will you have any cash left over after the exchange will be completed, or are you reinvesting all net equity)?
3. Are you assuming a new mortgage for as much as the liabilities you are surrendering?

If your answer is yes to these three questions, it is likely you will not have to report or pay tax on any gain in your exchange (assuming that the other requirements are met to qualify your exchange).

HOW TO AVOID OR MINIMIZE THE IMPACT OF BOOT

If it is unavoidable that you will be taxed on a portion of your gain from a like-kind exchange, the following strategies will assist you in avoiding or minimizing the impact of boot:

- After you complete your exchange, you can take out part of the boot as cash. Although you will have to pay tax on this amount, at least you will have the cash in your pocket to spend as you like.
- You are allowed to acquire more than one replacement property. If you find that you are going to have boot because you are not moving into a larger property, consider acquiring two or more properties to reinvest all your proceeds.
- Make capital improvements to the replacement property to avoid boot and equalize the values of the relinquished property and the replacement property. This is often referred to as an *improvement exchange*. Special rules may apply. See your tax advisor for details.

The following are some boot examples:

	Relinquished Property	Replacement Property
Value	$150,000	$300,000
Net equity	$ 25,000	$ 25,000
Debt	$125,000	$275,000

Here the taxpayer is moving up in value, reinvesting all the net equity and increasing the debt or mortgage on the replacement property. Thus, no gain will be recognized (taxpayer has received no boot).

	Relinquished Property	Replacement Property
Value	$150,000	$300,000
Net equity	$ 25,000	$ 0
Debt	$125,000	$300,000

Here the taxpayer has reinvested only $25,000 of the net equity into the replacement property. Thus, there is $25,000 of boot received here, and this $25,000 will be taxable gain to the taxpayer.

	Relinquished Property	Replacement Property
Value	$150,000	$100,000
Net equity	$100,000	$100,000
Debt	$ 50,000	$ 0

Here the taxpayer's replacement property is lower in value than the relinquished property. Furthermore, although all net equity has been reinvested in the replacement property, the new debt on the replacement property is not equal to the relinquished debt. Thus, the taxpayer has $50,000 of mortgage boot and $50,000 will be taxable gain to the taxpayer.

How to Permanently Eliminate the Gain on the Transfer of Property Through a Like-Kind Exchange

An extremely powerful tax planning tool to permanently eliminate the taxes on the gain for property exchanged via a like-kind exchange is to continue exchanging the property until you die. The gain at death will be completely eliminated and your heirs will pay no tax on any appreciation that has occurred over the years. This is because your heirs, at your death, receive what is called a *step up in basis* on the property. The basis in the property is "stepped up" to the property's fair market value (instead of the actual adjusted basis of the property in the hands of the deceased) on the date of your death. Be aware that this is the current law, but Congress is considering a major overhaul to the estate tax rules. Any changes may also involve changes to the step-up-in-basis rules.

> ### Example
>
> John has done several 1031 exchanges over the years. On the date of John's death, his basis in the last property exchanged is $150,000 (the property that will go to his heirs). The fair market value of the property on the date of John's death is $650,000. John's heirs' new basis in the property they inherit is the fair market value, or $650,000. If John's heirs sell the property for $650,000 (its fair market value), they will pay no tax! All the appreciation in the property that has been rolled over for the past several years is eliminated on transfer to John's heirs.

Holding Period to Qualify as Investment or Business Property

As stated earlier, only property held for investment purposes or for the productive use in your trade or business qualifies as property entitled to like-kind exchange treatment. To properly accomplish a like-kind exchange, how long do you have to hold property before it will qualify as business or investment property? The answer is that there is no definitive time period. The IRS will look at a number of factors in determining the taxpayer's intent in acquiring the property. Time is one important factor, but all facts and circumstances will be analyzed.

The IRS has explained that a minimum holding period of two years is sufficient to qualify the property as investment property.[21] However, this does not mean that a shorter holding period will not qualify. We recommend holding the property for at least 12 months as a reasonable minimum. A minimum of 12 months usually helps show that the taxpayer's intent was to hold the property as an investment. Again, the IRS will analyze a number of factors, time being only one of them, to determine the taxpayer's intent in holding the property. Note that this holding period requirement applies to both the relinquished property and the replacement property.

Converting Personal-Use Real Estate to Business or Investment Use

We are often questioned as to whether you can convert a personal residence into a qualifying business or investment use for like-kind exchange purposes. The answer is yes, you can. A property purchased with the initial intent to build a personal residence can be treated as an investment property if the owner decides to forego her plans to build a personal residence and instead use it for investment or business purposes. A personal residence can also be converted to investment property if the owner abandons the personal use and then changes it to investment or business use. The holding period discussed earlier will also apply. In many cases, you would not want to do this, since the personal residence exclusion would normally be available to allow you to exclude up to $500,000 of capital gain in the year of the sale under IRC Section 121 (see our discussion in Chapter 1). However, if you have more gain than the exclusion allows, you might want to consider the option of doing a 1031 exchange.

Example

Sara bought her home in 1984 for $50,000; she has used it as a personal residence since that time. It is now worth $500,000. If she sells the property, she will owe capital gains taxes of $30,000 (based on her gain of $450,000 less the $250,000 exclusion = $200,000 in gains × 0.15). Instead of paying these taxes, she decides to convert the residence to a rental property and rent it for at least one year. She then can use a like-kind exchange in the future to defer the taxes.

Converting Business Property to Personal-Use Property

Conversely, you might also want to take a piece of business or investment property that was the replacement property in an exchange and convert such property into a personal residence. A recent tax development has been implemented that rules on this specific issue. Under the new tax provisions, an investor who previously acquired his personal residence through a 1031 exchange will have to wait a minimum of five years before he can sell the property and exclude the capital gain. This applies to sales occurring after October 22, 2004. Thus an investor who exchanges into a rental house that is later converted to a personal residence must wait five years to exclude any gain under IRC Section 121.[22]

You still must have lived in the primary residence for at least two of the past five years before you can qualify for the tax exclusion.[23] The IRS will also scrutinize your intent in acquiring the replacement property, and if you had the intent to originally treat the replacement property as investment or business property, you can then convert it to a personal residence (if you meet the time requirements).[24] The gain deferred as a result of the exchange would then be eliminated under IRC Section 121 (up to a maximum of $500,000 for a married couple filing jointly).[25]

Example

John exchanges a piece of rental property for another piece of rental property. John rents the property for two years but then decides he will move into the rental property as his primary residence. John's original plan for the

(Continued)

replacement property was to hold it as long as possible and rent it out for appreciation purposes. Due to extenuating circumstances, John was forced to move into the rental property and make it his primary residence. John closed on the replacement property on January 10, 2009. John cannot sell the property and exclude the gain until at least January 11, 2014.

Losses

Losses from a like-kind exchange will not be recognized, even though money or nonqualifying property is received.[26] The loss increases the basis in the property received. Obviously, for this reason, if you have a loss, a like-kind exchange should be avoided.

Example

Jordan buys a rental property for $250,000; one year later it is worth $230,000. If she uses a like-kind exchange with respect to this property, she will not get the immediate tax benefit of the $20,000 loss because she will not be able to deduct this loss on her tax return. Instead, this $20,000 loss will increase her basis in the property she receives by $20,000.

Real Estate Dealers

As discussed in Chapter 5, real estate held as "stock in trade or other property held primarily for sale," that is *dealer property*, is excluded from like-kind exchange treatment. *Stock in trade* describes property that is included in the inventory of a dealer and is held for sale to customers in the ordinary course of business. Any gains from the sale of dealer property are subject to ordinary income tax rates.[27] Dealers cannot use favorable like-kind exchanges for their real estate holdings. Dealer status is discussed in Chapter 5.

Business Entities

On the other hand, any form of business that is holding property as investment property (not dealer property) can receive the tax benefits of Section 1031. These forms of ownership include:

- C corporations.
- S corporations.
- Partnerships (general or limited); note that partnership interests cannot be exchanged.[28]
- Limited liability companies.

Transfer to a Business Entity Immediately Following an Exchange

Many taxpayers want to move replacement property acquired via a like-kind exchange into a business entity for asset protection and tax purposes. Doing so poses special concerns, and taxpayers should be aware of the rules regarding moving the replacement property, which was acquired in the taxpayer's personal name, into a business entity.

Corporations

In *Regals Realty Co. v. Commissioner*,[29] the taxpayer, a corporation, acquired replacement property via a like-kind exchange. Months later, the corporation then decided to move the property to another corporation that in turn issued stock in exchange for the property. The Tax Court held that the exchanging party did not intend to hold the replacement property for investment and so disallowed the exchange. It thus appears that transfer to a corporation can impair the investment intent needed to qualify for a like-kind exchange. Additionally, for other tax reasons, it is usually never advisable to hold appreciating real estate in a C corporation; you should speak to your tax advisor before doing so.

Partnerships and LLCs

Contribution of replacement property to a partnership and/or LLC that is a partnership for tax purposes immediately after an exchange is allowed and does not, in contrast to a transfer to a corporation, impair investment intent.[30]

Additionally, it is important to note that whichever entity (LLC or partnership) exchanges property, not the individual owners, must also acquire the replacement property. Title must remain consistent in this regard, and the entity cannot distribute the proceeds to the LLC members or partners and allow them to buy their own property. If some LLC members or partners want to exchange and others do not, it would be advisable to dissolve the LLC or partnership before attempting to sell the property; then each member can exchange or sell his undivided interest.

Tenant-in-Common Interests and Like-Kind Exchanges

A *tenant-in-common* (TIC) interest in real property is a co-ownership in a piece of property with two or more owners. TIC interests on replacement properties in like-kind exchanges are becoming more common. A taxpayer can take the sale proceeds from the relinquished property in a like-kind exchange and invest the proceeds into a large commercial property with multiple owners. The taxpayer will receive a separate deed to the property, representing the taxpayer's undivided interest. There are a number of benefits of TIC ownership:

- *Appreciation*. Large commercial properties frequently have more appreciation opportunities than do smaller rental properties. Thus by exchanging into a TIC property you will have the opportunity to build your real estate portfolio more quickly.

- *Steady cash flow income and more security.* Commercial tenants generally provide more rental security than residential tenants, as well as steady cash flow income.

- *Flexibility of choice of properties.* More opportunities generally exist to exchange into commercial properties than into residential rental properties.

- *Annual depreciation and expense deductions.* Annual depreciation and expense deductions for interest, taxes, insurance, and the like are available (as they are for residential rental properties) to be taken as a deduction against rental income.

Note that to exchange into a TIC property via a like-kind exchange and receive the beneficial tax deductions related to rental properties, you must own at least 10 percent of the entire property. If you own less than this amount, you will lose the ability to deduct expenses related to the property on your tax return for the year. Consult with your tax advisor if you are interested in learning more about TIC properties and like-kind exchanges, since certain IRS requirements must be met. Care must be taken in structuring such exchanges and in analyzing the TIC interest to make sure it will qualify for the like-kind exchange. There are also numerous companies that can assist you with this type of like-kind exchange.

Last-Minute or Broken Exchanges

What happens if you were unaware of the availability of a like-kind exchange until after you have already closed on the sale of the relinquished property? Is there any option open to you at this point? You may be able to restructure the exchange using the *rescission doctrine*. To use this doctrine, you would form an agreement with the buyer of the relinquished property to rescind the sale. You would then agree to complete the transaction over again. The following requirements are necessary:

- The rescission must occur between the original parties to the agreement.

- The rescission must restore the parties to the original agreement to the positions they were in before the agreement occurred, with no further obligations.

- The rescission must occur within the same tax period as the original agreement.[31]

The rescission doctrine is a beneficial tax tool that allows taxpayers to obtain a fresh start for exchanges that have been broken due to unforeseen circumstances. Besides the preceding requirements, your lender may have additional ones. Ask your lender or QI for details.

Related-Party Issues

Special rules apply to like-kind exchanges between related parties. Under the related-party rules, exchanges between related parties will be disqualified from nonrecognition treatment if either the party relinquishing the property or the party receiving the replacement property disposes of the property within two years of the exchange. The gain or loss will be forced to be recognized as of the date of the disqualifying disposition. Related parties include the following (this list is not inclusive):

- Your spouse.
- Your brother.
- Your sister.
- Your parent.
- Your child.
- A corporation or partnership in which you have more than 50 percent ownership.

Example

Tom exchanges his rental property for his sister's rental property. At the time of the exchange the fair market value of Tom's rental property is $300,000 and its adjusted basis is $150,000. Tom's sister's rental property has a fair market value of $320,000 and an adjusted basis of $40,000. Tom's realized gain is $170,000 (fair market value of Tom's sister's rental of $320,000 less Tom's adjusted basis of $150,000 in his rental property). Tom's sister realized a gain of $260,000 (the fair market value of Tom's rental property of $300,000 less the adjusted basis of Tom's sister's rental property of $40,000).

Under the like-kind exchange provisions, Tom will not recognize any gain as long as he does not sell the replacement property for at least two years. Tom's basis in the new rental property (replacement property) is $150,000 (the same as the basis in the relinquished rental property). Tom's sister will also not recognize any gain as long as she does not sell the property within two years. Her basis in the received rental property is $40,000.

If Tom sells the rental property within two years of the exchange, his exchange will be disqualified. Tom must report the entire gain of $170,000 in the year of the sale. Tom's sister must also report on her return in the year of sale the $260,000 (even though she did not sell her property within two years). Tom's new basis is $320,000 (old basis plus gain recognized). Tom's sister's new basis is $300,000 (old basis plus gain recognized).

The two-year holding period begins on the date of the transfer of property as part of the exchange (usually the closing date for real estate). In addition, the two-year holding period is extended in some limited circumstances.[32] The two-year period is extended for any period of time during which the risk of loss of the holder of the property is substantially diminished by one of the following:

- The holding of a put (option) with respect to such property.
- The holding by another person of a right to acquire such property.
- A short sale or any other transaction.[33]

The Tax Court has noted that these categories are not exclusive. Rather, the extension of the two-year holding period refers to any other transaction for which the risk of loss is substantially diminished. To determine whether or not the two-year period is extended, it is necessary to determine whether the result of the subsequent transaction, whatever form it may take, is to substantially diminish the risk of loss at any time during the two-year period.[34]

Here are some exceptions to the related-party rules (such kinds of property dispositions will not be disqualified due to the related party rules):

- Dispositions due to the death of either related person.
- Involuntary conversions.
- Dispositions if it is established to the satisfaction of the IRS that neither the exchange nor the disposition has as its main purpose the avoidance of federal income tax.[35]

Tax Tip

The IRS requires related parties to a file Form 8824 for the two years following the year in which the exchange occurs as well as for the year of the exchange. If gain is realized as a result of a later disposition, the original return is not amended. Instead, the gain is recognized on the return for the year in which the disqualifying disposition occurred.[36]

Basis of Property Received

Note that the basis of the received property in the exchange is the same as the basis of the relinquished property. This is important for people who will be renting out the acquired property for depreciation purposes. After you complete Form 8824 for the exchange, your basis in the acquired property will be calculated and shown on Line 25.

Example

You exchange a piece of rental real estate with an adjusted basis of $250,000 for other rental real estate. The fair market value of both properties is $500,000. The basis of your new property is the same as the basis of your old property ($250,000, increased by any money paid or improvements or the like made to the property).

Refinancing

To have access to the equity tied up in the property, you should not refinance the relinquished property right before the exchange. If you do this, you must have a valid business reason for doing so or your exchange will be disqualified. The IRS has ruled that refinancing the relinquished property directly before completing the exchange constituted taxable boot to the taxpayer.[37] Instead, we recommend that you complete the exchange first, then refinance the replacement property to obtain the cash equity. You will then have the ability to do what you like with the proceeds and not have to worry about any adverse tax concerns.

Sale Expenses

How are sale expenses treated in a like-kind exchange? Certain expenses can be deducted from the exchange proceeds without resulting in any tax consequences. These expenses include the following[38]:

- Real estate commissions.
- Title insurance premiums.
- Legal and professional fees.
- Closing and escrow fees.
- Transfer taxes and notary fees.
- Recording fees.
- QI fees.
- Loan fees (relinquished property only).
- Title charges.
- Termite inspections.
- Courier fees.
- Escrow repairs.
- Survey fees.

Expenses that should not be deducted from the exchange proceeds include the following list. Instead, these items should be taken as a Form 1040/Schedule E adjustment and/or expense. Any points, discounts or origination fees are to be amortized over the life of the loan. The following are not deductible from the exchange proceeds:

- Points, discount and origination fees.
- Loan fees and application fees (replacement property only).
- Property taxes.
- Utilities.
- HOA fees.
- Hazard insurance.
- Prepaid rents and security deposits.
- Credit reports.
- Appraisal fees.
- Prepaid interest.
- Prepaid insurance.
- Lender reserves.

The following is a recap of six steps to follow to successfully complete your like-kind exchange (in the following order):

1. Engage a qualified intermediary to assist you with your exchange.
2. Ensure that the sale contract on the relinquished property is assignable and that the buyer is aware of such assignment.
3. Ensure that the exchange contract states the following:
   a. The seller of the relinquished property is performing a like-kind exchange.
   b. The buyer of the property is notified of the assignment.
   c. The buyer is released from any liabilities or expenses from the exchange.
4. The QI's like-kind exchange agreement should be executed before the closing.
5. The taxpayer must properly identify the replacement property under the 45-day rule.
6. The taxpayer must close on the replacement property within 180 days of the close of the replacement property or her tax return due date, whichever is earlier.

Tax Tip

Make sure that your tax advisor checks for the requirements for your exchange in the state you live in. Certain states have requirements that differ from the federal requirements to qualify for a like-kind exchange. For example, some states require that the replacement property be located in the same state as the relinquished property. Failure to follow these rules on the state level can disqualify your like-kind exchange for state purposes.

When *Not* to Use a Like-Kind Exchange

In certain circumstances, using a like-kind exchange does not make sense. One such circumstance is when you anticipate selling the property at a loss. Obviously, one of the main reasons for utilizing a like-kind exchange is to defer gain on the sale of the property. Another reason is that you might want to take advantage of selling at the low long-term capital gains rate of 15 percent (the current rate as of this writing). President Obama's tax policy is scheduled to raise long-term capital gain rates to at least 20 percent (to take effect in 2010). Last, remember that the basis of the relinquished property will be carried over and become the basis, for depreciation purposes, of the property being acquired. If the relinquished property had a basis of $50,000 and you acquire a new rental property for $350,000, the basis for depreciation purposes on the new property is only $50,000. You might want to consider the type of yearly depreciation deductions you will receive on the newly acquired property, because such deductions can result in a nice yearly tax deduction.

Conclusion

The rules associated with like-kind exchanges are relatively straightforward as far as the timing and sequence of events are concerned. The tax reporting, however, is far from straightforward. After reviewing this chapter, you should now be aware of the immense tax benefits that are available to taxpayers who want to exchange, rather than sell, their rental real estate properties. You should also be aware that these tax benefits come with a price in that you must satisfy all the specific rules to avoid a disqualification of your exchange. Given the lack of exceptions to these rules, we strongly recommend that you engage a qualified intermediary as early in the process as is possible. Most QIs know these rules and will assist you in making sure that no deadlines are missed.

The like-kind exchange provisions should be understood by all real estate investors due to the beneficial tax advantages they present. The successful use of these exchanges can result in thousands of dollars of tax savings in the year of the exchange. In addition, with proper tax and estate planning, it might be possible to completely avoid capital gains taxes in the future, all legally and according to IRS rules and regulations. Thus you can get the best of both worlds: current tax deferral along with future tax elimination.

CHAPTER 5

The Dealer Issue

There are specific tax rules associated with dealers—taxpayers who engage in real estate transactions on a full-time basis. This chapter discusses some of the rules concerning real estate investors who engage in a sufficient amount of activity in any year that they are considered to be dealers for tax purposes.

Being labeled a real estate dealer can have some very serious and usually negative tax consequences. Thus it is extremely important that you understand what a dealer is and how you can avoid this designation, if possible. If you are indeed a dealer, you can avoid some of the negative tax consequences of being one; toward that end this chapter discusses tax planning and business formation strategies.

What Is a Dealer?

A *dealer* is a person who holds real estate in the ordinary course of his or her business and anticipates very quick turnover and profits. The classic dealer is a person who engages in several "fix and flips" (a term used to describe buying a property, fixing it up, and, hopefully, selling the property very quickly) in one year. An *investor*, on the other hand, holds real estate for long-term appreciation or investment purposes. Whether or not you will be classified as a dealer is based on a "facts and circumstances" test. The Tax Court has set forth several factors that need to be analyzed to determine whether the dealer designation is appropriate. Note that interpreting the following factors moves us into one of the grayest areas of the tax laws:

- The amount and substantiality or number and frequency of real estate sales.
- The net profits received from sales for the year.
- The steps the owner has taken to sell the property through advertising, hiring a broker, and so on.
- The time spent on real estate compared to the owner's other jobs.
- The owner's intent for holding property determined at or near the time the owner initially purchases the property.
- The overall time and effort spent buying and selling.
- The extent of improvements made to the real estate.
- The length of time the property was held.
- Whether or not the taxpayer is a licensed real estate agent.
- The amount of gain, if any.
- The seller's reluctance to sell the property.
- The use of a business office for the sale of property.[1]

Example

Alex buys a home on January 2, 2009, for $100,000 because he believes it could be worth $150,000. He begins work on the property immediately and within two weeks he lists the property for sale at $150,000. He put $15,000 of improvements and repairs into the property, and within two months receives a full-price offer. Alex made $35,000 on this real estate deal and did several other similar deals throughout 2009. Alex would most likely be labeled a dealer due to his intentions when he purchased the properties. The amount of gains realized, the short-term holding periods, the number of deals he did, the quick advertising of his properties for sale, and the full-time nature of his work with respect to the real estate were all factors here.

Tax Consequences of Being a Dealer

Unfortunately, there are some negative tax consequences if you are labeled a dealer. Here are the primary negative ramifications:

- Dealer profits are not entitled to long-term capital gains rates. Instead, such profits are taxed at ordinary income rates, currently capped at a maximum of 35 percent. This is the case because the real property is presumed to be part of the business inventory and not held as an investment.[2]

- Dealer profits are subject to self-employment taxes (Social Security and Medicare taxes), currently taxed at 15.3 percent. These are taxes that are in addition to the federal income tax rates stated previously.[3]

- Dealers are not entitled to transfer property through a 1031 (like-kind) exchange (discussed in detail in Chapter 4).[4]

- Dealers cannot use the installment method of sale (discussed in detail in Chapter 6).[5]

- Dealers are not entitled to take depreciation deductions.[6]

- Dealers who report their profits and expenses on a Schedule C (as a sole proprietor) have a higher audit risk than do those taxpayers who do not file a Schedule C. This is one of the reasons we recommend that a dealer set herself up with a business entity (such as a limited partnership or corporation) for her real estate transactions.

With all these negative consequences, is there anything good about being a dealer? There is one very positive tax consequence: Dealer losses are not subject to the $3,000 capital loss limitations or any of the passive loss limitations to which investors are subject. Thus if a dealer has $100,000 of net losses for the year, $100,000 of these losses can be taken as ordinary losses on the tax return to offset any other ordinary income of the dealer (such as wages, interest, or the like). If an investor has $100,000 in losses for the year, only $3,000 of these losses can be taken in the year of sale to offset any ordinary income of the investor. Any balance left over must be carried forward and used in future years. In addition, one other slight benefit is that a dealer is permitted to claim an expense deduction, rather than using depreciation, for any ordinary and necessary costs incurred with respect to the property (because the properties are considered to be "inventory").

As you can see, being categorized as a dealer can be a tax nightmare. The one primary advantage that a dealer has is usually not enough to overcome all the significant negative factors stated previously. Also, most real estate dealers will not have losses from year to year, because their business is buying and selling real estate for short-term profits.

Let's discuss each of the previous points in more detail via an example to illustrate the problems with being a dealer.

Example

John holds property for one year and one day. John has a net gain of $40,000. If John sells the property as a dealer, he will have to pay ordinary income tax (John's tax bracket is 25 percent) on the profits as well as Social Security and

(Continued)

Medicare taxes (15.3 percent). John's total tax bill as a result of the sale would be approximately $16,120 (without any additional tax deductions), not including any state income taxes due on the sale. If John sold the property as an investor, he would only have to pay the 15 percent long-term capital gains tax on the profits. His total tax bill would be $6,000.

As shown in the example, John paid an additional $10,120 in tax simply because he sold the property as a dealer. John also cannot transfer the property through a like-kind exchange if he is a dealer, and he cannot take depreciation deductions if the property is held at any time as a rental.

Finally, as a dealer, if John wanted to sell this property on the installment sale method, he would be forced to pay tax on the entire gain in the year of sale, as opposed to paying tax only on the portion actually received.

Of course, the long-term capital gains rate might not be an issue if John is holding his property short term, since real estate investors who "flip" properties (that is, own the property for much less than one year) must report the sales as short-term capital gains and pay taxes at their ordinary income tax rates. However, real estate investors holding their property short or long term will certainly want to take advantage of some of the other benefits that are not available to real estate dealers as well as avoid the negative consequences.

Let's review a few court cases to see how courts have resolved the dealer issue for specific taxpayers.

The taxpayer in one particular case was classified as a dealer. The Tax Court's decision was based on the following factors[7]:

- The taxpayer devoted his time to residential development of real property on a full-time basis.
- The taxpayer entered into contracts for the construction of homes.
- The taxpayer had complete control over the homes and lots regarding price, type, and so on.
- The taxpayer handled the negotiations with buyers.
- The taxpayer attended the closings.
- The taxpayer's activities were exclusive, extensive, and full time.

The IRS will often challenge real estate transactions in an attempt to classify the taxpayer as a dealer. Given the difference in tax rates between capital gains (long-term gains taxed at 15 percent) and ordinary income tax rates (up to 35 percent), along with self-employment taxes (another 15.3 percent), there are often strong reasons for a taxpayer to fight the designation. Thus the Tax Court is often called in to resolve the dispute.

In one such case, the taxpayer sold a 1,050 acre parcel of land (he held 1,776 acres of land total) through his limited liability company. The property was acquired for residential development. The Tax Court held that the gain on the sale was a capital gain. The Tax Court noted here that the frequency and substantiality of sales are the most important factors in determining whether a sale was made in the ordinary course of business. The court held that the taxpayer did not hold the property in the ordinary course of business for the following reasons[8]:

- The taxpayer acquired the property with the intent and purpose of holding it for investment and appreciation.
- The sales of the property were unsolicited. The taxpayer did not hold broker or real estate licenses and did not advertise the property for sale.
- The taxpayer held the property for four years before selling off parcels. The taxpayer had only two sales of real estate during these four years.

The court noted that even though the taxpayer received substantially all his income in the year of sale from the sale of the property, this still did not mean that the taxpayer was selling in the ordinary course of his business. Thus, he received the more favorable capital gains tax rates.

In another case, the Tax Court was faced with a situation in which the taxpayer bought and sold real estate continuously and substantially from 1984 to 1986. The court determined that the taxpayer was a dealer and that the sales were in the ordinary course of his business for the following reasons[9]:

- The taxpayer employed 30 to 40 people to help manage his real properties.
- The taxpayer relied on brokers, escrow agents, and other agents to help execute the sale of his properties.
- The taxpayer sold 321 properties during a two-year period.
- The proceeds from the taxpayer's sales of properties exceeded $17.5 million.

Interestingly, the Tax Court stated that the lengthy holding period of the properties (an average of 58 months) was not dispositive of whether or not the taxpayer was a dealer. The court noted that not all gains from appreciation of real estate over a substantial period of time will be treated as capital gains.

The Supreme Court has also ruled on the dealer issue. The Court stated that property is "dealer property" or "primarily held for sale to customers" when that is the "principal purpose." In other words, when the property is "of first importance" or "principally" offered to the sale of customers as its chief purpose, it is considered dealer property.[10] The Court in this case (*Malat*) stated the following:

> The purpose of the statutory provision with which we deal is to differentiate between the "profits and losses arising from the everyday operation of a business" on the one hand (*Corn Products Co. v. Commissioner*, 350 U.S. 46, 52) and the realization of "appreciation in value accrued over a substantial period of time" on the other (*Commissioner v. Gillette Motor Co.*, 364 U.S. 130, 134). A literal reading of the statute is consistent with this legislative purpose. We hold that, as used in Section 1221(1), "primarily" means "of first importance" or "principally."[11]

Thus, based on the *Malat* case, if the "primary purpose" for purchasing the real estate is not for resale (i.e., as in a rental or investment property), the property is not dealer property. Many courts have stated that the purpose of acquiring the property is the most important factor in determining whether the property is dealer property.

In some cases the taxpayer might want to be classified as a dealer. For instance, one taxpayer wanted to be classified as a real estate dealer to use losses from real estate activities to offset other business income. The Court of Appeals found that the taxpayer was not in the trade or business of a being a real estate dealer. Thus, the taxpayer was precluded from offsetting his profits from his Schedule C business by his rental losses in calculating his self-employment tax. The court found that the taxpayer merely held real estate for investment or speculation and received rental income and thus was not a real estate dealer.[12]

The dealer issue is difficult because there is no definitive test to resolve the "dealer versus investor" dispute. Instead, the taxpayer's intent becomes very relevant in making this determination. However, it is often very difficult to know what the taxpayer's intent was with respect to any given real estate transaction. One way of measuring intent is to examine the frequency of sales. The Tax Court has stated that "the frequency of the taxpayer's sales is highly probative in the real estate context" because the presence of frequent sales ordinarily belies the contention that the property is being held "for investment or for personal purposes" rather than "for sale." In one such case, the facts revealed that the taxpayers sold only four properties over a 20-year period. The court stated that the "infrequency of sales is highly probative that the properties were held for personal or investment reasons rather than for sale."[13] The court concluded that the taxpayer's real estate activities, therefore, did not constitute real estate dealer activities.[14]

Some cases involve taxpayers who have jobs outside the real estate arena. One case involved a successful accountant who worked full time on the practice of that profession. He purchased 11 and sold 9 parcels of undeveloped land in four years. The court found that the taxpayer acquired such properties to hold and to sell later, when he could realize a satisfactory profit. The Tax Court found, therefore, that the taxpayer was not a real estate dealer. Specifically, the Tax Court noted the following[15]:

- The taxpayer did not hold himself out as a dealer in real estate.
- The taxpayer was not a licensed real estate broker.
- The taxpayer was not associated with a real estate company that advertised itself as such.
- The taxpayer was not listed in the phone book as a real estate dealer and did not maintain a separate office in which to conduct his real estate transactions.

In another such case, the Tax Court ruled that the taxpayer was engaged solely in investment activities in acquiring and selling real estate. The court noted the following[16]:

- The real property in question was not sold for four years after its acquisition.
- There were a total of three sales of real property, with the first two merely incidental to the final sale, which disposed of over 90 percent of the initial tract of land.
- The real estate was unimproved and the taxpayer made no attempt to improve or subdivide it.
- The court also noted that, although the real property might have been acquired with the ultimate intention of reselling it, this did not result in a determination that the property was held primarily for sale in the ordinary course of business. The court stated that the property must not only have been "held primarily for sale" but also for sale in the "ordinary course of business."[17]

Tax Tip

You can be an investor and a dealer at the same time.[18] That is, you can own some property as dealer property and other property as investment property. If you are unavoidably a dealer, you should be careful to keep separate your dealer property and your investment property. That way, only the dealer property will be subject to the negative tax consequences we've discussed. One way to successfully separate your dealer property and your investment property is by setting up various business entities to hold and separate the various properties. We discuss different business entity structures in Chapter 11.

Tax Planning Strategies

Now that you know what a dealer is for tax purposes (and hopefully you can now begin to make an informed decision about whether or not your real estate activities constitute dealer activities), what type of tax planning strategies will benefit you most? First, we discuss how to avoid being classified as a dealer so that you will not be subject to the negative tax consequences. Second, we discuss what business structures you should use to alleviate some of the negative tax consequences if dealer status is unavoidable.

Avoiding Dealer Status

Let's review again the factors the IRS looks at to determine dealer status and how you can structure your real estate dealings to avoid this classification:

- *The amount and substantiality or number and frequency of the sales.* You should try to hold properties for as long as possible to limit the number of sales for the year. It might be possible for you to use multiple business entities to keep sales in each entity at a minimum. In addition, you might want to place all your short-term sales into one business entity so that the dealer status only applies to this entity and not the rest of your holdings.

- *The net profits received from the sales for the year.* You might be able to minimize large profits by using multiple business entities to sell properties. However, you need to keep in mind that you must have a nontax reason for using multiple business entities. For many real estate investors, this is not difficult to do, since asset protection issues are often of paramount concern due to the risks real estate ownership brings with respect to lawsuits.

- *The steps the owner has taken to sell the property through advertising, hiring a broker, or the like.* You need to be sure to separate any investment property from dealer property into different business entities. You also should be sure to keep an accurate paper trail showing you tried to rent the property (if this is the case). In addition, you should make sure you document any unsolicited sales offers to support your position that you were not actively seeking to sell the property.

- *The time spent on real estate compared to other jobs the owner has.* You should get in the habit of keeping a time log to show your limited time spent on the properties compared to your other job(s). A time log is also needed for other reasons, including material participation rules. Many real estate investors have nonreal estate jobs and thus do not engage in real estate activities on a full-time basis. However, it is up to you to prove this to the IRS if your return is selected for audit.

- *Intent in holding the property.* Whether or not you are a dealer is often determined by your intention at the time you purchase the property. Thus, if you rent the property or try to rent the property before selling it, you will not likely be a dealer with respect to this property. You need to keep copies of any rental advertisements you use with respect to the property. If the property is vacant land, you can show your investment purpose by holding it as long as possible, to show you were seeking capital appreciation.

- *Time and effort in buying and selling.* Again, you need to maintain time logs and try to minimize the time you spend on real estate activities. The more time you spend, the more likely you will be classified as a dealer."

- *Extent of improvements made.* Do as little development as possible to the property. The IRS is aware of the "fix and flip" mentality of many real estate dealers, as the buy, renovate, and sell pattern is fairly common. If you are intending to rent the property and need to make improvements, this will not create a problem, since your intention was to make the improvements for rental purposes (investor) and not for a quick sale (dealer).

- *Length of time the property was held.* To avoid dealer status, you need to try to hold onto properties for as long as possible before selling them.

- *Whether the taxpayer is a licensed real estate agent.* Avoid holding yourself out as a real estate agent, broker, or dealer. Never hold yourself out as a dealer to the public.

- *Seller's reluctance to sell.* You should be sure to document your business dealings to show that you tried to rent the property before selling but that keeping the property was not practical. Keep documentation showing why the investment property was sold (for example, you moved, you needed cash because of a job loss, or the like), even though your original intent was to hold onto the property as an investment. In many instances, a sale will be the result of an unsolicited offer (too good to refuse).

Example

Caitlin purchased a four-unit apartment building for $250,000 on July 1, 2009. She kept the three current tenants and immediately advertised the vacant unit for rent. On September 1, 2009, Sam approached Caitlin and offered to buy the building for $325,000. Caitlin had no intention of selling the property, but the offer was too good to pass up. Caitlin would not be considered a dealer with respect to this sale.

- *Use of a business office for the sale of property.* Use a home office, if possible, instead of an outside office for your real estate transactions. In addition, you should not have a full-time office staff to assist in your real estate dealings. The more employees you have, the more likely you will be considered to be in the real estate business and thus be classified as a dealer.

Tax Tip

For the sale of nondealer property, you will report the sale on Form 4797 and Schedule D. Use Part I of both tax forms for the sale of property held longer than one year. Use Part II of both forms to report the sale of property held for less than one year.

Tax Alert

Acquiring a piece of property and renting it for a short period of time before selling it does not automatically categorize you as an investor. The most important thing the courts and IRS will look at is your intent or primary purpose for acquiring the property. For example, if your intent was to sell the property in the ordinary course of your business but you rented it for a couple months to avoid dealer status and you are challenged, you could lose investor status.[19]

Dealer Status and Number of Sales

We are frequently questioned as to "how many" properties need to be sold in any year before the taxpayer is categorized as a dealer. Many of our clients have been to real estate seminars and they are actually told that a set number of sales for the year will allow them to completely avoid dealer status and will guarantee them investor status (for example, they might tell you that if you sell five properties or fewer for the year, you are not a dealer). As discussed previously, whether or not you are a dealer is a "facts and circumstances" test. There is no set number that you can use to guarantee your status one way or another. Of course, if you only have a few sales for the year and the factors discussed previously do not point to you being a dealer, having only a few sales may very well secure your status as an investor. The point is that a set number of sales for the year is not definitive and will not control the answer to this question.

Dealer Entity Structuring

As previously discussed, if you are a real estate dealer, you absolutely do not want to buy and sell in your own name as a sole proprietor. If you do, you will be forced to file a Schedule C for your real estate activities, which will increase your overall audit risk, increase your taxes, and provide no asset protection. Instead, there are two types of entity structures that will serve you best: the limited partnership and the corporation (in limited circumstances). As stated previously, you will want to separate your dealer properties from your investor properties and keep them in different entities. Investors usually hold their properties in a limited liability company, not in a limited partnership or corporation. Setting yourself up as an entity will also reduce your audit risk, since corporations and limited partnerships are audited much less frequently than sole proprietorships. Business entities and their advantages for real estate investors are discussed in more detail in Chapter 11.

Conclusion

The "dealer versus investor" issue is very common for active real estate participants. Thus, it is very important that you understand the factors the IRS and the courts use to determine which category you fit into. To avoid the dealer designation, you should be sure to document your intention with every parcel of real estate you purchase. Did you buy the property to rent to others? Did you buy it to hold for long-term capital appreciation? Did you buy it because it was undervalued and you could make a quick profit? The answers to these questions, along with your actions immediately following the purchase, such as a quick "for rent" or "for sale" advertisement, will go a long way toward resolving the dealer issue.

CHAPTER 6

Installment Sales

When you sell your rental or investment property, the tax laws require you to report the sale and any net gain or loss on your Form 1040 (Schedule D; see copy in Appendix A).

Many real estate investors successfully use installment sales as a way to defer capital gains taxes, at the same time facilitating real estate sales (no bank or other lender besides the seller is involved). In addition, many sellers want to be able to defer capital gains taxes while generating a future income stream. The installment sales method permits a seller to accomplish both of these worthwhile goals. This chapter relates only to gains that occur as the result of a sale, since losses must be claimed in full (if at all) in the year of the sale and cannot be deferred over time via the installment sale method.[1]

What Is an Installment Sale?

An *installment sale* is simply a sale in which the seller receives at least one payment after the year of the sale.[2] In many cases, an installment sale is the result of the seller financing the buyer's purchase of a property. If the seller receives the payments over more than one year, she is permitted to elect not to use the installment sale method. If she chooses to opt out of this method, she must report all the income in the year of the sale, even though all payments were not received in this year. Although there could be some reasons for opting out (such as different tax brackets for short-term gains in different years, or perhaps the desire to utilize a large capital loss that is being carried forward from prior years), we generally do not recommend this option, since the installment sale method has the distinct advantage of being able to defer taxes on the sale until the payments are actually received.

Dealer Sales

If you are classified as a dealer for purposes of your real estate transactions, you are not permitted to use the installment sale method to report any of your sales. This rule applies to any sales in which you offer real property for sale to customers in the ordinary course of your trade or business (which would be real estate sales). For further information on whether you are considered a dealer for tax purposes, see Chapter 5.

Tax Calculations with Installment Sales

The tax calculations concerning installment sales often get complicated. This section discusses the basic requirements for computing and reporting the installment sale income. Installment sales are reported on Form 6252, a copy of which can be found in Appendix A. For each payment that you receive, you must determine how much of the payment represents: (1) interest; (2) return of principal or basis in the property; and (3) net capital gain. The amount reported for each of these three elements is important because there are completely different tax treatments for the three. The interest is reported like any other interest as ordinary income. An amortization table will be necessary in these situations so that the interest can be handled appropriately on the tax return. The return of capital (or basis) is not taxable at all, whereas the capital gains taxation is often reported as long-term capital gains (if the real estate was held for more than one year) and taxed at a 15 percent rate (short-term gains are still taxed at ordinary income tax rates, like any other properties held one year or less).

To compute your overall installment sale gains, the following formula should be utilized:

1. Gross sales price for property: $_____

2. Adjusted basis in property (see below): $_____

3. Selling expenses (see below): $_____

4. Depreciation recapture (see below): $_____

5. Add Lines 2, 3, and 4 (this is the adjusted basis): $_____

6. Subtract Line 5 from Line 1: $_____

If the amount on Line 6 is zero or less, you cannot use the installment sale method.

7. Enter sales price for property: $_____

8. Divide Line 6 by Line 7:   _____%

Line 8 represents the gross profit percentage. The gross profit percentage is needed to be able to compute how much of your payments are taxable.

The *adjusted basis* represents the amount of what your investment in the property represents for tax purposes. This amount is often the amount that you paid for the property. However, there are different rules for this number if you received the property as the result of a gift, inheritance, or like-kind exchange. The basis can also be increased if you make any major improvements to the property. We discussed these basis considerations in Chapter 1.

The *selling expenses* represent any amounts paid to others as a result of the sale of the property. Here are some common selling expenses:

- Real estate broker commissions.
- Attorney fees.
- Title charges (at closing).

If the property that was sold represents rental property that was subject to depreciation, you must recapture (include in income) any depreciation that was claimed or could have been claimed. This *depreciation recapture* must be done in the year of the sale (all is taxable in the year of sale). The depreciation is recaptured and taxed at a flat rate of 25 percent. Thus, even though you may receive payments for several years after the year of the sale, all depreciation must be recaptured in the actual year of the sale.

Example

Sara bought an investment home (which she rented out) for $200,000 in July 2007. In July 2009 she wanted to sell the property on the installment sale method. The price of the 2009 contract was $300,000. She claimed $10,000 of depreciation on the property and had selling expenses of $15,000 on the sale. Here is her overall calculation for installment sale purposes:

1. Gross sales price for property: $300,000
2. Adjusted basis in property: $200,000
3. Selling expenses: $ 15,000
4. Depreciation recapture (see below): $ 10,000
5. Add Lines 2, 3, and 4 (this is the adjusted basis): $225,000
6. Subtract Line 5 from Line 1: $ 75,000
7. Enter sales price for property: $300,000
8. Divide Line 6 by line 7:   25%

In this example, Sara would pay taxes on 25 percent of any payments received (after factoring in interest) at the 15 percent long-term capital gains rate for each year that payments are received. The interest rate should be specified in the real estate sales contract and note and should be at a fair market rate, especially if a related party is the purchaser. In addition, an amortization table should be used to compute the overall interest payments.

Installment Sales Between Related Parties

There are special rules if an installment sale is made between related parties. Though an installment sale is possible between related parties, there are special rules if the related party disposes of the property before all installment payments are due. In this instance, you must report all the income in the year in which the related party disposes of the property. Unfortunately, the rules here vary depending on the type of property sold. The following are considered related parties for purposes of the rules concerning installment sales involving depreciable property:

- A person and all entities that are controlled by such person (such as corporations and limited liability companies).

- A person and a trust in which the person or his or her spouse is a beneficiary. (Exception: This rule does not apply if the beneficial interest is a remote contingent beneficial interest.)

- An executor of an estate and a beneficiary of the estate, unless the sale is the result of a specific bequest in the will.

- Two or more partnerships in which the same person owns (either directly or indirectly) more than 50 percent of the capital interests or profits of the partnerships.

If you sell depreciable property to a related person (as defined previously), you generally cannot use the installment sale method unless you can demonstrate to the IRS that the avoidance of taxes was not one of the primary purposes of the sale. This is a difficult, but not impossible, burden to overcome. In most instances, the taxpayer will need to demonstrate a nontax avoidance reason for the installment sale. Typical nontax reasons include fiscal responsibility issues (see the following example) and other potential financial reasons.

Example

Robert owned 44 percent of a company that was approached for purchase by a competitor. Robert's attorney knew that Robert was prone to problems with handling money and set up a trust to handle the stock sale. Robert and his wife reported the stock sale on the installment sale method and the IRS challenged it. The Tax Court ruled that even though this was a related-party transaction, the use of the trust was for reasons other than tax avoidance (namely, fiscal responsibility for Robert's spouse and children).[3]

For purposes of later disposition rules (in which the buyer sells the property prior to making all required payments), related persons are much more broadly construed and include the following:

- Members of a family, including husband and wife, children, parents, grandparents and grandchildren, and brothers and sisters.
- A trust and its beneficiaries.
- A partnership and its partners.
- An estate and its beneficiaries.
- A trust and the grantor or owner of the trust.
- Corporations that are part of a controlled group of corporations (as defined in Section 267(f) of the Internal Revenue Code).
- The fiduciaries of two or more trusts if the same person who set up the trusts is the grantor of the trusts.
- The fiduciary and beneficiary of two or more trusts if the same person who set up the trusts is the grantor of both trusts.
- An executor of an estate and a beneficiary, unless the sale is the result of a specific bequest in the will.
- An S corporation and a C corporation if the same persons own more than 50 percent of the stock in each corporation.
- A corporation and partnership if the same persons own more than 50 percent of the stock in the corporation and 50 percent of the capital or profits in the partnership.
- Any two S corporations if the same person(s) owns more than 50 percent of the stock in each S corporation.
- The grantor and fiduciary, or the fiduciary and beneficiary, of any trust.
- An individual and a corporation if the individual owns more than 50 percent of the corporation's stock.
- A tax-exempt educational or charitable organization and a person who directly or indirectly controls the educational or charitable organization.
- A fiduciary of a trust and a corporation when the trust or the grantor of the trust owns, either directly or indirectly, more than 50 percent of the stock of the corporation.

Example

Caitlin sells her property to a related party for $800,000 using the installment sale method. She computes her gross profit percentage at 50 percent. These payments are to be made over 16 years at $50,000 per year (plus any applicable interest). When she receives $50,000 in the first year, she will pay tax on $25,000 of this income (50 percent of $50,000). If the related party subsequently disposes of the property in year two, Caitlin will be required to report the balance of $750,000 as income in year two. If she continues to receive payments in the future per the terms of the installment agreement, none of the principal would be taxable because it was all taxed in year two. She would, however, need to pay taxes on any interest received in these future years.

Advantages of an Installment Sale

There are several advantages of an installment sale from the seller's perspective. Here are the primary advantages:

- The seller can effectively control the timing and taxability of the sale proceeds. In addition, the seller may also be able to lower the overall tax rates if he is in a lower tax bracket in the future (either via planning using current tax laws or if future tax rate decreases occur).

- The seller is able to defer taxation on some of the capital gains associated with the sale of the property. The ability to do this is based on the terms of the note and the creativity and needs of the seller. For instance, using an interest-only note for 10 years with a balloon payment due at the end of the 10-year period effectively defers the capital gains for 10 years. The interest payments are taxed as ordinary income during the years they are received. Be aware, however, that a "reasonable" interest rate must be set to avoid problems with the IRS and what is known as *implied interest*. See IRC Section 483.

- The seller may be able to convert unproductive property into an interest-earning or income-generating property by creating an income stream from the property. This is often the case from vacant land or some other real property that is not currently being used to its maximum economic benefit for the owner.

- The seller is able to leverage money by not paying current taxes on the sale. This is the case because funds that would otherwise go to pay taxes can now be utilized to fund other investments, thus providing a source of leverage with respect to the funds.

- Buyers like installment sales in which there is owner financing with respect to the sale. The use of a seller-financed deal typically means fewer costs for the buyer, as there is no third-party lender involved. This means that many common lending fees, including points, administrative costs, and appraisal fees, are not required. In addition, it may be easier to sell the property and obtain a higher sales price due to the possibility of seller financing.

Tax Tip

A seller can allocate the interest rate and sales price based on what best suits him (and assuming that the buyer agrees). For instance, the receipt of interest generates ordinary income that is taxed at the seller's ordinary income tax rates (up to 35 percent), whereas capital gains are currently capped at a federal rate of 15 percent (assuming that the property was a long-term capital gain in that it was held more than one year before it was sold). Thus a seller may find it advantageous to receive a higher sales price from the buyer to obtain the favorable capital gains rates in exchange for a lower overall interest rate (which is taxed as ordinary income).

Disadvantages of an Installment Sale

Although installment sales are beneficial to most taxpayers, there are some disadvantages that you should be aware of prior to negotiating and entering into an installment sale. The following is a short list of the most common negative ramifications of using an installment sale from the seller's perspective:

- The buyer may default on the property and the seller will need to foreclose. Although the seller will eventually get the property back via the foreclosure, there are numerous state and local rules that must be followed to do so. These rules vary considerably from place to place, but they generally involve legal proceedings to gain possession of the property. Furthermore, although the timeframes involved in the foreclosure process have generally sped up, the seller is still faced with several months of legal maneuvering before possession is retained.

- There may also be problems concerning the timing of the payments received in the future. This can work both ways. On one hand, the buyer may pay off the note earlier than required. In this instance, the seller will have to pay more in capital gains taxes sooner than was expected. This is often the result of a downward change in interest rates (a buyer is likely to refinance a seller-carried note of 9 percent if the current commercial interest rates fall to 7 percent). There are ways to limit this possibility, including the use of a prepayment penalty. In addition, the seller has the ability to restructure the note and drop the interest rate to make the buyer less likely to want to refinance with a commercial lender.

- The seller could run into financial difficulties. It might be very difficult for him or her to be able to sell the note on the market (or get the buyer to pay off the note early) due to a lack of commercial liquidity concerning privately financed notes.

- There also could be problems if the buyer lets the property fall into a state of disrepair and then finally abandons the property. Not only would a foreclosure be necessary, but the seller would be receiving a property back that is worth less than the original sales price. It is possible to anticipate this problem in the drafting of the sale documents by allowing the seller the opportunity to inspect the property on a periodic basis. If this is done, the seller can require the buyer to make reasonable repairs (or face the possibility of an acceleration clause coming into play and calling the remaining amount as currently due under the note).

Opting Out of Installment Sale Reporting

You are not required to report an installment sale on the installment sale method. Instead, you may make an election to report the entire sale proceeds in the year of the sale rather than waiting until all payments are received. Although this might sound counterintuitive, there are some reasons it could be advantageous.

First, you may have a large capital loss carryforward deduction from a prior year, and opting out will not result in any capital gains taxes being due and payable. For instance, if you lost $100,000 in the stock market in 2009, you would be able to use only $3,000 of this amount per year against other ordinary income (such as wages, interest, dividends, and business income). If you sold an investment property under the installment sale method in 2010 and had a net total capital gain of $50,000, you could opt out of the installment sale method and choose to report the entire $50,000 gain in 2010. This would be totally offset by the remaining $97,000 of capital losses carried forward, and no taxes would be due and payable.

Second, you may have a net operating loss that is about to expire due to timeframes involved in carrying the net operating loss forward. Rather than lose this loss carryforward, you may be able to use it by opting out of the installment sale method for reporting the gains.

Finally, if you expect your tax rates to change in the future, either as a result of your income increasing or an expectation that Congress will raise taxes, accelerating the income may make very good financial sense.

To opt out of the installment sale method, you do not need to fill out Form 6252. Instead, you would report this sale on Schedule D or Form 4797, depending on the type of property that was sold. You make the election by the due date of your return, including extensions. If you miss this date, all is not necessarily lost, especially if this error is caught soon. The IRS permits you to amend your tax return within six months of the due date of your return, including extensions. At the top of your amended tax return, be sure to state the following: "Filed pursuant to Section 301.91200-2." Once you make this election, you must get the IRS's consent if you want to revoke it. This revocation is not guaranteed, and the IRS does not grant revocations on a routine basis.

Installment Sale of Your Primary Residence

If you decide to sell your primary residence using the installment sale method, you still may be able to exclude all or part of your gain. This will still depend on whether you satisfy the two-year ownership and use rules, along with the maximum exclusion amounts of $250,000 or $500,000, depending on marital and filing status. If you are eligible to exclude part of the gain, any amount that you exclude is not included in the gross profit percentage from the calculations, as shown previously.

Example

You are single and bought your home for $300,000 in 1999 and want to sell it for $700,000 in 2009. It was used as your personal residence for each of these years, and thus you qualify for an exclusion of the gains. Here is how you could calculate the installment sale using $250,000 of excluded gains:

1. Gross sales price for property ($700,000 –
   $250,000 sale price exclusion): $450,000
2. Adjusted basis in property: $300,000
3. Selling expenses: $ 25,000
4. Depreciation recapture: $ 0
5. Add Lines 2, 3, 4 (this is the adjusted basis): $325,000
6. Subtract Line 5 from Line 1: $125,000
7. Enter sales price for property: $450,000
8. Divide Line 6 by Line 7:   27.77%

In this example, Line 1 was listed as $450,000, which represents the $700,000 sales price less the amount of the exclusion ($250,000). Only 27.77 percent of any future payments of capital gains via the installment sale method would be taxed. The rest of the proceeds (not including interest) would represent a return of your original investment and would not be taxed.

Use of Escrow Account for an Installment Sale

In some instances the seller will require the buyer to pay all funds into a nonfundable escrow account, for which the funds are paid to the seller over a period of time. For tax purposes, this is not considered an installment sale, and the entire purchase price must be reported and taxed in the year of the sale. If the escrow account is established in a future year (after the year of the initial sale), the amount paid into escrow is considered a payment in full in the year the escrow account is established.

Example

You sell your real estate for $500,000 and receive $100,000 down, and the balance of the $400,000 is placed into an irrevocable escrow account. All $500,000 is considered to be received in the year of the sale, and no installment sale tax treatment is permitted.

Example

This scenario is the same as the previous example except that the $400,000 in payments is set up to be received over four additional years. This is an installment sale, and only $100,000 of the sale proceeds is reportable in the first year. If in year three an irrevocable escrow account is established, you must consider all payments in year three to have been made in that year, even though you may not actually get the funds for an additional two years.

Considerations Related to Installment Sales

In general, the seller will be able to control most of the terms of the installment sale in an attempt to alleviate any potential large problems down the road. Thus, you as the seller need to think like a commercial lender in terms of the lending process. You must be at ease with the buyer's ability to repay the loan, the value of the property and its acceptability in being used as collateral to secure the loan, and the specific provisions of the note itself. Although this can involve many different factors, most sellers are often concerned with the following:

- *The overall term (length) of the loan.* This decision depends simply on how soon you want to be paid in full. You could draft the loan for a short period (in months or a few years) or make the loan an "interest-only" loan for 30 years (in which case none of the capital gains would be taxed for 30 years, whereas the interest received would be taxed on an annual basis as received).
- *The overall loan-to-value ratio for the loan.* A *loan-to-value ratio* is simply the amount of the loan in relation to the overall sales price. Many commercial lenders do not want this value to exceed 80 percent, to limit their overall risk with the loan. Thus, if the sales price is $500,000, most

lenders would want to loan no more than $400,000 (80 percent of $500,000). The spread between the loan and property value is protection for the lender in the event of a foreclosure or a downturn in local property values. The lower the percentage for the loan-to-value ratio, the less risk for the seller. Often the local market or current economic conditions will dictate an acceptable level of risk with respect to this ratio. In addition, the type of property, such as residential versus commercial, will also come into play. This overall risk must be balanced with the tax ramifications, since a lower loan-to-value ratio will be better from a risk perspective, but a higher loan-to-value ratio (achieved with a lower down payment) will be better for tax deferral and planning.

- *Structuring the terms of the note, to reduce the chances of a foreclosure.* You should consult with a local real estate attorney to assist in drafting the terms of the note, at least for the first note that is done (and to review any notes done on the second and future installment sales). There are potentially major legal differences, depending on the geographic area of the property.

Certain clauses should always be considered. These include, among numerous other possibilities:

- Clauses for prepayment penalties (what happens if the buyer wants to pay off the note early?).
- Late fees and penalties (how much should you charge, and when are fees and penalties applicable?).
- Assumption clauses (what happens if the buyer wants to sell? can the new buyer assume the note?).
- Inspection provisions (to make sure the property is being kept in good working order; what happens if it is not?).
- Attorney fees (in the event that legal action is necessary to enforce one or more terms of the note).
- Due on sale or transfer clauses (what happens if the property is sold or otherwise transferred?).
- Insurance and tax requirements (so that the buyer pays the property taxes and keeps homeowners insurance in full place during the terms of the loan).

Default Under Installment Agreements

As we previously stated, one of the main problems with an installment sale is the possibility that the buyer will default on the installment sale and you will receive the property back. In general, you will keep the same adjusted basis in the property after you repossess it as you had before the original installment sale was made. This will have the net effect of limiting the amount of income you must report. If you do need to repossess the property after the sale, the tax calculations in the following formula will need to be made so that all income is properly accounted for and reported.

1. Enter the total of all payments received or treated as received prior to any repossession: $_____
2. Enter total gain already reported as income: $_____
3. Subtract Line 2 from Line 1: $_____
4. Enter gross profit on original sale: $_____
5. Enter costs of repossessing the property: $_____
6. Add Line 2 and Line 5: $_____
7. Subtract Line 6 from Line 4: $_____
8. Enter the lesser of Line 3 or Line 7. This is the taxable gain from the repossession: $_____

For purposes of the calculation for Line 1 (payments received or treated as received), the following are considered to be payments made by the buyer:

- Cash-down payments or deposits (even if made in a prior year).
- Cash at closing.
- Payments of any installment payments due for the current year.
- Options paid if considered to be part of a down payment.
- Early payments of future-year required payments.
- Fair market value of other property received in lieu of actual cash payments (a barter type of arrangement).
- Excess of any mortgages over the seller's basis in the property.
- Payments made by the buyer for taxes, liens, or other expenses if done for the benefit of the seller.
- Cancellation of debt to the buyer from the seller.
- Selling expenses of the seller paid by the buyer.

Example

Jack sells his property for $500,000 to Sam using the installment sale method. Jack's gross profit percentage is 50 percent. Sam pays the initial $100,000 and a portion of year two's payment ($25,000) and then defaults on his second payment in year two. Jack repossesses the property and needs to determine his taxable amount to report using the installment sale method and the repossession. He incurs $10,000 of legal fees in evicting Sam and repossessing the property.

1. Enter the total of all payments received or treated as received prior to any repossession: $125,000
2. Enter total gain already reported as income: $100,000
3. Subtract Line 2 from Line 1: $ 25,000
4. Enter gross profit on original sale: $250,000
5. Enter costs of repossessing the property: $ 10,000
6. Add Line 2 and Line 5: $110,000
7. Subtract Line 6 from Line 4: $140,000
8. Enter the lesser of Line 3 or Line 7; this is the taxable gain from the repossession: $ 25,000

Jack's basis in the property is now computed by adding the adjusted basis in the installment agreement to the repossession costs and the taxable gain on the property. To compute his adjusted basis in the property, he needs to multiply the unpaid balance of the installment sale by the gross profit percentage. This amount is subtracted from the unpaid balance of the installment sale. Here is how this would compute:

1. Unpaid balance of installment sale: $375,000
2. Gross profit percentage: 50%
3. Multiply Line 1 by Line 2 (adjusted basis): $187,500
4. Repossession costs: $ 10,000
5. Taxable gain on the property: $ 25,000
6. New adjusted basis of property (add Lines 3, 4, and 5): $222,500

If Jack decides to sell the property again, he can use the amount of time he held the property prior to transferring it to Sam as part of his holding period. Any period of time that Sam owned the property would not be counted for purposes of determining whether the overall capital gain was long or short term.

Conclusion

The use of the installment sale method can produce some favorable tax consequences for real estate sellers. However, with the positive attributes come some potential pitfalls. We hope that you understand all the ramifications of using installment sales prior to actually using this method with any of your real estate sales. By thoroughly understanding how installment sales work, you will be able to integrate them into your real estate holdings and use them when the situation dictates.

CHAPTER 7

Passive Activity Rules Related to Real Estate

The passive activity loss limitations may limit the amount of a tax deduction you can take related to your real estate activities. Thus it is essential that you understand these limitations and that you engage in tax planning techniques to minimize the negative impact these rules can have.

Generally, you can deduct passive activity losses only from passive activity income. Any excess losses are then carried forward from year to year indefinitely until the passive losses can be utilized (either through eventual disposition of the property or through future passive income).

Tax Tip

The at-risk rules also must be applied before you can deduct any losses on your tax return. The at-risk rules are discussed in more detail later in this chapter.

The passive activity rules apply to:

- Individuals.
- Estates.
- Trusts.
- Corporations.
- Owners of partnerships, LLCs, and S corporations.[1]

What are passive activities? IRS Publication 925 defines a passive activity as:

- A trade or business in which you do not materially participate during the year.
- Rental activities, even if you do materially participate in them, unless you are a real estate professional.

Passive income does not include the following:

- Income from a nonpassive activity.
- Income from oil or gas property (unless the taxpayer holds the interest in this income-producing activity in an entity that limits personal liability, such as a limited partner interest in a limited partnership or stock in a corporation or other entities that, under state law, limit personal liability).
- Income from patents and copyrights.
- State, local, and foreign income tax refunds.
- Cancellation of debt income.
- Income from a covenant not to compete.
- Personal service income, including:
  - Salaries.
  - Wages.
  - Commissions.
  - Self-employment income.
  - Deferred compensation.
  - Social Security income.
  - Retirement benefits.
  - Guaranteed payments from partnerships or LLCs for personal services.
- Portfolio income, including:
  - Interest.
  - Dividends.
  - Annuities.
- Royalties not received in the ordinary course of a trade or business. The following activities are not passive activities:
  - A trade or business in which you do materially participate for the year.
  - A rental property that you also use for personal purposes for more than 14 days, or 10 percent of the number of days during the year that the property was rented for fair market value.
  - Rental real estate activities for real estate professionals (discussed later in this chapter).

To determine whether you materially participated in an activity for the year, you must meet one of the following tests:

- You participated in the activity for more than 500 hours for the year.
- Your participation in the activity was substantially all the participation of all individuals who participated in the activity for the year. (This test involves activities for which fewer than 500 hours were needed for the year.)
- Your participation in the activity was more than 100 hours for the year and you also participated in the activity at least as much as any other individual for the year.
- The activity is a significant participation activity in which you participated for more than 500 hours for the year. A *significant participation activity* is a trade or business in which you participated for more than 100 hours for the year and in which you did not materially participate under the other material participation tests, other than this test.
- The activity is a personal service activity in the field of law, health, engineering, architecture, accounting, actuarial science, performing arts, consulting, or any other trade or business in which capital is not an income-producing factor and you materially participated for any three preceding tax years (that is, this is likely to be your job rather than an investment).
- You materially participated in the activity for any 5 of the prior 10 years. This time does not have to be consecutive.
- Under the facts and circumstances, you participated in the activity on a regular, continuous, and substantial basis for the year. This time cannot be fewer than 100 hours for the year.

Note that you cannot count your time in managing the activity to determine whether you materially participated if you paid a management company to manage the activity or if any other person spent more time managing the activity than you did.

Participation

The IRS defines *participation* as "any work you do in connection with an activity in which you own an interest."[2] The work must be of the type that is customary for that type of business and not done to avoid the passive activity limitations. Your participation in the activity will include your spouse's participation, even if your spouse had no ownership interest in the activity.[3]

Participation as an investor does not count toward the participation rules. To count your time as participation, you must be directly involved in the day-to-day operations of the business.

Rental activities are considered passive activities, even if you do materially participate for the year. There is an exception to this rule for individuals who qualify under the real estate professional provisions discussed later in this chapter. A *rental activity* is defined as "an activity in which tangible property (real or personal) is used by customers and the gross income is for such use of the property under a contract or lease."[4]

The Active Participation Exception

There is an exception to the general rule that passive activity losses can be deducted only against passive activity income for rental real estate activities. This rule applies to rental real estate activities in which you actively participate for the year. If you actively participate in your rental real estate activity, you are allowed to deduct up to $25,000 ($12,500 for married taxpayers who file separately) of losses from the activity on your tax return every year. This $25,000 can be taken as a deduction to offset ordinary income from wages, interest, S corporation income, and so on. This is a special allowance that can result in a very nice tax deduction on your return. There are some limitations to this special allowance.

Tax Tip

Married taxpayers are entitled to the full $25,000 exception per year if they qualify. Single individuals are entitled to $25,000 per year. If you are married and file separate tax returns and lived apart from your spouse the entire year, you are allowed to deduct only $12,500 for the year. If you are married and file separate returns and lived with your spouse at any time during the year, you cannot use the special allowance to reduce any ordinary income or tax on ordinary income.

Example

Tom and Jane, married taxpayers, have $90,000 in wages, $1,500 from interest and dividends, and $29,000 from rental activities losses. Tom and Jane actively participated in their rental activities for the year. Tom and Jane's modified adjusted gross income for the year is less than $150,000. Tom and Jane can take a $25,000 rental activity loss on their tax return for the year. This $25,000 will directly offset the $90,000 in wages they earned for the year. The remaining $4,000 of rental losses will be carried forward, to be utilized in a future tax year.

Modified Adjusted Gross Limitation

The $25,000 maximum special allowance ($12,500 for married individuals filing separate returns) is reduced by 50 percent of the amount of your modified adjusted gross income that exceeds $100,000 ($50,000 if you are married filing separately). If your modified adjusted gross income is $150,000 or more ($75,000 if you are married filing separately), you will be completely disqualified from using the special allowance. If you are disqualified, you can carry the disallowed loss forward until it can be used in the future.

Modified adjusted gross income is calculated as follows:

Adjusted gross income (as shown on Line 37 of your Form 1040 and not including rental real estate losses), less:

- Taxable Social Security and Tier 1 Railroad retirement benefits.
- Deductible Contributions to IRAs and Section 501(c)(18) pension plans.
- The exclusion from income of interest from qualified U.S. savings bonds used to pay qualified higher education expenses.
- The exclusion from income of amounts received from an employer's adoption assistance program.
- Passive activity income or loss included on Form 8582.
- Any rental real estate loss allowed because you materially participated in the rental activity as a real estate professional.
- Any overall loss from a publicly traded partnership.
- The deduction for one-half of the self-employment tax.
- The deduction allowed for interest on student loans.
- The deduction for qualified tuition and related expenses.

The result equals modified adjusted gross income.

Example

Jim and Sara, married taxpayers, had the following income in 2009:

- $100,000 wages
- $25,000 rental losses
- $1,500 dividends
- $1,000 interest

Jim and Sara's modified adjusted gross income is $102,500. Neither Jim nor Sara is a real estate professional; therefore, they can deduct only $23,750 of

(Continued)

the rental losses they have incurred for the year. The remaining $1,250 will be carried over to the next tax year. The calculation is as follows:

Modified adjusted gross income:	$102,500
Less amount not subject to phase-out:	$100,000
Amount subject to phase-out:	$ 2,500
Multiply by 50% ($2,500 × 0.50):	$ 1,250
Reduction to special $25,000 allowance:	$ 1,250
Maximum special allowance:	$ 25,000
Minus reduction:	$ 1,250
Adjusted special allowance:	$ 23,750
Rental loss:	$ 25,000
Adjusted special allowance:	$ 23,750
Amount to carry forward to next year:	$ 1,250

If their modified adjusted gross income was less than $100,000, Jim and Sara could use the entire $25,000 loss in 2009.

Real Estate Professionals

As stated previously, any rental real estate activity, even if you materially participated, is generally considered a passive activity subject to the passive activity limitations. Real estate professionals who materially participated in rental real estate activities for the year do not fall under the passive activity limitations. Instead, real estate professionals are not subject to the $25,000 loss limitation, and all losses from their rental real estate activities can be deducted in full. This means that all your losses from rental real estate activities for the year can be taken against ordinary income such as:

- Wages.
- Interest and dividends.
- Pension and retirement income.
- Sole proprietorship income.
- S corporation distribution income.

Example

Tom is a full-time real estate agent. He earned $170,000 in wages in 2009. He also had a $60,000 loss from rental real estate activities in 2009. If Tom meets the real estate professional requirements stated in a moment, he will be able to deduct the entire $60,000 loss from his rental real estate activities against his $170,000 in wages. If Tom is not a real estate professional, none of the $60,000 in losses can be deducted, since Tom's modified adjusted gross income exceeds the $150,000 threshold stated previously. Instead, all of the $60,000 loss would need to be carried forward to future tax years.

Tax Tip

If you meet the real estate professional requirements for the year, you will treat all your losses for the year as regular losses. You will also complete Line 43 of Schedule E and attach it to your Form 1040, as well as make an election to be treated as a qualifying real estate professional and attach the election to your return, as explained shortly.

To qualify as a real estate professional, you must meet the following two requirements:

- More than half the personal services you performed in *all* trades and businesses for the year were performed in real property trades or businesses.

and

- You performed more than 750 hours of services for the year in real property trades or businesses in which you materially participated.

Note that any personal services performed as an employee in real property trades or businesses will not count unless you are more than a 5 percent owner of your employer via stock ownership or capital or profit interest.

Qualifying real estate businesses include:

- Real property development.
- Construction.
- Rental properties.
- Real property leasing.
- Real property management.
- Real property conversion.
- Real property brokerage.

A closely held C corporation will satisfy the test if, during the tax year, more than 50 percent of the gross receipts for its tax year came from real property trade or businesses in which the corporation materially participated.

If you are filing a joint tax return for the year, you will not count your spouse's personal services to determine whether you meet the real estate professional requirements. You can, however, count your spouse's participation in an activity to determine whether you materially participated in an activity. If either spouse (on a jointly filed tax return) qualifies as a real estate professional, both spouses will benefit in that there are no limitations to the amount of losses that can be claimed.

Example

Tom works in real estate activities 50 hours for the year. Tom's wife works in real estate activities 51 hours for the year. Tom can add his wife's 51 hours to his 50 hours to meet the 100-hour material participation requirement. However, Tom would not qualify as a real estate professional under these facts since he does not meet the annual 750-hour test.

Example

This scenario has the same facts as the previous example except that Tom is a full-time real estate broker who works 2,000 hours per year (50 weeks × 40 hours/week). He would thus qualify as a real estate professional because more than $1/2$ of all his services for the year were for real estate activities and the total time was more than 750 hours.

Calculating Your Time

As stated previously, to qualify as a real estate professional you must meet two tests: the half-time test and the 750-hour test. You should first calculate whether you will meet the material participation test, stated previously, before you go on to calculate the more difficult time tests discussed here.

Example

Tom is a real estate agent and earned $170,000 in 2009. Tom worked 1,100 hours for the year as a real estate agent. He also worked 200 hours managing his rental real estate properties. Tom also worked as a part-time musician for 100 hours for the year, for which he earned $10,000. Tom calculates his time as follows:

50 percent test: 1400 total hours worked × 50% = 700 hours

750-hour test: 1300 > 750 hours

Tom meets the 750-hour test because he has worked 1300 hours in real estate businesses for the year. He also spends more than half his time in real estate businesses (1300 total hours worked in his real estate business is more than half his time of 700 hours worked for the year). Thus Tom can deduct all his rental real estate losses for the year, even if they exceed $25,000 and even if his modified adjusted gross income is higher than $150,000.

Note that if you are a real estate professional, each interest you have in a rental real estate activity will be treated as a separate activity unless you make an election to treat all your rental real estate activities as one activity. The election is binding on all future tax returns unless you have a material change in facts and circumstances. You must provide a written statement on your tax return if you want to revoke this election.[5]

Tax Tip

The election to treat all your activities in rental real estate as one single activity must be attached to your tax return in the year you are making the election. A text statement that reads as follows should be attached to the return:

Pursuant to IRC Section 469 (c)(7), the taxpayer, *<your name>*, a qualifying taxpayer under IRC Section 1.146-9(g)(3), elects to treat all activities in real estate as one activity.

The failure to make this election and attach it to your tax return can result in serious negative tax consequences. Namely, the IRS can treat all your interests in rental real estate activities (which you meant to group together) as multiple activities. This would result in the requirement to show that you met the two time tests for each of your rental real estate activities individually, an extremely difficult task!

Proof of Participation

You need to keep a written log of your daily activities to show that you met the time requirements as a real estate professional or under the material participation tests stated previously. The IRS states that any "reasonable method" will be accepted as proof. Your summary should include the amount of time spent per day on the activity and what you did. Note that in Tax Court many taxpayers have lost the argument that they were real estate professionals when they did not keep such a log. Do not let this happen to you. Keep a working log with you at all times. Just as you are required to keep a mileage log for auto expenses, you must keep a log of your real estate activities. "Ballpark guesstimates" of your time spent on real estate activities are not allowed.[6]

The IRS is targeting real estate professionals; thus, any taxpayer claiming this status on her tax return needs to be aware of heightened IRS scrutiny. The IRS is now auditing more and more real estate professionals, and they are using internal guidelines and technical advice memoranda to disqualify many hours of real estate professional activities. The IRS is using this advice and internal guidance to review every hour of activity that taxpayers claim and then disallowing many hours so that the taxpayer cannot meet either the 750-hour test or the one-half-time test. If you are claiming this status on your tax return, be aware that certain items on your tax return can red-flag your return for an audit:

- One or both taxpayers show a high wage amount on the Form 1040. This indicates that the taxpayer(s) have full-time job(s) and usually will not be able to spend more than half their time on real estate.

- The taxpayer(s) show rental properties that are out of state and a property manager is utilized. The IRS will check the Schedule E on the tax return and check whether both the property management expense lines are completed, as well as where the property is located. The IRS is currently making the claim that any time spent with property managers does not count toward real estate professional time since it indicates that the taxpayer did not materially participate in the property. This is another good reason to hold your rental property in a separate entity (discussed later); doing so will eliminate the Schedule E from your personal tax return (and instead will be reported on a separate tax return).

- Large travel expenses are listed on Schedule E. The IRS is currently making the argument that time spent looking for new properties does not count as real estate professional time and instead is considered investment time.

- The election to aggregate is not made. The IRS will check to see whether an election is made to treat all rental activities as a single activity for material participation purposes. If this election is not attached to the tax return, the IRS will require that the taxpayer spent 500 hours on each rental property.

- One or both taxpayers are limited partners in a limited partnership that has real estate rentals. The IRS will check to see whether you are a partner in a limited partnership and at the same time claiming the real estate professional status. Limited partners are not allowed to actively participate in the business of the limited partnership and thus are not allowed to claim the real estate professional status.

- The occupation line on the tax return does not state that either taxpayer is in real estate. The IRS is checking the occupation line on the tax return (Page 2 of the 1040, next to the signature line) to see whether the taxpayer and spouse have indicated that they are real estate professionals.

Obviously, it is crucial that you work with your tax advisor to minimize the impact of the previously stated factors on your audit risk. If you have been selected for audit and your real estate professional status is being challenged, it is urgent that you contact a competent tax professional immediately. Due to special concerns with this kind of audit, you will not want to go it alone!

Former Passive Activities

If you change your activity from passive in one year to nonpassive in another based on the material participation rules, you can deduct the prior year's disallowed losses from the activity up to the amount of your current year's income. Any remaining prior-year losses that are being carried forward will continue to be carried forward like any other passive loss.

Example

Jordan is a passive real estate investor and has $40,000 of passive losses from her 2008 tax return that she could not claim. In 2009, she decides to work her real estate activities on a full-time basis. Thus, on her 2009 tax return, she is permitted to use the $40,000 of prior disallowed losses to reduce her other income.

Dispositions

If you sell a piece of property that was a passive activity, such as a rental property, the gain on the disposition is generally passive activity income. This is true if, at the time of the disposition, the property was used in a passive activity.

If the property was used in more than one activity (that is, passive and nonpassive) for the 12 months prior to the disposition, the gain on the disposition must be allocated between the activities on a basis that is "reasonable." An allocation of such gain will be considered to reasonably reflect the activity if the fair market value of your interest in the property is not more than the lesser of:

- $10,000.

or

- Ten percent of the total of the fair market value of your interest in the property and the fair market value of all other property used in the activity immediately before its disposal.[7]

There is an exception to the rule if you have disposed of substantially appreciated property. The gain is passive activity income if the fair market value of the property at disposition was more than 120 percent of its adjusted basis and either of the following apply:

- Your use in the property was passive for 20 percent of the time that you had an interest in the property.

or

- Your use in the property was passive for the entire 24-month period before its disposition.

If neither of these conditions apply, the gain is not passive activity income. It is portfolio income only if you held the property for investment for more than half the time you held it as nonpassive income.

How to Capture and Deduct Prior-Year Carryforward Losses

As stated earlier, passive losses not utilized in the year they were incurred due to the modified adjusted gross income phase-out rules discussed previously must be carried forward until either the phase-out does not apply or you have passive income to utilize against the carryforward losses. Any passive activity losses that have not been allowed in prior years, however, are allowed in full in the year you dispose of your entire interest in the property of a passive activity. Your entire interest must be disposed in the activity and all gain or loss must be recognized for the losses to be allowed. Also, you cannot dispose of the property to a related party.

Example

Tom has $100,000 of wages and owns one rental property. In 2009, he sells his entire interest in the rental property to an unrelated person for $150,000. His adjusted basis in the property is $100,000. Tom was carrying forward passive losses of $25,000 from prior years. Tom's deductible carryover loss for 2009 is $25,000, calculated as follows:

Sales price:	$150,000
Minus adjusted basis:	$100,000
Equals capital gain:	$ 50,000
Less carryover loss:	$ 25,000
Equals capital gain:	$ 25,000

The carryover losses thus allow Tom to reduce his overall capital gain to $25,000. The tax savings here would be $3,750 ($25,000 × 0.15) if the property was held on a long-term basis and more if it was a short-term capital gain.

Carryforward losses are to be taken first against the gain recognized on the disposition of an interest in a passive activity. If the suspended losses exceed the gain recognized on the disposition of an interest in a passive activity, the excess is used against the following types of income, in the following order:

- Net passive activity income or gains.
- Nonpassive income or gains.

Example

Tom sells a rental property to an unrelated party for $250,000. Tom's adjusted basis is $225,000. Tom is also carrying forward passive losses of $30,000. Tom's realized gain is $25,000. His deductible carryover loss is $30,000. Tom also has $5,000 of rental income from another rental property he owns. The calculation is as follows:

Sale price:	$250,000
Minus adjusted basis:	$225,000
Equals capital gain:	$ 25,000
Less suspended losses:	$ 30,000
Equals capital loss:	($ 5,000)

The remaining $5,000 loss that exceeds the gain on the sale can now be used to offset other income: first, passive income or gain, then nonpassive income or gains. Since Tom has $5,000 of other rental income (considered passive income), he can now utilize the remaining $5,000 to wipe out this $5,000 of passive rental income.

Tax Tip

One of the best ways to utilize any passive losses that you are carrying forward is to dispose of a piece of passive real property and recognize a gain. As shown previously, you can then offset any gain on the sale from prior-year passive loss carryovers. Otherwise, it could take you several years to utilize the losses being carried over. Smart tax planning will help you utilize such losses, which would otherwise take you years to recover.

You will generally use two forms to report the sale or other disposition of real property: Form 4797 and Schedule D.

> **Compliance Tip**
>
> Form 4797: Sales of Business Property is used to report the dispositions of property held in a trade or business. For real estate purposes, rental real estate is considered to be held in a trade or business.

> **Compliance Tip**
>
> Schedule D: Capital Gains and Losses is used to show the sale of capital assets. Capital assets are assets held for investment purposes, such as stocks and some real estate.

> **Compliance Tip**
>
> Form 8582 also must be completed to determine the passive activity limitations for any rental properties that have losses for the year. It must also be used to report any carryforward losses from prior years. Real estate professionals do not need to complete Form 8582, because all their losses from rental real estate activities are allowed for the year. Only individuals subject to the passive loss limitations will complete Form 8582.

> **Tax Tip**
>
> The forms can be confusing to prepare. We do not recommend you prepare these forms yourself unless you are an experienced tax preparer. Do yourself a favor and save yourself headaches by having a competent tax professional prepare your tax return and these forms for the year.

At-Risk Limitations

The at-risk rules limit any losses you can take for the year from most activities to the amount you have at risk in the activity. The at-risk rules must be applied first before any passive loss limitations are determined.

Any loss that is disallowed because of the at-risk limitations is to be treated as a deduction in the next tax year. If your losses from an at-risk activity are allowed, they are subject to recapture in later years if your amount at risk in the activity goes below zero.

Definition of Loss for the At-Risk Rules

A *loss* is defined as:

The excess of allowable deductions from the activity for the year (including depreciation or amortization allowed or allowable and disregarding at-risk limits) over income received or accrued from the activity during the year. Income does not include income from the recapture of previous losses.[8]

What this means is that a real estate investor cannot lose more than he or she has invested into the property. These rules cover individuals, partners, and shareholders of corporations.

Example

Tom buys a rental building for $150,000. He puts down $10,000 in cash and gives the seller a $140,000 nonrecourse note. Because Tom has only invested $10,000 for which he is liable, he is only allowed to take a deduction up to this amount. Tom will only be allowed to take up to $10,000 of losses total from any deductions the property has that generate losses (depreciation, taxes, and so on). If Tom instead took out a recourse note, one for which he is personally liable, he would have been able to take losses of up to $150,000 that he personally invested and for which he is liable.

Tax Tip

Use Form 6198, At-Risk Limitations, to determine how much of your loss you can take as a deduction for the year. Form 6198 must be attached to your tax return if:

- You have a loss from an activity that is subject to the at-risk rules.

and

- You are not at risk for some of your investment in the activity.

Dispositions and Installment Sales

If you sell a piece of real estate using the installment sale method and the real estate had passive losses that were being carried forward, the losses being carried forward can be utilized to offset any gain from the installment sale over a period of time. The losses are allowed only to the extent that they bear the same ratio as the gain, as calculated in the year of the installment sale.

This means that if you sell a piece of passive activity property, such as a rental property, that has losses being carried forward, the losses must be spread out over the installment contract period instead of being deductible in full in the year of sale. This does, however, give you some planning options with installment sales, since the passive activity losses that were carried forward will get to be utilized.

Conclusion

The passive activity rules can be very confusing due to the numerous material participation rules and exceptions. However, do not let this deter you. As long as you are aware that these rules exist, you can know exactly what you need to do to get around any limitations. Thus, after reading this chapter, it should be apparent that an accurate time log is indispensable if you need to prove the extent of your participation in real estate activities. Furthermore, you should now be aware of what you must do to qualify as a real estate professional. Once you understand how these rules apply to your personal tax situation, you will be able to plan so that you can use all tax losses in the most advantageous ways possible.

CHAPTER 8

Trusts, Trusts, Trusts!

Land Trusts, Private Annuity Trusts, and Charitable Remainder Trusts for Real Estate Investors

Real estate investors often use trusts for tax planning, asset protection, and business planning reasons. Furthermore, in today's world, the number of lawsuits is growing at an alarming rate. Asset protection has become increasingly popular as a way to avoid the serious consequences of lawsuits and to protect one's wealth. Trusts are often used by real estate investors as part of a defense mechanism to help preserve their wealth by avoiding taxes and minimizing their risks of lawsuits. There are several varieties of trusts. In this chapter we discuss the trusts that are often used in connection with real estate activities.

Land Trusts

A land trust can be a very powerful tool in an overall asset protection plan for your real estate holdings. When properly utilized, land trusts can provide more benefits for your real estate than you might have thought possible.

A *land trust* is a device by which legal title and beneficial title to real property are divided between a trustee and a beneficiary. Generally, the purpose of a land trust is for privacy of ownership of real property and not for tax planning purposes. The reason is that land trusts are disregarded for tax purposes and thus provide no additional tax savings. The real property that is placed into a land trust will first need to be transferred to a trustee who will hold legal title to the property but who will not retain control or have management decisions over the property. The beneficiary of the land trust will retain the management and control of the property.

The beneficiary still has rights to possession, profits, management, and the like, as though he still owned the property. The trustee cannot make any decisions without written direction from the beneficiary. The beneficiary's interest is personal property, not real property, since the trustee has legal and equitable title to the property.

Many states have enacted specific land trust statutes specifying that the beneficial interests under a land trust are personal property and not real property. Most states that have enacted land trust laws have modeled their laws after Illinois, since land trust law emanates from that state. Illinois also has the most extensive case law regarding land trust usage, and because of this case law Illinois has been slowly chipping away at the privacy and other benefits a land trust provided. It is for this reason we recommend that a land trust be formed in a state other than Illinois. Other states such as Virginia, Nevada, Florida, and Delaware have favorable land trust statutes; we recommend forming a land trust in one of these states.

Land trusts are created through two agreements. First, a deed in trust will convey legal title to the trustee. Second, a trust agreement will designate the arrangement between the trustee and the beneficiary. The trust agreement will limit the trustee's authority and will protect the beneficiary's authority over the property. The trustee cannot act without written direction from the beneficiary or face personal liability.

Land trusts are used for several purposes and have the following four advantages:

1. *To preserve the anonymity of the owner of the real property.* Land trusts preserve the anonymity of the real property owner because the owner's name never appears on the public records of the property. Only the trustee's name will appear. The trustee of the property is frequently an entity the beneficiary owns (such as an LLC or corporation). However, the trustee can be any person or entity the beneficiary designates. The trustee cannot disclose the name of the beneficiary without a court order. You, as beneficiary, never need disclose that you own the property, because you do not! If you have tenants on your property that is held in a land trust, this can be very powerful, since lawsuits are frequently generated by tenants against owners of property simply because tenants think owners are wealthy. You can simply hold yourself out as property manager and not owner of the property. A land trust gives you the ability to keep your real estate ownership private, thus providing a deterrent to lawsuits.

2. *To avoid transfer taxes.* A land trust can also help you avoid transfer taxes in certain states or counties. Most counties charge transfer fees whenever title to real estate is transferred from one owner to another. However, a land trust is not considered real estate; instead, it is considered personal property. Thus, in some states or counties, sellers and buyers can avoid transfer taxes when real property is transferred to a land trust.

3. *To aid in the administration of the beneficiary's estate.* Land trusts can help avoid lengthy probate because the trust agreement, not the will, governs the ownership of the property. Thus, the property will not be included in the probate estate. Title to the property will immediately vest on the beneficiary's death based on the trust agreement.

4. *To avoid the due-on-sale clause of a mortgage.* Land trusts are not subject to the due-on-sale clause in real estate mortgage contracts. A *due-on-sale clause* allows a mortgage lender to call the entire unpaid loan balance due and payable immediately, should the property securing the loan be sold, transferred, traded, gifted, or otherwise disposed of without the lender's prior written consent. Property transferred into a land trust is not considered to be "sold, transferred, traded, gifted or otherwise disposed of" under most state laws. Thus, the transfer of the property into a land trust will not trigger the due-on-sale clause. However, you should research this issue for your state's laws because the laws differ from state to state.

These are only some of the benefits of forming a land trust!

You can form your land trust in a state different from where the property is located. This is recommended because it provides an additional deterrent from creditors locating the trust and its property. For example, if you have property located in Colorado (where there is no specific land trust statute), you could form your land trust in Virginia (a state that has beneficial land trust laws). However, be sure to make your trustee (at least for the first year) a person or company residing in the state you use for your trust, so you can show a nexus to that state if you were ever sued.

Certain factors need to be considered when deciding who your trustee should be. First, you should always use a trustee with a different last name than your own. If you are forming a land trust in a state different than the one in which the property is located, you can utilize a trustee service (if you do not know anyone with a different last name to act as trustee). These services are located across the country and usually are relatively inexpensive. Ultimately, though, the trustee needs to be someone you trust. A friend or family member who lives out of state and has a different last name is ideal as well.

We strongly recommend that you set up your land trust in conjunction with a business entity such as a corporation or LLC. Ultimately, a creditor will be able to attach your beneficial interest if it is held in an individual name as opposed to a business entity. A land trust can only provide maximum asset protection if it is formed where the beneficial owner is a business entity.

Most attorneys and professionals across the country are not familiar with land trusts. Caution is urged in forming a land trust, and you should only hire a professional who has experience with these kinds of trusts.

A land trust is "disregarded" for tax purposes, which means that it is not recognized by the IRS as being separate from its owner for tax purposes. Therefore, no separate tax return needs to be completed for land trusts. Land trusts are economical to administer and to maintain, since there are no separate tax returns required, there are minimal setup fees, and there are no annual fees to maintain a land trust unless you hire an outside trustee service to act as the land trust's trustee.

> **Tax Tip**
>
> Since a land trust is disregarded for federal tax purposes, no separate IRS form will need to be completed to show any gain or loss from real estate held or sold by a land trust. You will simply report the sale as though it were held in your own name or held in the name of one of your business entities.

Note that land trusts can be problematic when you are trying to refinance a property. Many lenders do not want to loan money when the borrower is not named on the title. The way to solve this problem is to transfer the title for the property to the borrower immediately before and transfer title back to the trust immediately after the refinance. However, for many investors, the time and expense involved in doing this could make a land trust an undesirable device, especially if refinancing of the property is foreseeable in the near future.

Private Annuity Trusts

A *private annuity trust* is a device in which the seller of real property can defer capital gains taxes and create an income stream for life. Private annuity trusts are usually favored by taxpayers who are about to sell highly appreciated real estate and want to defer large capital gains taxes on the sale. They are also beneficial for owners who do not need the immediate cash from the sale of their property but who instead opt to take payments on the sale in the future.

Private annuity trusts are often formed between parents and their children. The appreciated asset will be transferred to the private annuity trust in exchange for the private annuity contract. At the time of the transfer, no capital gains tax is recognized, and the taxes are deferred until the payments are actually received (when the trust sells the property). The proceeds from the sale of the property can be invested for the benefit of the trust. The trustee can invest the proceeds as she sees fit, as long as the trustee is acting in the best interests of the beneficiaries. The trustee will be a person you designate (such as a family member), which means that you will retain control of the trust. Make sure that you also completely trust your trustee's judgment in handling the trust's investments. Hiring a professional to act as trustee is another option if you have no family members you want to designate as trustee.

The trustee will determine how the sale proceeds are to be distributed. If the trustee decides to invest the sale proceeds of the asset, the proceeds can produce wealth within the trust through certain investments and the compounding of interest. Private annuity trusts are similar to self-directed IRAs in that the trust can designate how it wants to invest in any funds within it. The trustee of the trust can decide which investment it likes or does not like. Virtually any type of investment is available. You will want to make sure that the trust agreement designates this flexibility in investing.

At first glance, the private annuity trust may look just like an installment sale (that is, property is sold and payments are received in the future with a deferral of taxes). However, unlike an installment sale, private annuity trusts have less risk because there is no risk of having to foreclose on the property or risk of the buyer paying the note off early. These risks and disadvantages of installment sales are discussed in more detail in Chapter 6.

With a private annuity trust, the seller can defer the payments, just like on an ordinary annuity, up until the age of $70\frac{1}{2}$. The seller pays no tax until the payments are actually made and actually received by the beneficiary.

Example

Dave owns a piece of rental real estate that he has held for more than one year with a fair market value of $350,000 and an adjusted basis of $100,000. If Dave sells the property today, he stands to pay federal and state taxes of approximately $50,000, along with any depreciation recapture that will be taxed at 25 percent. Dave is ready to retire and thus he has no desire to like-kind exchange the property and continue as a landlord. He also does not have an immediate need for the money from the sale. Dave has two children, so he decides to set up a private annuity trust, making his two children its beneficiaries. Dave defers the payments on the contract until he reaches 70 years of age. Dave's children sell the property after it is transferred to the trust. The proceeds of the sale are placed in a trust account, where the money will grow until Dave's payments begin at age 70. Dave will recognize no gain on the sale until he actually starts receiving the payments.

Tax Tip

Private annuity trusts are relatively unknown, and you will not find many advisors who are familiar with them. The IRS has strict regulations governing private annuity trusts. Thus, it is important to engage a professional who is familiar with such regulations if you are interested in creating a private annuity trust.

The private annuity trust is an irrevocable nongrantor trust. You will need to contact a professional experienced in the formation of private annuity trusts to help you create a private annuity trust. Note that once it is created, you must not transfer to the trust property that is listed for sale or in the process of being sold. The property should be transferred to the trust first in exchange for the annuity contract, and then the property should be listed for sale. The IRS could otherwise disallow the deferral of the taxes if the property is transferred into the trust shortly after it is listed for sale or before the property's closing.

> **Tax Tip**
>
> The annuity contract cannot give the seller of the property any control or interest in the property being transferred to the trust. The IRS will disallow the tax benefits if the seller does not relinquish all control and interest over the property to the trust. To retain control would render the trust to be a grantor trust, which you definitely do not want to happen to this type of trust arrangement.

The costs to create and administer a private annuity trust will vary from state to state, but the following list will give you estimates of the costs:

- *Formation.* An attorney will need to be hired to create the trust and the annuity contract. Attorney fees will average about $3,000 for this service, although the fees vary greatly depending on the attorney's experience level and the location of the law practice.

- *Administration.* If you need to hire a professional to act as trustee, the fees will be based on the value of the trust's assets. The trustee will usually charge a fiat fee based on this value. Fees range from 1 percent to 2 percent and up, depending on the type of services the professional provides. If your trustee is a relative, such fees can be avoided or greatly reduced.

- *Tax preparation.* The trust will need an annual tax return. Fees will vary depending on the tax preparer. Generally, trust returns start at $500 and go up depending on the complexity of the return and the experience of the tax return preparer.

Charitable Remainder Trusts

A *charitable remainder trust* (CRT) is a tax planning device that can help you eliminate taxes on your real estate sales. Like private annuity trusts, CRTs are designed for individuals who have no immediate need for the proceeds from the sale of their real estate holdings but instead would like to create a steady income stream in the future.

CRTs have the following tax advantages:

- They can eliminate capital gains tax on the sale of appreciated property.

- They can provide an income stream to the transferor of the property to the trust.

- They can create a charitable contribution deduction to the transferor of the property to the trust.

Tax Tip

Note that CRTs, once created and funded, are irrevocable. Do not fund assets into the CRT that you might someday need.

A CRT is created to hold assets that are eventually donated to a charity of your choice. Instead of selling your appreciated real estate (or any other appreciated asset you own), you will transfer the real estate to the CRT. The trust will then sell the property and invest the proceeds. Most charities set a minimum amount for any gifts or contributions for use with a CRT. For many charities, the value of the gift must not be less than $25,000 or $50,000 before the charity will want to work with a CRT, due to the added complexity of these types of trusts. You will then be entitled to an income stream from the investment during your life, and the charity you designate will be the beneficiary when you die.

Example

Tom has appreciated real estate with a fair market value of $500,000. His adjusted basis is $100,000. Tom is considering a CRT because he has no need for the immediate proceeds from the sale of the property, and he wants to avoid the capital gains taxes he will have to pay on the property's disposition. If he sells the property without a CRT, he will pay capital gains taxes of $60,000 ($500,000 − $100,000 = $400,000 × 0.15 = $60,000). By transferring the property to the CRT, Tom can avoid the capital gains taxes. In addition, he can get a charitable donation tax deduction based on IRS tables and actuary formulas. He will also get the benefit of an income stream when he retires. The charity, however, will receive the assets when he dies.

The CRT must have at least one noncharitable beneficiary and one remainder man. The noncharitable beneficiary can be the donor to the trust. The remainder man is the charitable organization that is chosen to receive the proceeds at the end of the trust. The donor can also decide to change the remainder man later. A CRT is created first with the CRT agreement, which specifies how the trust is to be administered and how the income is to be paid out. A trustee will be designated. The trustee can be the same person as the donor/beneficiary of the assets into the trust. The trustee can also be the charity or a third party. The trust will pay an income stream or annuity to the beneficiaries of the trust, as specified in the trust document. The charity will eventually receive whatever is remaining in the trust at the death of the noncharitable beneficiary. The remainder man must be a qualified charity under IRC Section 170 and IRC Section 501(c)(3).

CRTs are popular because they can help investors avoid the capital gains taxes on appreciated assets. For individuals who have no need for the immediate cash from a sale and who also have a desire to make a charitable contribution, a CRT can be a nice tax planning tool. Appreciated assets transferred into the CRT are not considered a "sale" to the CRT (only a transfer); therefore no gain is recognized on the transfer. The trust realizes a gain once the assets within the trust are sold, but the trust does not recognize any gain (i.e., pay tax on it) because it is exempt from taxation.[1]

Once the appreciated assets are transferred to the trust, the trust will start paying back an annuity or income stream to the beneficiary for a period of time as specified in the trust document. The beneficiary can be the donor or even an entity such as an LLC or corporation. More than one beneficiary can be designated, but all beneficiaries must exist at the time of the trust creation.

The time period of the annuity of the CRT can be either for the beneficiary's life or any number of years (not to exceed 20 years). The annuity to the beneficiary is taxed on a tier system determined by the income earned in the trust as follows:

- Ordinary income.
- Capital gains.
- Other income (such as tax-exempt income).
- Return of principal.[2]

The amount of income paid to the donor/beneficiary is based on a percentage of the value of the trust's assets. Generally, the amount paid cannot exceed 50 percent or be less than 5 percent.

Appreciated assets, usually consisting of real estate, stocks, or other securities, are typically the kinds of assets transferred into the trust because one of the purposes of creating a CRT is to avoid the capital gains taxes on the sale of appreciated assets. The trustee can decide whether the trust will sell the assets within it. Once sold, the trust can then take the proceeds from the sale and invest them as he or she sees fit. The trustee is not allowed to engage in self-dealing when making investment decisions (that is, you cannot designate the proceeds to a charity that you own) and must also follow state laws governing trust investments.

Tax Tip

An advisor who specializes in CRTs should be engaged to create the trust, since the IRS has issued technical requirements for CRT instruments that must be closely followed. If a mistake is made, the entire CRT may be void and not provide the benefits you had anticipated.

The donor will receive a tax deduction in the year of the transfer. The amount of the deduction is based on two things: the estimated value to the charity and the kind of charity. The amount of the tax deduction will also be based on the remainder value to the charity. Your tax advisor can help you determine the amount of the deduction you can take.

The remainder man should not be a private foundation, because the IRS can disallow your tax deduction based on the fair market value of the asset and can instead recategorize the deduction based on your cost basis in the donated asset (usually resulting in a much lower deduction). You are allowed to designate more than one remainder man to receive the trust assets.

There are two different types of CRT: the charitable remainder annuity trust (CRAT) and the charitable remainder unitrust (CRUT). IRS regulations require that a CRT be one of these two types of trusts.

A CRAT is designed so that the donor receives a fixed amount of income from the trust each year of the donor's life or for a fixed period of time. Whatever property is left in the trust after the donor dies will be passed to the charity. The payments can be designated to the donor, the donor's spouse, or the donor's children or grandchildren. Payments are a fixed amount of the initial value of the trust assets or a fixed sum as determined by the trust agreement. The payments must be no lower than 5 percent and no more than 50 percent. The payments cannot be changed once determined.

A CRUT is designed so that the donor receives a percentage of the fair market value of the trust assets each year for the donor's life or for a fixed period of time. Whatever property is left in the trust after the donor dies will be passed to the charity. The payments can be designated to the donor, the donor's spouse, or the donor's children or grandchildren.

Your individual facts and circumstances will determine which type of trust you should choose to set up. Your professional advisor can assist you in determining which structure is best for you.

Conclusion

This chapter was intended to simply make you aware of the most common types of trusts for real estate investors. It was not intended to provide you with all rules and requirements associated with each of these trusts. Instead, due to the technical requirements and complexity of trusts in general, we strongly suggest that very experienced counsel be obtained to assist in the creation of these trusts. In addition, trusts are also used in connection with a personal estate plan, for which individual consultations are advisable for all taxpayers.

CHAPTER 9

Individual Retirement Accounts

All taxpayers should strongly consider using individual retirement accounts (IRAs) as an integral part of their overall real estate investment strategies. Basically, an IRA is a personal savings plan that offers numerous tax advantages for money that is set aside for your retirement. Depending on the type of plan, there are three main advantages to an IRA:

1. You might be able to deduct the amounts you contribute to an IRA during the year of the contribution.

2. You will be able to gain tax deferral on the earnings that accrue in the IRA (meaning that you do not pay income taxes on the earnings during the year in which the earnings are received).

3. You might not need to pay any taxes on the funds when they're withdrawn, again depending on when the withdrawal takes place and the type of retirement plan.

Although we do not discuss each of the IRA plans in detail in this book, we want to cover the basic features of these plans and how they can be utilized in conjunction with real estate holdings and transactions.

IRA Rules and Plan Types

The following rules apply to all types of IRAs:

- The custodian of the IRA must be approved by the IRS and must be a bank, a federally insured credit union, a savings and loan association, or another entity approved by the IRS to act as a custodian.

- The account must be fully vested at all times.
- There is a maximum annual amount that can be contributed, and the custodian is prohibited from accepting more than this amount in any given year. This does not include rollovers, which are not subject to the annual maximum contributions.
- You must have earned income during the year to make any contributions (or be able to rely on your spouse for "compensation" if you are married and file a joint tax return).
- You must contribute cash or roll over other IRA funds.
- Life insurance policies cannot be purchased by an IRA.
- An IRA is generally prohibited from investing in collectibles (such as antiques or stamps). It can, however, invest in certain U.S. gold and silver coins and certain types of bullion (gold, silver, platinum, and palladium).
- The custodian must follow the mandatory distribution rules concerning ages, timing, and amounts to be distributed.
- The custodian of the IRA is legally required to provide a full disclosure agreement outlining the terms by which it will be acting as the custodian of your account.

The following chart outlines some of the differences between some IRAs.

Tax Issue/ Question	Traditional IRA	Roth IRA	SEP-IRA
What is the maximum amount I can contribute each year?	For 2009, $5,000 per year or $6,000 if you were at least 50 years old by the end of 2009. There are no income limitations on who can make a contribution.	For 2009, $5,000 per year or $6,000 if you were at least 50 years old by the end of 2009. There are income limitations on who can contribute to these types of plans.	The amount of the contribution will depend on the amount of compensation received as an employee or from a trade or business. In general, for 2009 you can contribute the maximum of 25% of your overall compensation or $49,000, whichever is less.
Is there an age limit to making a contribution?	Yes. You cannot make any contributions if you have reached age 70½.	No.	No.

Tax Issue/ Question	Traditional IRA	Roth IRA	SEP-IRA
Can I deduct my contributions?	Possibly. The answer depends on your filing status, your income, whether you contribute to a retirement plan at work, and whether you receive any Social Security benefits.	No.	Yes.
How do I report my contributions to the IRS?	No reporting is necessary unless you make a nondeductible contribution. If this is the case, file Form 8606 with your tax return. (See copy in Appendix A.)	None.	Any reporting is done via your Form W-2 or deducted on your regular business tax return or Form 1040.
When do I need to start taking distributions?	You must receive minimum distributions by April 1 of the year following the year in which you reach age $70^1/_2$.	There are no rules that require a distribution from a Roth IRA.	You must receive distributions by April 1 of the year following the year in which you reach age $70^1/_2$.
How are distributions taxed?	All distributions are taxed as ordinary income. If you made nondeductible contributions, the amounts that you contributed but could not deduct are not taxed.	Distributions are not taxed in most cases (some early withdrawals may be taxable).	All distributions are taxed as ordinary income.
What forms do I need to file if I receive a distribution?	None unless you have made a nondeductible contribution in the past. If this is the case, you must file Form 8606. (Copy included in Appendix A.)	Form 8606 must be used to report distributions. (Copy included in Appendix A.)	None.

For most taxpayers, the benefits of a Roth IRA are hard to beat. All income earned through the Roth IRA is tax free in that when the funds are withdrawn, there is no income tax due on any of the profits, in most instances. This very favorable feature is offset by the fact that a contribution to a Roth IRA is not tax deductible. For many taxpayers who have built up value in a traditional or regular IRA, a decision must be made at some point as to whether or not to convert your regular IRA to a Roth IRA. Assuming that the income limitations can be met (to fully utilize the Roth IRA provisions currently, you earn less than $105,000 of adjusted gross income for single taxpayers and $166,000 for married taxpayers filing jointly), the tax ramifications must be calculated to determine whether this is financially worthwhile. Most financial planners can easily make these calculations for you to assist with this decision.

Contribution Limits for Retirement Plans

The annual maximum amounts that can be contributed depend on the type of plan and the year in which the contribution is made. Here is a chart of these amounts.

Age/Plan	2004	2005	2006	2007	2008	2009
Roth and regular IRA, up to age 50	$ 3,000	$ 4,000	$ 4,000	$ 4,000	$ 5,000	$ 5,000
Roth and regular IRA, age 50 or more	$ 3,500	$ 4,500	$ 5,000	$ 5,000	$ 6,000	$ 6,000
Simple IRA or simple 401(k), up to age 50	$ 9,000	$10,000	$10,000	$10,500	$10,500	$11,500
Simple IRA or simple 401(k), age 50 or more	$10,500	$12,000	$12,500	$13,000	$13,000	$14,000
401(k), 403(b), 457, up to age 50	$13,000	$14,000	$15,000	$15,500	$15,500	$16,500
401(k), 403(b), 457, age 50 or more	$16,000	$18,000	$20,000	$20,500	$20,500	$22,000

The numbers for the tax years beginning with 2010 will likely change depending on the annual inflation rate in place during these years.

Self-Directed Individual Retirement Accounts

One of the most attractive features of an IRA is the ability to transact real estate deals within it. If done properly, it is possible to avoid paying any taxes on the receipt of rental income or on the capital gains (either short or long term) when the real estate is sold. The ability to use an IRA to self-direct real estate deals has been around since 1975, when the Employee Retirement Income Security Act of 1974 (ERISA) became effective.[1] To take advantage of these tremendous potential tax savings, you must establish an IRA with a nontraditional custodian (for instance, most IRA funds are administered by mutual funds, banks, and/or brokerage firms). You need to locate a firm that can act as your fiduciary that is not one of these more common IRA custodians. Fortunately, there are several firms that specialize in this type of investment assistance.

In most instances, there is little noticeable difference in buying or selling real estate from your IRA as opposed to buying or selling in your personal name. For example, the offer and acceptance portions of the contract phase are the same, as are the escrow, title, and closing issues. The only real difference is that the IRA custodian is acting on your behalf in handling the transaction due to the fact that the IRA, not you, is the purchaser or seller of the property. The custodian earns some money on these transactions, so be sure to review and compare charges among various self-directed custodians before deciding which one to use.

Example

Sara has $100,000 in her current regular IRA. She has these funds with ABC Bank and is currently earning 4 percent per year. She wants to take advantage of holding real estate in her IRA and directs her bank to transfer $75,000 to XYZ Investments (an approved IRA custodian). She never takes possession of the funds and instead has the bank make a direct transfer to XYZ. She then locates an apartment building worth $500,000 and is able to work out a deal with the owner whereby she puts 15 percent down and the owner carries a note for 15 years. She has all rent payments paid into the IRA fund and makes all expense payments from the IRA, including the debt service, taxes, and other expenses. After 15 years, the IRA has fully paid for the property, all rents are tax free in the years received, and any capital gains are tax deferred when the IRA sells the property. She will pay taxes on these amounts only when she receives distributions, perhaps at a time when her income is lower due to retirement and her tax bracket is correspondingly lower.

Example

Caitlin is engaged in the business of buying properties, fixing them up, and selling them on a short-term basis (she holds them less than one year). She is paying many thousands of dollars every year in taxes because these sales are short term and thus do not qualify for the favorable long-term capital gains

(Continued)

rates. She is also labeled a real estate dealer and thus has self-employment tax issues as well. Rather than owning all these properties in her own name, she decides to utilize a self-directed IRA to make all the purchases and sales. By doing so, Caitlin defers all capital gains taxes (if done in a regular IRA) or her capital gains are tax free (if done in a Roth IRA). She thus has more funds available for real estate investing because she is now saving 25 to 35 percent in taxes every year.

Necessary Steps to Using an IRA for Real Estate Transactions

Here is what must be done to use this advantageous method of deferring or avoiding taxes on the funds earned as the result of real estate sales and related activities:

- Locate a plan or administrator that handles these types of transactions.

- Determine the type of IRA (such as a regular or Roth) to use for this type of activity.

- Fund the account. Be aware that the normal contribution limits still apply to self-directed IRAs. Thus, to realistically be able to utilize this strategy, you most likely will need to transfer funds from an already established IRA so that you will have sufficient funds available to invest. This is a major difference from a traditional investment in that it is relatively easy to locate investment vehicles for your $5,000 annual contribution if you are buying stocks, bonds, or mutual funds. For real estate, the typical down payment is greater than the amount of the maximum annual contribution.

- Buy the real estate within your self-directed IRA.

Example

Morgan wants to buy a single-family residential rental in Iowa. The purchase price is $150,000. She has $200,000 in her current IRA. She finds ABC Company to handle her self-directed IRA, since ABC is an authorized custodian for self-directed IRA accounts. She directs her current IRA custodian to transfer $200,000 to ABC. There are no tax implications to this transaction because it is a direct rollover from one IRA to another; thus Morgan never takes possession of the funds. Morgan then directs ABC to purchase the property by completing a buy authorization form provided by ABC. All closing documents, including title reports, are reviewed and determined to be in good order. Following approval, the custodian (ABC) signs all closing documents. The closing follows and the deed is recorded and sent to ABC as the custodian for Morgan. The tenants of the property are directed to make all rent payments to ABC for the benefit of Morgan's IRA. Any utility, tax, or other expenses are also sent to ABC, and ABC makes the payments directly, keeping track of all income and expenses as it acts on behalf of Morgan.

Buying Notes or Liens in an IRA

It is certainly possible to purchase notes, including mortgages and tax liens, via your self-directed IRA. A *tax lien* is basically a lien by a governmental agency asserting that certain taxes have not been paid. These governmental agencies then sell these liens and provide the buyer with a tax lien certificate. There are entire investment seminars and books devoted to these types of purchases; thus the mechanics are not discussed in this book. However, when you buy one of these certificates, the government is reimbursed for the amount of its lien, and you, as the purchaser of the certificate, get the current owner of the property to reimburse you, often at very favorable interest rates.

The process is virtually identical to the actual purchase of real estate except that only the paper, not the property, is being purchased. The interest earned on any notes is also tax deferred or tax free, depending on the type of IRA utilized.

Prohibited Transactions with Real Estate in an Individual Retirement Account

There are limitations on the type of real estate transactions you can structure using your IRA. In general, you do not have the same amount of flexibility in using an IRA as you would with a regular real estate deal. The following types of transactions are considered "prohibited" transactions and cannot be accomplished using a self-directed IRA:

- The sale, exchange, or lease of any real estate between the IRA and any disqualified person (defined in a moment). Thus, your IRA generally cannot purchase a rental property that you currently own or that is owned by a business entity that you own or otherwise control.
- The lending of money or other credit between the IRA and a disqualified person. This also includes using IRA property for collateral or security for a non-IRA loan.
- Any act or deal by a disqualified person and the IRA in which the disqualified person is acting as a fiduciary and uses the IRA for her own personal account.
- Any furnishing of services or goods by a disqualified person and the IRA.

- Any use of the income or assets of the IRA by a disqualified person. This means that you generally cannot buy a rental property in your IRA and then use it for yourself and your family.
- The receipt of any funds or other consideration by the disqualified person (who is a fiduciary to the IRA) in connection with any income or assets of the IRA.

A *disqualified person* is:

- Any individual who also acts as a fiduciary to the IRA.
- A person who provides services to the IRA plan.
- An employer that provides the plan for its employees.
- An employee organization for which the employees are covered by the plan.
- A direct or indirect owner of the business establishing the plan (and who owns 50 percent or more of the business, either indirectly or directly).
- A 10 percent or more partner of a partnership offering the plan.

In addition to these individuals, a family member of any of these disqualified persons may also be considered a disqualified person, along with business entities such as corporations or partnerships that a disqualified person controls. The rules are very severe if the plan deals with a disqualified person, and this must be avoided to keep your plan in good standing with the law. If you find that you have engaged in a prohibited transaction, the sooner that it is corrected, the better. If it is not corrected, it is possible that you could face a 100 percent tax on the transaction.

The Use of Financing in an IRA

An IRA is not permitted to be used as collateral for a personal loan. Thus you could not purchase a vehicle and use your IRA account as collateral. However, an IRA is permitted to borrow money to use with respect to an asset in the IRA, such as real property. But like most other tax matters, this is not as simple as it would first appear. Special rules are involved when you are considering using financing in your IRA in an attempt to leverage the funds in your IRA. This works by having the IRA put as small a down payment on the property as possible and financing the balance. There is a special rule for what is known as *unrelated business income*, or UBI. UBI is basically income that is not specifically related to the direct business activities of the IRA. Unfortunately, income from debt-financed property is considered UBI.[2] In general, the income from UBI cannot exceed $1,000 per year without incurring adverse tax consequences. If the income exceeds this amount, you must pay taxes on this income and file IRS Form 990-T for the IRA with the IRS in Ogden, Utah. This form does not get filed directly with your personal tax return.[3] Fortunately, there are ways to plan for this situation and not be required to pay any taxes on the UBI.

The most common way to avoid UBI is to make sure that all income from the property is zeroed out (or at least comes out to less than $1,000) by using expenses and depreciation with respect to the property. For many rental properties, this is not a problem, since the depreciation more than eats up any paper profits. If you use this method and there is still a profit that exceeds $1,000, it may be possible to use any surplus to pay down the debt. Once the debt is paid off in full, UBI does not become an issue, because the property is no longer debt-financed property and the UBI rules no longer apply.

Conclusion

We wanted to include this short chapter on self-directed IRAs for real estate transactions to rebut the popular myth that an IRA cannot be used for real estate ventures. Once you are aware that this is an option, you can seek out a custodian to handle these types of transactions for you. The Internet is a good starting point to locate a custodian. If you decide to go this route, you should make sure that you consult with a qualified financial planner to make sure that you have sufficient diversification and risk assessments in place. If all your retirement funds are in real estate and there is a severe downturn in real estate values, your portfolio could take a large hit (as we have seen with the very recent real estate and stock market declines). It is certainly possible to build a great deal of wealth using your self-directed IRA. We hope that you are able to use some of these accounts to provide an outstanding retirement for your future.

CHAPTER 10

Depreciation Issues with Real Estate

Depreciation is the reduction in value of any given asset over its useful period of life. This is often a theoretical exercise with real property in that the property may actually be appreciating in value when the depreciation deduction is claimed. However, for most personal property, including cars, computers, appliances, and so on, depreciation is a very real expense. The tax deduction for depreciation is intended to account for any decreases in value over time due to normal wear and tear and technological advancements. Inasmuch as the largest expense you will incur for your real estate transactions is for the initial purchase of the property, along with major improvements during your ownership period, you should pay particular attention to this major tax deduction. It is strongly recommended that you obtain the very lengthy IRS Publication 946 to assist you with this important tax deduction. In general, depreciation applies to property that is expected to last for more than one year and that could wear out over time.

You are permitted (actually required) to deduct your depreciation costs on an annual basis and will need to know the following three items to determine how much you are permitted to deduct:

1. Your overall basis in the property.
2. The recovery period (in years) for the property.
3. The depreciation method to be used.

How Is Basis Computed?

For many items associated with rental property, the basis is simply the cost you pay for the asset. In addition to the actual purchase price, the cost of the item includes any sales taxes paid, shipping charges, and installation charges. For real property, the cost also includes the vast majority of closing or settlement costs. These costs include any legal, recording, title, surveying, or other fees generally associated with the final closing for the purchase of the property. (We covered many basis issues in more detail in Chapter 1.)

Basis of Personal Property Converted to Business Use

For any property that you owned prior to the rental activity and used for personal reasons, the basis is computed by determining the lower of the fair market value at the time it is converted to rental property use or the original cost basis.

Example

Jordan has a spare refrigerator at her home that she bought in 2007 for $1,000. She places it in one of her rental properties on January 2, 2009. It was worth $200 when she placed it into her rental unit. The basis for depreciation purposes is $200.

Example

Jordan has a desk in her basement that she bought at a garage sale for $50 in 2008. She wants to place the desk in a furnished rental property and finds out it is an antique worth $2,000. She must use the lower value ($50) for depreciation purposes.

There are also other instances in which you cannot use the actual cost as the basis for depreciation purposes. A complete discussion of different ways to compute tax basis can be found in IRS Publication 551. These include:

- *Property received as a gift.* Your basis in this type of property is the original cost basis of the person from whom the gift was received.

- *Property received as an inheritance.* Your basis on this type of property will depend on how the assets were valued for purposes of any estate tax reporting obligations. Although there are a few possible methods of calculating this amount, the most common are either the value of the asset on the date of death or the value on the estate's alternative valuation date. This information needs to be obtained from the executor or personal representative of the estate.

- *Property received in exchange for other property.* This is often accomplished as the result of a like-kind exchange under Section 1031 of the Internal Revenue Code. In general, the basis for property received in a like-kind exchange is the adjusted basis of the property originally given up. We discussed these basis issues in greater detail in Chapters 2 and 5.

- *Property transferred from a spouse (often as the result of a divorce).* The basis is computed by using the basis from the spouse. More information for computing tax-related issues for divorced taxpayers can be found in IRS Publication 504.

- *Property received in exchange for services rendered.* Generally, the amount of the barter or exchange that you report as income is the amount of your basis. This will generally be the fair market value of the property or the services rendered, absent any evidence to the contrary.

Furthermore, there are instances in which you may be able to increase your original cost basis to permit additional depreciation. These include adding any additions or improvements to the property (such as finishing a basement or adding a bedroom), local assessments done by governmental agencies (such as getting assessed a fee for the local city installing new sidewalks, curbs, or other municipal improvements), restoration costs after a natural disaster, and the costs associated with bringing new utility lines to the property. Finally, taxpayers who live in any community property state (Arizona, California, Idaho, Louisiana, Nevada, New Mexico, Texas, Washington, and Wisconsin) have special rules concerning computing basis in the event of one spouse's death. In this instance, the basis is generally split in half as the result of one half of the asset's value being including in the deceased spouse's estate.

If you actually construct a building that becomes your rental property, the cost basis is computed by adding together the costs of the land, labor, materials, professional fees (including architects, contractors, and attorneys), building permits, utility meter connections, and any other amounts spent on completing the buildings.

What Is the Recovery Period for Property Subject to Depreciation?

Depreciation is calculated using IRS tables based on an asset's "useful life." You can begin to depreciate property when you place an asset into service. This date is often different from your actual purchase date. Property is considered placed into service when it is ready and available for use in connection with your rental property.

The following are common assets used in connection with real property:

- *Three-year depreciation.* This includes computer software used in your rental activity, such as QuickBooks to keep track of your income and expenses.

- *Five-year depreciation.* This includes appliances such as stoves and refrigerators, along with furniture used in connection with a rental property. This period of depreciation also includes automobiles, computers and related electronic equipment, and carpeting.

- *Seven-year depreciation.* This includes office furniture, fixtures, and equipment. It is also the "catch-all" provision in that any property that does not have a specific class life is lumped into the seven-year period.

- *Ten-year depreciation.* This includes single-use agricultural buildings, such as a grain bin on a leased farm.

- *Fifteen-year depreciation.* This includes roads, shrubbery, and fences. It also includes driveways, parking lots, and most landscaping, along with swimming pools and hot tubs as well as qualified leasehold improvements placed into service between October 22, 2004, and January 1, 2010.

- *Twenty-seven-and-a-half-year depreciation.* This includes residential rental property (any buildings or structures but *not* the value of the land), along with any structural components such as furnaces, water pipes, and the like.

- *Thirty-nine-year depreciation.* This includes commercial rental properties and the home office (business use of your home). Again, this does not include the value of the land.

A chart showing the various depreciation rates for the 27.5- and 39-year properties follows. Here are the depreciation rates for personal property using the 200 percent declining balance method with a half-year convention (the most common and advantageous method for claiming depreciation for personal property).

		Recovery period (in years)			
Year	3-Year	5-Year	7-Year	10-Year	15-Year
1	33.33%	20.00%	14.29%	10.00%	5.00%
2	44.45%	32.00%	24.90%	18.00%	9.50%
3	14.81%	19.20%	17.49%	14.40%	8.55%
4	7.41%	11.52%	12.49%	11.52%	7.70%
5	—	11.52%	8.93%	9.22%	6.93%
6	—	5.76%	8.92%	7.37%	6.23%
7	—	—	8.93%	6.55%	5.90%
8	—	—	4.46%	6.55%	5.90%
9	—	—	—	6.56%	5.91%
10	—	—	—	6.55%	5.90%
11	—	—	—	3.28%	5.91%
12	—	—	—	—	5.90%
13	—	—	—	—	5.91%
14	—	—	—	—	5.90%
15	—	—	—	—	5.91%
16	—	—	—	—	2.95%

Example

Cam buys a new computer for $1,000 on January 1, 2008, which he uses exclusively in his rental property business. He determines that this item needs to be depreciated over a five-year period. He is able to claim the following deductions for this depreciation.

2008:	$ 200.00
2009:	$ 320.00
2010:	$ 192.00
2011:	$ 115.20
2012:	$ 115.20
2013:	$ 57.60
Total:	$1,000.00

If your rental property includes both residential and commercial rental units, as is common in many urban areas, to use the more favorable 27.5-year period you must be able to show that at least 80 percent of the total rent receipts came from residential units.[1] If the total rent receipts are less than 80 percent residential, you must use the 39-year period for depreciation.

Any values attributed to land cannot be depreciated. To determine the amount of your purchase price that is attributable to land, it is often necessary to use the property tax assessor's information or a certified appraisal.

> ### Example
>
> Alex buys a rental property for $200,000. According to the assessed value at the local county's assessor's office, the property is assessed at $20,000, with $14,000 attributed to the buildings and $6,000 to the land. Given that the building is 70 percent of the assessed value, Alex may use 70 percent of his purchase price, or $140,000, as his basis for purposes of depreciation.

What Methods of Depreciation Are Available?

For property placed into service after 1986, the Modified Accelerated Cost Recovery System (MACRS) method is most commonly used. MACRS is described in detail in IRS Publication 946. The basis and recovery period are determined as described previously. The only other item that must be determined is the date the asset was placed into service. This date is determined by the date on which the property was ready and available for a specific use in the rental activity.

> ### Example
>
> Michael buys a new refrigerator for his rental property unit. He makes the purchase in December 2008 but does not actually receive the refrigerator until January 2009. Even though the refrigerator was purchased in 2008, he cannot start to depreciate this asset until January 2009 (when it was ready for use in the rental unit).

> ### Example
>
> Michael buys a furnished rental property unit on March 1, 2009. He needs to make minor repairs and completes these on April 25, 2009. He lists the property for rent on May 1, 2009, and a tenant occupies the property on July 1, 2009. He is permitted to begin depreciating the property on May 1, 2009, since this is the date it was placed into service (it was available for rent on this date).

The IRS has also established certain conventions to follow with respect to depreciation of property. For most rental activities, this involves the use of the half-year convention. This rule simply assumes that you place all rental property into service on July 1 (the midpoint for the year). This method is also generally the most favorable method for using depreciation. This rule can be used as long as at least 60 percent of the costs associated with your personal property were placed into service prior to September 30 of the year at issue. If more than 40 percent of your property was placed in service during the last quarter of the year (October 1 through December 31), you must use the less favorable mid-quarter convention. The mid-quarter convention treats all property as being placed into service during the midpoint of the fourth quarter and would thus result in less overall depreciation being claimed for the initial year. Ultimately, you will receive the same overall depreciation under any of these methods, although the actual amounts will vary from year to year, depending on the depreciation convention you use.

Depreciation Rates for New Property

All real property is depreciated using a straight-line method. This simply means that you get the same tax deduction for each tax period that you have the property in service in connection with your rental property. This is different than most items of personal property, whereby the depreciation amounts vary from year to year. For example, an automobile generally depreciates the greatest in the first few years, and the IRS depreciation tables reflect this reality by allowing a greater tax deduction in the earliest years.

When real property is involved, the first issue to be considered is the allocation of the purchase price between land and buildings. Land cannot be depreciated, and this issue must be resolved in the first year you begin to try to rent the property. Once the value of the buildings is known, it may be depreciated over 27.5 or 39 years, depending on the type of property (residential or commercial). The building includes all structural components, including walls, ceilings, floors, electrical and plumbing, attached fixtures, air conditioning and heating, and anything else that is part of the structural components of the building itself.

Example

Alex buys a rental house for $200,000. The purchase contract does not list the amount of land and buildings associated with the purchase price. He checks

(*Continued*)

with the local property assessor's office and finds out that the land value is considered to be 25 percent of the total property taxes. He thus calculates the value of the land at $50,000 (25 percent of the $200,000 purchase price) and begins to depreciate the building using $150,000 as its depreciable basis.

The following chart shows the percentages to use with respect to residential and commercial real property depreciation.

Month First Used for Business	27.5-Year Property	39-Year Property
January (1)	3.485%	2.461%
February (2)	3.182%	2.247%
March (3)	2.879%	2.033%
April (4)	2.576%	1.819%
May (5)	2.273%	1.605%
June (6)	1.970%	1.391%
July (7)	1.667%	1.177%
August (8)	1.364%	0.963%
September (9)	1.061%	0.749%
October (10)	0.758%	0.535%
November (11)	0.455%	0.321%
December (12)	0.152%	0.107%

For any future years, the property will depreciate at an annual 3.636 percent for 27.5-year property and 2.564 percent for 39-year property.

Example

Jack buys a residential rental property on June 1, 2009, and immediately places it into service. He determines that the depreciable basis is $150,000. He can claim the following depreciation on the building: 2009, $2,955 (which is 1.97% of $150,000); 2010 and future years, $5,454 (which is 3.636% of $150,000).

In determining what value to use for depreciation purposes, you should include the following with respect to your building costs:

- Original contract purchase price.
- Settlement charges, including closing costs, abstract fees, title fees, escrow fees, legal fees, transfer taxes, survey costs, inspection fees, and recording fees. If you paid other costs at the closing, these also may be added to your original cost basis and used for depreciation purposes. As previously provided in Chapter 2, the following chart will assist you in determining your depreciable basis.

Item	Buyer Closing Costs	Where to Deduct Buyer Closing Costs	Seller Closing Costs	Where to Deduct Seller Closing Costs
Commissions	Added to basis	Form 4562	Sales expense	Schedule D or Form 4797
Items Payable in Connection with the Loan				
Loan origination (points)	Amortized	Form 4562	Sales expense	Schedule D or Form 4797
Loan discount (points)	Amortized	Form 4562	Sales expense	Schedule D or Form 4797
Appraisal fee	Amortized	Form 4562	Sales expense	Schedule D or Form 4797
Other loan costs	Amortized	Form 4562	Sales expense	Schedule D or Form 4797
Items Required by the Lender to be Paid in Advance				
Interest	Deductible	Schedule E or Form 8825	Deductible	Schedule E or Form 8825
Mortgage insurance (PMI)	Amortized; Form 4562	Sales expense	Schedule D or Form 4797	—
Hazard insurance	Deductible	Schedule E or Form 8825	Deductible; Schedule E or Form 8825	—
Reserves Deposited with Lender				
Reserves	Not deductible	—	Not deductible	—
Title Charges				
Title charges	Added to basis	Form 4562	Sales expense	Schedule D or Form 4797
Government Recording and Transfer Items				
Recording fee, deed	Added to basis	Form 4562	Sales expense	Schedule D or Form 4797
Recording fee, mortgage release	Amortized	Form 4562	Sales expense	Schedule D or Form 4797
Tax stamps/ transfer tax	Added to basis	Form 4562	Sales expense	Schedule D or Form 4797

Item	Buyer Closing Costs	Where to Deduct Buyer Closing Costs	Seller Closing Costs	Where to Deduct Seller Closing Costs
		Additional Charges		
Survey	Added to basis	Form 4562	Sales expense	Schedule D or Form 4797
Pest inspection	Added to basis	Form 4562	Sales expense	Schedule D or Form 4797
Closing fee	Added to basis	Form 4562	Sales expense	Schedule D or Form 4797

If you also use your rental property for personal purposes, such as if you buy a duplex and live in one of the units, you must reduce your overall cost basis by the amount of personal use. Thus, assuming that the two residences are approximately equal in size, you would be able to claim a depreciation deduction of 50 percent of the overall cost (not including the value of the land).

What Property Cannot Be Depreciated?

For some types of property, depreciation is not permitted. The following are some common examples with respect to assets used in connection with real estate:

- *Land.* Land is never depreciated because it does not wear out, become obsolete, or get used up.

- *Rented property.* You cannot claim depreciation unless you actually own the property. If you purchase property on credit, you are permitted to claim a deduction for depreciation, even if amounts are still owed on the purchase. You can also claim a deduction for any interest paid on the amount financed.

Component Depreciation

In many instances, when you purchase a residential rental property, you will often be purchasing personal property with the land and buildings. For instance, a seller may have the rental unit fully furnished or may include some appliances (refrigerator, stove, washer and dryer) with the purchase. You are permitted to depreciate all these personal property items with the cost of the building (and over a 27.5-year period). This is the easiest way to claim this depreciation. However, simply because it is the easiest method does not mean that it is the best method from a tax perspective. The Tax Court has ruled that a taxpayer is permitted to depreciate each asset (personal property) separately instead of lumping all assets into the valuation of the buildings.[2] This is known as *component depreciation* or *cost segregation.* By using this method of depreciation, you are maximizing a key tax deduction without actually spending more money and will see your overall tax bill decrease. This is the case because you are now able, with IRS and Tax Court approval, to correctly reduce the period of time that certain assets can be depreciated, thus increasing the overall depreciation deduction available to you.

The Tax Court has assisted with determining whether an asset is connected to a building (and thus cannot be depreciated alone) or can be considered personal property and depreciated as its own asset (with a shorter useful life and thus higher depreciation deductions every year). Here is the test it has developed[3]:

- *Can the property be moved?* If yes, it would tend to indicate it is personal property.

- *Is the property designed to stay in one place?* If yes, this would tend to demonstrate that the property is a part of a building and is not considered personal property.

- *Are there instances in which the property may need to be moved in the future?* If yes, the property is likely personal property.

- *Is the property easy to move?* Again, a yes answer would indicate that it is personal property.

- *How much damage to the structure would occur if the property was moved?* The greater the damage, the more likely it is a part of the building and not personal property.

- *How is the property affixed to the land?* The more it is permanently attached, the more likely it is a building component and not personal property.

Example

Jordan purchases a residential rental property and there is a window air conditioner in the unit. She must decide whether the air conditioner is part of the building and thus depreciable over 27.5 years or personal property that can be depreciated over 5 years. In going through the six elements of the previously mentioned test, she determines that the property can be moved, it is not necessarily designed to stay in one place, it can be moved in the future (if she sells the place and wants to keep the air conditioner), it is relatively easy to move, there would be no structural damage if it was removed, and it is not affixed to the land. After reviewing these factors, she determines that it is personal property and does not need to be depreciated over 27.5 years.

Although not every instance of personal property or building components has been previously decided, there are several IRS rulings and court cases to assist us with this determination. The following are a few more common instances of using these rules.

The following types of property have been found to be personal property:

- Kitchen appliances (stoves, refrigerators, etc.).
- Drapes, curtains, and window treatments.
- Fire extinguishers.
- Movable and removable partitions.
- Carpeting.

The following types of property have been determined to be building components and not personal property:

- Windows and doors.
- Sprinkler systems.
- Fire escapes.
- Central air conditioning and heating systems.
- Plumbing and plumbing fixtures.
- Chimneys, stairs, and fire escapes.
- Walls, paneling, and tiling.
- Electrical wiring and lighting fixtures.[4]

You can use component depreciation at any stage of your ownership, so if you did not do this the first year or two that you owned the property, you can begin using this during your actual period of ownership. Of course, the sooner you do this, the better from a tax deduction and savings standpoint. To use component depreciation, you must be able to do the following:

- Determine the entire purchase cost of the property. This is normally the contract price plus any other expenses, often the costs associated with the closing.
- Next, determine the value of any personal property for which you will be using component depreciation. You may find it helpful to work with an appraisal firm that specializes in component depreciation to fully maximize your overall deductions. In addition, it is often helpful to have your tax professional involved in this analysis, to fully maximize the tax benefits from the very beginning.
- Determine the values of the land and buildings with respect to the total purchase.
- Determine the amount of any land improvements included in the purchase price. This includes any landscaping, fencing, sidewalks, or the like. Many real estate investors skip this step and include these values in the overall

building basis. By doing so, however, they miss out on claiming depreciation for a 15-year period for these items and instead must use a 27.5-year period.

- Create depreciation schedules for the buildings, land improvements, and personal property.

You might want to obtain a copy of what IRS revenue agents (tax auditors and examiners) look for when they are faced with component depreciation. A copy of their *Cost Segregation Audit Techniques Guide* (January 2005) is available at www.irs.gov.

Example

Caitlin buys a residential rental property for $203,000. Her closing costs (including recording fees, escrow fees, title insurance, and other small items) are $2,000. She determines that the value of the personal property (including a refrigerator, stove, dishwasher, and blinds) is $5,000 based on its current fair market value (depending on age, condition, and make/model). She also determines the value of the land improvements (the fencing and sidewalk leading up to the front door) to be $2,000. She reviews the most recent property tax bills and determines that her assessed property value includes 25 percent for the value of her land. Here is how she would compute her depreciation deductions:

Purchase price:	$203,000
Closing costs:	$ 2,000
Total basis:	$205,000
Value of personal property:	$ 5,000
New basis:	$200,000
Value of building (75%):	$150,000
Value of land improvements:	$ 2,000
Building basis:	$148,000

Thus, Caitlin will be able to depreciate the personal property ($5,000) over 5 years, the land improvements ($2,000) over 15 years, and the building ($148,000) over 27.5 years. Had she not done these calculations, she would need to claim all depreciation over 27.5 years. She would still get the same amount of depreciation in the long run, but it would take her a full 27.5 years to fully maximize her depreciation deductions. In general, you will nearly always benefit from the shortest period of time needed to fully depreciate any assets. This is due to the fact that you are reducing current taxable income and thus delaying the actual payment of taxes (and perhaps changing how the income is taxed—that is, capital gains or ordinary income).

Depreciation in the Year of Sale

When you decide to sell your rental property, you are permitted to claim depreciation up to the date of sale. For instance, if you sell your property on July 1, you are permitted to deduct depreciation for the first six months of the year.

Section 179 Deductions

Section 179 of the Internal Revenue Code permits certain taxpayers to claim an expense deduction rather than depreciating certain types of assets. This is a very favorable provision for many small businesses in the United States because it permits a current-year deduction for the cost of the asset rather than waiting for several years to deduct the amount in full. Unfortunately, this favorable tax provision is not permitted with respect to assets utilized to produce rental income. Thus, you could not purchase a new refrigerator for your rental unit and claim a Section 179 tax deduction.

For most landlords, the only assets that can be expensed using Section 179 are those assets not located in the rental property. For instance, computer equipment or office furniture in your office may be expensed using Section 179. However, there are other limitations on using this favorable tax provision. These include:

- To use Section 179, you must actually purchase the property (new or used) for an active trade or business.
- Section 179 cannot be used for inherited or gifted property or with property that you have converted from personal to business use.
- You cannot use Section 179 to increase your loss on the property for the tax year at issue. Thus you can use this tax provision to zero out your income, but you cannot use it to produce a tax loss.
- The property must be used 50 percent or more for business purposes.

Must Depreciation Be Claimed?

You should claim deprecation on your rental property because if you do not claim this expense, your basis is still reduced by the amount that you could have claimed. Thus the tax law assumes that you will claim depreciation, and you will suffer any adverse tax results whether or not you actually claimed the expense. If the IRS is going to assume that you depreciated the property and you will suffer the adverse results if you do not claim it, you might as well get the benefit of the tax deductions over the years of use as a rental property.

Recapture Issues with Depreciation Claimed

When you sell your rental property, any depreciation that was claimed must be "recaptured," or added back to the sales price and taxes paid on the sale. The IRS requires the depreciation to be recaptured even if it was not previously claimed on any tax return. This is just another reason that this tax deduction should be claimed.

Example

Caitlin buys a rental property for $200,000 and claims $20,000 of depreciation over the time she owns the property. She then sells the property for $300,000. Her adjusted basis in the property is $180,000 (her purchase price less depreciation claimed; this number could be higher had she done any extensive improvements). Here is how her tax calculations would look:

Sales price:		$300,000
Less adjusted basis:		$180,000
Total gain:		$120,000
Gain due to depreciation:	$20,000 × 25% (recapture rate) =	$ 5,000
Gain due to capital gain:	$100,000 × 15% (federal rate) =	$ 15,000
Total federal taxes due:		$ 20,000

State or local taxes could also be due on this sale, depending on where the property is located.

Claiming the Correct Amount of Depreciation

If you failed to claim the correct amount of depreciation in a prior year (or failed to claim any depreciation at all when it was permitted), you are allowed to file an amended tax return to correct the error. This is done on Form 1040X. An amended tax return can be used to correct any mathematical errors in past years or to correct any improper methods of accounting with respect to the depreciation.

To file an amended return, you must do so within three years from the date you filed the original tax return (a timely filed return before April 15 is considered to be filed on April 15) or within two years if you actually paid the tax for this year. If you are outside this timeframe, you might need to file a change of accounting method with the IRS using Form 3115. (You must also get the IRS's permission to make the accounting method change to correct the depreciation. You cannot use Form 3115 to correct other tax errors when you are beyond the statute of limitations.)

Records Needed for Depreciation

The IRS will almost certainly review depreciation calculations in the event your return is selected for an audit. Thus, you must have the following documents available to support any amounts claimed for depreciation:

- Original purchase agreement (including closing documents and HUD-1 statements).
- Receipt and cancelled checks for any amounts spent on the property for the original purchase price or for any capital improvements.
- Valuation evidence for any personal property assets that you purchased and are claiming depreciation. This becomes especially important when you are using component depreciation, as we have previously discussed.

Conclusion

Claiming depreciation deductions is one of the best tax strategies available for rental property owners. Depreciation will often turn a cash-flow-positive property into a negative situation for tax filing purposes. Given that the IRS will attribute depreciation to you whether or not it was actually claimed, there is no reason not to utilize this valuable tax strategy.

We have seen many taxpayers fail to understand how depreciation can work to their ultimate benefit, especially with respect to the component depreciation. By fully understanding these tax rules, you will likely save yourself hundreds if not thousands of dollars every year—certainly a worthwhile goal!

CHAPTER 11

Business Entities and Real Estate Investors

Many real estate investors realize early on in their real estate careers that owning real estate and/or operating a rental real estate business in their own names is not generally a good idea. This is due to the litigious nature of our society and the relatively high risk that real estate ownership carries from a lawsuit perspective. What happens to your assets if a roofing subcontractor falls off the roof or a tenant slips and falls in your rental unit? Certainly, carrying liability or premises insurance will alleviate some of the risks and may be sufficient in many instances. But what if it is not sufficient? Fortunately, the use of various business entities can go a long way in assisting you with protecting your hard-earned assets. This chapter discusses these business entities in the context of the real estate arena. However, due to the differences in laws from state to state, it is important that you consult a qualified business law attorney or asset protection firm prior to establishing any business entities for your own real estate business.

The C Corporation

For most real estate investors, the use of a business entity will come down to a choice between a corporation and a Limited Liability Company (LLC). We will begin our discussion with corporations before moving on to the LLCs.

Definition

A *corporation* is simply a separate business entity (sometimes called an *artificial person*) that is organized under the laws of a state and is completely distinct from its owners. A *C corporation* is basically any for-profit corporation that did not make an election to be treated as an S corporation. It is called a C corporation because it is governed by Subchapter C of the Internal Revenue Code. All C corporations are treated as separate entities for tax purposes and must file an income tax return each year (Form 1120, a copy of which is included in Appendix A). Many real estate dealers have found that using a C corporation is an excellent method for combating some of the dealer tax ramifications. At the very least, some of the income may be taxed at a 15 percent tax rate, and the 15.3 percent self-employment taxes may be sufficiently reduced via controlled and planned salary payments (after other business expenses are paid).

How to Form a C Corporation

A corporation is formed by filing articles of incorporation with the secretary of state in the state where the corporation wants to do business. Once the articles are filed, the corporation is ready to begin doing business and should apply to the IRS for an Employer Identification Number (EIN) on Form SS-4 (copy included in Appendix A). The corporation should also have its bylaws voted on by the shareholders. Though the bylaws are not filed with any governmental agency, they are very important because they provide the means and ways for the corporation to operate on a day-to-day basis. The corporation may also register any trade names with the secretary of state if it will do business using a name different from its corporate name.

Who Can Own and Manage a C Corporation?

The owners of a corporation are called the *shareholders*. The corporation itself is run by the officers (president, vice president, secretary, and treasurer) and its board of directors. Generally, there are no limitations on who can be a shareholder, officer, or director of a corporation. Furthermore, in a one-person corporation, the same person may, in effect, occupy all corporate offices at once.

Personal Liability of Owners/Managers

Shareholders have no personal liability for the debts or acts of the corporation unless the corporation itself is disregarded as the result of a lawsuit (called *piercing the corporate veil*, a somewhat rare occurrence). A shareholder is always responsible for his or her own acts and can also lose all money contributed to the corporation to purchase the shares of stock.

Example

Michael invests $5,000 into ABC, Inc., a real estate company. The company runs into debt problems and must file bankruptcy. Assuming that Michael did not personally guarantee any of the corporate debts, Michael's loss is limited to his $5,000 original investment. Had Michael been operating as a sole proprietorship or general partnership, he could also be held personally liable for the business debts.

Special Tax Provisions and Rules

A C corporation must file its own tax return (Form 1120) every year, and it is taxed on its net profit (after business expenses have been deducted). Depending on the net income of the business, it might be advantageous for the business to be taxed at the corporate level, since the tax rate may be lower than it would be at the individual shareholder's tax rate level. For 2009, the following table shows the effective tax rate for C corporations.

Taxable Income	Tax Rate
$0–50,000	15%
$50,000–75,000	25%
$75,000–100,000	34%
$100,000–335,000	39%
$335,000–10,000,000	34%
$10,000,000–15,000,000	35%
$15,000,000–18,333,333	38%
$18,333,333 and up	35%

How to End a C Corporation

A corporation can stop doing business after a vote of a majority of shareholders to cease doing business. Once a decision has been made to stop doing business, the corporation must file articles of dissolution in the state where it filed its articles of incorporation. If the corporation sells its assets and distributes any money or other property to its shareholders, the shareholders may be liable for taxes on any property received (if the value of what was received is more than any amount paid for the stock in the corporation). Any gains will normally be taxed at the more favorable long-term capital gains rate (if the stock was held for more than one year). Finally, when the corporation ends, it must notify the IRS by filing a Form 966 (Corporate Dissolution or Liquidation).

Advantages of the C Corporation

- A corporation provides personal liability protection for all its shareholders. This liability protection is probably the most attractive reason to form a corporation.
- It is very easy for a shareholder to sell or transfer his shares of stock or to sell the entire company.

- There is a limited risk of loss. The only real risk of loss is the amount paid for the shares of stock. This is extremely important, since a shareholder who invests $10,000 in a corporation knows that no matter how poorly the corporation does, the most money that can be lost is the original $10,000 investment. Had the taxpayer instead invested the $10,000 in a sole proprietorship that then ran up $50,000 in business debts, the taxpayer could be liable for the $50,000 in debt in addition to losing his or her original $10,000 investment in the business.

- The corporation itself may be able to borrow or raise money without any personal guarantee of the owner(s). This will work if the corporation has a financial track record and is not a new company.

Tax Alert

A newly formed corporation may have trouble securing credit at the beginning of its operations because it does not have a financial track record. As such, a shareholder may be asked to personally guarantee a loan or other debt by co-signing on the loan with the corporation. By doing this, the shareholder is agreeing to become personally liable for the debt if the corporation does not pay.

- The corporation will not be affected by the death, bankruptcy, or incompetency of a shareholder. In many other forms of businesses, any one of these events could cause the business to end.

- The corporation is considered a separate legal entity under the law. This is important because it separates a taxpayer's business affairs from her personal affairs.

- The corporation can elect to have a fiscal year ending on some date other than December 31. This gives you some tax planning potential, since income and expenses can be accounted for using different year-end dates.

Example

XYZ, Inc., a C corporation, elects to end its tax year on February 28. If it pays Sam $10,000 in wages during January and February 2009, it can claim these wages as a tax deduction (assuming they are "reasonable") on its tax return, due May 15, 2009 ($2^{1}/_{2}$ months after is year ends). However, Sam will not need to report this $10,000 of wages until he files his 2009 personal tax return (due April 15, 2010, nearly one year after the corporation claimed a tax deduction).

- A corporation can adopt a medical reimbursement plan. This plan permits the corporation to reimburse its employees for their out-of-pocket medical expenses. This can be a very advantageous fringe benefit because the C corporation can deduct the reimbursements, and the employees do not have to claim these reimbursements as income. Such medical expenses are frequently lost without the benefit of having a C corporation to deduct them, since medical expenses are subject to the 7.5 percent adjusted gross income limitation on Schedule A (Itemized Deductions) on your personal return. The corporation needs to adopt the plan either in its bylaws or via a corporate resolution.

- The corporation can deduct premiums paid on group term life insurance policies with payouts of up to $50,000 per employee per year. This is a nice way to increase any life insurance policies you have. Any life insurance policies that have more than $50,000 of death benefits are taxable compensation to the employee. The IRS has established a cost of $2.76 of additional compensation for every $1,000 in additional policy limits.[1]

Example

Nick works for Bates, Inc., a C corporation. The corporation pays for the premiums on a $70,000 life insurance policy for Nick. Here is how Nick will be affected by this policy:

Total insurance coverage:	$70,000
Tax-free insurance:	$50,000
Taxable insurance coverage:	$20,000
Taxable compensation (20 × $2.76):	$ 55.20

In this example, Nick will need to pay taxes on the $55.20 of additional premiums paid on his behalf.

- A corporation may set up a dependent care assistance program. If it does so, up to $5,000 may be excluded from an employee's gross income, and the corporation is allowed to deduct such payments made on behalf of its employees. The corporation must adopt the plan, and the plan must clearly state what each employee is entitled to. Note that nondiscrimination rules state that the corporation cannot pay more than 25 percent of the benefits under the plan to owners or their spouses or dependents who own more than 5 percent of the business.

- A corporation that has 50 or fewer employees and has a high deductible medical plan for its employees can deduct contributions paid to Archer Medical Savings Accounts (MSAs) for its employees.

- A corporation that makes contributions to cafeteria plans or flexible spending arrangement plans on behalf of its employees can claim a tax deduction for these payments as a business expense.

- A corporation can also reimburse employees for educational expenses they incur. Any job-related courses are fully deductible by the corporation as business expenses. In addition, the employee does not have to claim the benefits as income. There is a $5,250 exclusion for employer-provided education assistance, including graduate-level courses, under a qualifying education plan. Any amount the corporation pays for an employee under the plan can be excluded from the employee's income, even if the courses are not job related. The corporation can deduct these expenses as regular business expenses. Again, no more than 5 percent of such benefits can be paid on behalf of owner-employees or their spouses or dependents.

Disadvantages of the C Corporation

- The corporation may be subject to double taxation, since the corporation itself pays taxes on its net income (Form 1120) and the shareholders pay personal taxes on any dividends they receive from the corporation (Form 1040). The double taxation occurs because the corporation does not get a tax deduction for any dividends it pays to its shareholders, so the same money is taxed twice. For this reason, many C corporations will try to not pay any dividends, which can create its own problem (see next disadvantage).

- The corporation may be subject to an accumulated earnings tax if it accumulates too much money (more than the business reasonably needs) and doesn't make any distributions in the form of dividends to its shareholders. For this reason, many larger corporations are forced to pay dividends and the double taxation issue comes into play. However, this is not often an issue for smaller corporations, since the amount of accumulated earnings from year to year is often quite small. Furthermore, it is generally very easy for a small corporation to retain earnings for future needs, including business expansion and/or the purchase of additional assets.

- There may be reasonable compensation tax issues. Reasonable compensation tax issues may apply to C corporations that pay their shareholders (who are also employees) salaries that might be too high. Under the Tax Code, the business is permitted to deduct "a reasonable allowance for salaries or other compensation for personal services actually rendered."[2] If the IRS determines that the salaries are too high, it may try to reclassify wages or other forms of compensation as dividends. If the IRS does this, it can effectively trigger double taxation issues (the corporation is denied a salary expense deduction and must pay additional tax, whereas the shareholders must also pay tax on the dividends that the IRS has now imposed).

- There are costs to form the corporation and keep it going on an annual basis. These costs are paid to the state where the business is incorporated. In addition, there might be legal fees to pay if the business uses an attorney to prepare the documents to form the corporation or needs to pay for resident agent or other state-specific services.

- Any losses that the corporation incurs stay with the corporation (the shareholders cannot deduct the losses personally on their Forms 1040, as they could if the business was a sole proprietorship).

- The corporation pays tax on its net profits as a separate taxable entity. The tax rates for corporations range from 15 to 39 percent, depending on the corporation's taxable income. This rate could be higher (or lower) than the corporate owner's individual tax rates.

- The corporation may have additional bookkeeping obligations and must obtain an EIN from the IRS.

- Unlike a sole proprietorship, a C corporation must withhold and pay Social Security taxes on any amounts paid as wages to minor children (under age 18).

Use of a C Corporation in Real Estate Activities

In general, a C corporation is not entitled to the capital gains tax rates on the sale of capital assets held longer than one year. Given the current 15 percent long-term capital gains rate for individuals, this is not good news. For this reason, you will not want to hold any long-term assets including rental properties in a C corporation. However, given that a C corporation has low tax rates on the first $50,000 of net taxable income (15 percent federal rate for income tax) as well as other non-taxable fringe benefits that other forms of entity do not have, holding a short-term asset in a C corporation might be a strategy to consider. Many real estate investors also use a C corporation to act as a management company for their real estate investments.

Example

Caitlin buys a property for $100,000 on August 1, 2008, and spends $25,000 to fix it up. On March 1, 2009, she sells the property for $175,000. If she holds this property in a C corporation, her tax bill will be $7,500 ($50,000 net profit times 15 percent federal tax rate). Assuming her personal tax bracket is 28 percent, the same sale done in her personal name without the C corporation would result in a tax of $14,000 ($50,000 net profit times 28 percent federal tax rate). By using a C corporation, she could potentially save $6,500 in federal income taxes.

Example

This scenario involves the same facts as the prior example, but the holding period is changed to more than one year. In that case, both the C corporation and Caitlin personally will pay taxes at a 15 percent rate. However, if the C corporation had any other income (such as from other property sales or management fees), the tax rate would quickly escalate from the 15 percent rate.

Note that to take advantage of the lower tax rate stated previously, the income generated from the sale of the property must be left in the C corporation to be taxed. If all funds are needed by the owners (for example, to pay living expenses), the benefit of the lower tax rate will be diminished. The corporation could also be subject to an accumulated earnings tax for keeping funds within the corporation. Your tax advisor can assist you with these potential issues.

C corporations are ideal for property management companies or to manage other business entities (such as being the manager of a limited liability company or the general partner of a limited partnership). As the prior examples indicate, it might also be appropriate for a limited number of short-term (less than one year) property sales. You generally will not want to hold rental properties in a C corporation due to the lack of a favorable long-term capital gains tax rate as well as the lack of ability to transfer rental losses to your personal tax return to offset your other income.

The S Corporation

For some real estate dealers and investors, the use of a C corporation will not adequately meet their overall tax planning needs, but the corporate entity is still attractive for other non-tax reasons. For these taxpayers, the use of an S corporation may make a lot of sense.

Definition

An *S corporation* is identical to a C corporation except that it makes an election with the IRS on Form 2553 to be treated as an S corporation. (A sample of Form 2553 is included in Appendix A.) The election must be made by the 15th day of the third month of a newly formed corporation's first year in order for the corporation to be able to take advantage of the S election during its first year. If this requirement is not met, there is a one-year delay for the election to be valid (that is, it will be valid for the second tax year but not the first tax year). Congress created S corporations as a way for small businesses to incorporate and get some tax advantages that C corporations do not have. All shareholders must agree to the S election before the election can be effective. Many small corporations that meet the criteria for S corporation status usually benefit from making the S election.

How to Form an S Corporation

An S corporation is formed exactly the same way as is a C corporation in that it must file its articles of incorporation with the secretary of state. It must also create its bylaws. The only additional step is that it must file its S election with the IRS on Form 2553. The S corporation must also obtain an EIN from the IRS.

Who Can Own and Manage an S Corporation?

There can be a maximum of 100 shareholders in an S corporation (a C corporation can have as many shareholders as it wants).[3] In addition, only individuals, estates, and certain trusts can be shareholders. It is not permissible for other business entities, such as C corporations or limited liability companies (taxed as partnerships), to be shareholders of an S corporation. A single-member LLC that elects to be "disregarded" for tax purposes is permitted to be a shareholder in an S corporation.

Personal Liability of Owners/Managers

The personal liability of any owners of an S corporation is exactly the same as those of a C corporation. Refer to the discussion in the section on C corporations.

Special Tax Provisions and Rules

The main difference between a C and an S corporation is the way the corporation is taxed. An S corporation is required to file a tax return (Form 1120S), but it does not pay any income tax on its net business income. Instead, the shareholders pay tax on the corporate income based on their percentage of ownership in the corporation. This income is reported to the shareholders on Schedule K-1 and is finally reported on Schedule E of the shareholder's personal (Form 1040) tax return.

Example

Suppose the S corporation had a net income of $50,000 in 2009 and there were two 50 percent shareholders in the corporation. Each shareholder would receive a Schedule K-1 at the end of the year showing $25,000 in income that they need to report on their personal tax return ($50,000 × 0.50 = $25,000). Each shareholder, not the corporation, would be required to pay income taxes on the $25,000 of income that is attributed to them individually.

In addition, with proper tax planning, the owners of an S corporation can limit the amount of self-employment taxes that they must pay. This is a very nice feature of an S corporation, since the ability to avoid having to pay employment taxes on some of its income gives an S corporation a distinct advantage over sole proprietorships and other business entities.

Example

Assume that a sole proprietorship business had a net income of $80,000 in 2009. It would pay self-employment taxes of $11,304, which are calculated as follows:

1. Net profit: $80,000
2. Multiply Line 1 by 92.35%: $73,000
3. Multiply Line 2 by 15.3%: $11,304
4. Total employment taxes: $11,304*

If this business was organized as a S corporation and paid out half its income ($40,000) as wages instead of the full $80,000, it would pay the following in employment taxes:

Employer share of Social Security (6.2%): $2,480

Employee share of Social Security (6.2%): $2,480

Employer share of Medicare (2.9%): $1,160

Employer unemployment (FUTA): $ 56

Total employment taxes: $6,176

Although this example is rather simplistic, it is obvious that some very real tax savings can be obtained by structuring payments as wages of S corporation owners and avoiding the large amount of self-employment taxes that would be due if the business were organized as a sole proprietorship.

*The individual owner would also be entitled to a deduction on his or her individual income tax return in an amount equal to 1/2 of the self-employment taxes due and payable ($5,652 in this example, which is 50 percent of $11,304). This would reduce his or her income tax by an amount of $565 to $1,978, depending on his or her tax bracket (currently 10 to 35 percent).

Example

Tom's S corporation, for which he is the 100 percent owner, grosses $150,000 for the year. Tom has $100,000 of expenses, including $50,000 of wages he has paid to himself. Thus, Tom's S corporation has a $50,000 net profit, which will be treated as a distribution to Tom for tax purposes. The K-1 Tom receives for the year will show the $50,000 as ordinary income, and Tom will have to pay federal and state income tax on this amount. However, this $50,000 of income is not subject to self-employment taxes (currently at a rate of 15.3 percent). Thus, Tom has just saved approximately $7,500 for the year in self-employment taxes.

Note that 100 percent of the profits of a limited liability company are subject to self-employment taxes. Also, if we look at the prior scenario with a C corporation, for Tom to be able to receive the benefit of the profits of the corporation, 100 percent of the profits would have to be paid as wages to Tom. Wages are also subject to self-employment taxes.

Tax Tip

The IRS states that S corporations must pay "reasonable compensation" to their employees. The IRS will scrutinize the compensation paid (in an audit), especially if the S corporation shows that no wages were paid. The IRS is savvy to the fact the shareholders in an S corporation can avoid the payment of self-employment taxes by paying no wages to its shareholders and instead paying distributions. You can still maximize the benefit of having an S corporation by paying distributions; just make sure some wages are paid and that the wages are reasonable.

What is reasonable compensation? Unfortunately, there is no set answer. Much like the definition of a real estate dealer, the definition of reasonable compensation is based on a number of facts and circumstances. However, there are some guidelines to follow:

- Research compensation paid in your industry based on your job description: You need to keep written proof of such research in case your compensation is challenged.
- Do not pay out the distributions to owners on a weekly or biweekly basis, because such payments will start to look like wages. Instead, you should pay the distributions on a quarterly, half yearly, or yearly basis. Likewise, you should pay the wages on a weekly or biweekly basis to make sure that wages look like wages.

How to End an S Corporation

An S corporation ceases doing business in exactly the same way that a C corporation cases doing business; see the discussion under the C corporation.

Advantages of an S Corporation

- An S corporation, like a C corporation, provides personal liability protection for its shareholders.
- An S corporation avoids the double-taxation problems of a C corporation, since the S corporation never needs to declare any dividends to its shareholders.
- There are no accumulated earnings tax issues with S corporations.

- An S corporation does not need to deal with the reasonable compensation tax issues in the same manner that a C corporation does. Reasonable compensation tax issues may apply to C corporations that pay their shareholders (who are employees) salaries that may be too high. With an S corporation, there may be reasonable compensation issues for corporations that pay salaries that are too low (to avoid employment taxes).

- It is generally easy to transfer or sell ownership in a corporation or to sell the entire corporation. However, depending on the percentage of ownership being transferred, there may not be a great market to purchase the shares (unlike the New York Stock Exchange).

- The corporation does not pay any tax on its profits. However, some states impose a corporate tax on S corporations. All taxpayers should research any potential state income tax issues prior to making the election, since the laws vary greatly from state to state. With respect to federal taxes, any profits (or losses) that the S corporation may incur flow through to the shareholders' individual income tax returns, and the shareholders pay any tax owed or get the benefits of the loss that the corporation suffered. Each shareholder receives a Schedule K-1 from the corporation at the end of the corporation's tax year, informing the shareholder how much profit or loss she must report to the IRS.

- An S corporation can be set up with only one owner (shareholder).

- The shareholders of the S corporation can deduct losses from the S corporation on their personal tax returns up to the amount they contributed to the S corporation (called the *shareholder's basis*).

Disadvantages of an S Corporation

- A corporation can be expensive to set up (may need to hire a lawyer and pay filing fees).

- There is an additional form to file (Form 2553) that a C corporation does not have to file.

- There is a maximum of 100 shareholders for an S corporation. For purposes of this rule, a husband and wife are treated as one shareholder.

- An S corporation can issue only one class of stock. (Unlike a C corporation, an S corporation cannot have common and preferred classes of stock.)

- The S corporation shareholders are taxed on the income of the corporation, even if the shareholders do not actually receive the income. The reason for this is that most S corporations do not distribute the profits to the shareholders at the end of the year but instead retain the earnings to provide for the financial needs of the business for the next year. There is nothing in the rules that says that an S corporation cannot distribute to its shareholder at least enough money to cover the shareholder's new income tax bill. However, please keep in mind that you must be paid a "reasonable" salary if you perform personal services for the S corporation and cannot thus take all your compensation in the form of a distribution.

- There are some restrictions on who can be a shareholder in an S corporation. For instance, most corporations, partnerships, LLCs, and any other entity that is not an individual cannot be a shareholder.

- The owners of the S corporation must be paid wages if they perform services for the corporation, so there may be employment tax returns that need to be filed (Forms 940 and 941; copies provided in Appendix A).

- Like a C corporation, there could be additional bookkeeping requirements. In addition, the S corporation must obtain an EIN from the IRS.

- The passive activity rules may apply to an S corporation. These rules limit a shareholder's loss when an S corporation has a loss, and not a profit, for any given tax year. When a loss occurs, the loss can be used by the shareholders to reduce the other taxable income, but only if the shareholders "materially participated" in the business. This area of the Internal Revenue Code is hopelessly complex, but generally a person is considered to have materially participated in a business if he worked more than 500 hours for the business during the year of the loss, worked more than anyone else did for the business (but fewer than 500 hours), or worked at least 100 hours and at least as much as anyone else. It is recommended that you consult a competent tax professional whenever the IRS uses the passive activity rules against you.

- Owners of more than 2 percent of the stock of an S corporation are taxed on the value of medical payments plans, group term life insurance, and other fringe benefits. (Owners of C corporations are *not* taxed on these fringe benefits.)

- Unlike a sole proprietorship, an S corporation must pay Social Security taxes on wages paid to minor children (under age 18) who are working for the business.

Use of an S Corporation for Real Estate Activities

An S corporation can be used in lieu of a C corporation when you want the corporate asset protection but not the separate taxpaying requirements. However, an S corporation is generally not a favored entity for holding real estate either short-term or long-term. Like a C corporation, an S corporation also has limits on fully deducting rental property tax losses. Tax losses in an S corporation are limited to the shareholder's basis in the S corporation's stock. The basis does not include third part debt, such as a mortgage. S corporations work well for labor-intensive business activities, such as operating a real estate brokerage agency or a property management company.

> ### Example
>
> David forms an S corporation to hold a piece of rental property. He purchases the property for $300,000 and takes out a mortgage on the property for $290,000. The $10,000 cash David put as a down payment on the property becomes his stock basis in the company. David then transfers the property to the S corporation and the S corporation obtains the $290,000 mortgage. David's stock basis does not include the $290,000 mortgage even though David has signed personally on the note. If the property has a tax loss of $20,000 on the tax return, David is only allowed to deduct $10,000 of the loss on his personal tax return. The remaining $10,000 will be carried over until David's stock basis is increased.

The Limited Liability Company (LLC)

Perhaps the most valuable business entity for real estate investors is the limited liability company, or LLC. This entity often provides the greatest flexibility and ease of use, along with providing some very nice tax and asset protection benefits. Most real estate investors with rental properties will title such properties in a LLC.

Definition

A LLC, is a mix between a corporation and a partnership. It is similar to a corporation because it limits the personal liability of its members, but it is taxed like a partnership.

How to Form an LLC

A LLC is formed by filing articles of organization with the secretary of state in the state where the LLC wants to do business. In addition, like a corporation, a LLC must have an *operating agreement* (called *bylaws* for a corporation). This document is not filed with any governmental agencies and is used solely to assist the LLC in its day-to-day operations.

Who Can Own and Manage an LLC

The owners of an LLC are called *members*. The LLC can be run by one or more of its members, or it can hire an outside manager to run the company. Many taxpayers with multiple business entities use a C corporation as the outside manager of the LLC. There are generally no restrictions on who can own an interest in an LLC. In addition, it is permissible for an LLC to have only one owner or member.

Personal Liability of Owners/Managers

The members of an LLC have the benefit of limited liability, which basically means that they are responsible only for their own personal acts and not for the debts or obligations of the LLC itself (unless they personally guaranteed a LLC debt). The members can also lose any investments they make in the LLC if the LLC goes bankrupt or otherwise becomes insolvent. These rules are basically the same as the rules for corporations.

Special Tax Provisions and Rules

An LLC can elect to be taxed as a corporation or partnership or disregarded for tax purposes. If the LLC has two or more members (owners), it will generally elect to be taxed as a partnership (to avoid the double-taxation problems of a C corporation or the various restrictions for S corporations). If there is only one member of the LLC, it can elect to be disregarded for tax purposes. Unfortunately, this does not mean that it will not need to file any tax returns or pay any tax on its net profits. Instead, it can report its income and expenses on a Schedule C or E, the exact same way that a sole proprietorship or rental real estate owner reports its income and expenses. . The net earnings of an LLC may be subject to self-employment tax, whether it elects to be taxed as a partnership or is disregarded for tax purposes, unless it elects to be taxed as a corporation. Of course, if it elects to be taxed as a corporation, the corporate tax rules will apply to the LLC.

How to End an LLC

In some states, an LLC can end when one of its members dies, retires, resigns, is removed, or files for bankruptcy, unless the remaining members vote to keep the LLC up and running. To voluntarily end an LLC, the members must file articles of dissolution with the state in which it filed its articles of organization.

Advantages of an LLC

- There is no double-taxation issue if the LLC is taxed as a partnership. Like a partnership or S corporation, any income that an LLC earns is taxed on the individual members' tax returns, and the LLC does not need to declare dividends or generally pay any income tax.

- A single-member LLC can be disregarded for tax purposes, thus easing the tax reporting requirements. However, we frequently recommend that single-member LLCs be avoided for asset protection purposes, since they generally receive less favorable asset protection than LLCs taxed like a partnership (with two or more members). There are differences in liability protection among the various states, and this issue must be considered before making an election on an overall choice of business entity.

- A LLC provides personal liability protection for its members.

- There are no accumulated earnings tax problems (like an S corporation but unlike a C corporation).

- There are no reasonable compensation tax issues, unlike a C corporation or possibly an S corporation. An LLC is not required to pay wages or salary to its owners.

Disadvantages of an LLC

- An LLC can be expensive to set up, since you may need to hire a lawyer to draft the documents and pay any state filing fees. This is basically the same disadvantage as for corporations.

- An LLC may cease to exist if a member files bankruptcy, dies, or becomes incapacitated.

- The net profit of an LLC is often considered income from self-employment and thus is subject to self-employment taxes. Thus, you will want to be sure to make a proper tax election with your LLC, depending on your overall circumstances. However, simply owning real estate in an LLC will not trigger only self-employment taxes if such taxes were not due if the real estate was not owned in an LLC.

- There may be limitations on the use of fringe benefits such as medical payment plans and group term life insurance (similar to the rules with S corporations).

- The members of an LLC are taxed on their share of the LLC's net income, even if the LLC did not actually distribute the income to its owners. This is very similar to one of the disadvantages of an S corporation. Like an S corporation, there is no rule to preventing the LLC from distributing a portion of the income to the members to cover the member's income tax bill as a result of having to include the LLC income on the member's Form 1040.

- A member may need to get the consent of other members before he can sell or otherwise transfer his ownership interest in the LLC.

Use of an LLC for Real Estate Activities

Many real estate taxpayers utilize one or more LLCs in their overall real estate activities. An LLC is an excellent vehicle for holding title to real estate. Many actively run real estate businesses, including brokerages, use the LLC due to its ease of use, even if there is more than one member and a partnership tax return (Form 1065; copy included in Appendix A) is required. An LLC is also used often for rental real estate activities, commercial or residential. In fact, we believe that it is often the best entity to hold title to rental properties. You also may want to consider forming multiple LLCs to hold title to rental properties you own for additional asset protection.

The Limited Partnership

One of the oldest and best methods of gaining some very attractive asset protection comes via a limited partnership. As the following discussion will show, there are also some situations in which a limited partnership makes a lot of sense for a real estate investor or dealer.

Definition

A *limited partnership* is a way for two or more people to conduct business together for profit without having to go through the process of incorporating the business. It must file organizational documents with the state in which it wants to do business. Keep in mind that there are major differences between a limited partnership and a general partnership. All partnerships must file tax returns (Form 1065) at the end of the year, with each partner receiving a Schedule K-1 indicating how much income must be reported on the partner's personal tax return. The basic difference between a general partnership and a limited partnership is that certain limited partners in a limited partnership are able to limit their personal liability with respect to partnership debts. Because the laws vary considerably from state to state, it is highly recommended that a lawyer be contacted before setting up a limited partnership. We limit our discussion in this section to limited partnerships, since we do not advise any taxpayers to utilize a general partnership for their real estate activities due to the unlimited exposure the partners would have to the operation of the general partnership.

How to Form a Limited Partnership

A limited partnership is formed when the partners (two or more) file a certificate of limited partnership in the state where the partnership wants to do business. Once this certificate is filed, you must obtain an EIN (using Form SS-4) from the IRS.

Who Can Own and Manage a Limited Partnership

The owners of the limited partnership are called *partners*. The partners are either general or limited. There must be at least two partners before a partnership can be formed. The general partner of the limited partnership is responsible for the management of the company. The limited partners are merely investors in the partnership and do not participate in the day-to-day management of the partnership. Instead, they are *passive* participants, whereas the general partner or partners are *active* participants.

Personal Liability of Owners/Managers

All general partners are personally responsible for the debts of the limited partnership. The limited partners, on the other hand, do not have such responsibility. Given this liability issue, it is often advisable to use a business entity, such as a corporation or LLC, to act as the general partner.

Special Tax Provisions and Rules

A limited partnership is not subject to paying any income tax. However, it is required to file a Form 1065 to report all income and expenses, and the individual partners receive a Schedule K-1 from the partnership. Thus the partners (both general and limited) are required to pay any taxes on their portion of the net profit. The partners may also benefit if there is a loss from the partnership, since they may be able to use the loss to offset other income that they or their spouses received during the year. The general partners may also be liable for self-employment taxes on their portion of the net income from the partnership. This is the case if the general partner is an individual and not another business entity.

How to End a Limited Partnership

It is generally quite easy to end a limited partnership; all that is required is for the partnership to file a certificate of dissolution with the state where the limited partnership was established.

Advantages of a Limited Partnership

- There are no double-taxation issues with a limited partnership, since the partnership itself does not pay tax. Instead, like an S corporation, any profits or losses that a limited partnership incurs flow through to the individual partners' tax returns.

- There are no accumulated earnings tax problems (the way you could have with a C corporation).

- There are no reasonable compensation tax issues (as you could have with a C or S corporation).

- Partners may be able to deduct any losses from the partnership on their personal tax returns, at least in an amount up to what they contributed to the partnership (called the *partner's basis*).

Disadvantages of a Limited Partnership

- The general partner in a limited partnership has potentially unlimited liability. (A judgment against a partnership can force a general partner to use her personal assets to satisfy the partnership's debts.) For this reason, we do not recommend having an individual as the general partner of most limited partnerships.

- Like an S corporation and an LLC, the (general and limited) partners are taxed on profits of the partnership, even if they don't actually receive their share of the profits. However, the partnership is permitted to distribute enough money to cover the additional tax liability as a result of including the partnership income on the partner's personal tax return.

- The income a general partner must report on his personal tax return may be subject to self-employment taxes. This is another reason that we do not recommend that the general partner be an individual.

- A partner may have a very difficult time selling or transferring her interests in a limited partnership. The reason for this is that most people do not want to be partners with other people who they do not know or trust. Also, many written partnership agreements contain provisions that prohibit the sale of one partner's interest in the partnership without the written consent of the other partner(s). These prohibitions on the transfer of an ownership interest are also often contained in a separate document called a *buy/sell agreement*. Buy/sell agreements are also commonly utilized in the corporate arena for similar reasons.

- There may be limitations on the availability of maximizing fringe benefits, such as medical payment plans and group term life insurance.

- It may be very difficult for the partnership to borrow funds on its own unless one or more of the partners are willing to co-sign on the loan (and to accept personal responsibility for the loan in the event of a default).

- The passive activity rules (discussed in Chapter 7) may apply to the partnership.

Use of a Limited Partnership for Real Estate Activities

Limited partnerships are generally an excellent way for multiple investors to invest together in a real estate project. Each of them (limited partners, not a general partner) can effectively limit their overall risk of loss to the amount invested, thus providing valuable limited liability protection. In addition, many families use limited partnerships as a way to provide some beneficial estate and tax planning strategies because there may be opportunities to obtain valuation discounts and some income shifting. Of course, a competent estate planning attorney should be consulted prior to utilizing a limited partnership for estate tax or planning purposes. Finally, many real estate dealers have also found that using a limited partnership is a beneficial method of conducting dealer activities. This is because profits earned in a limited partnership are not subject to self-employment taxes (unlike dealer income earned in a sole proprietorship, LLC, or C or S corporation).

Tax Tip

We do not recommend you hold your rental real estate in a limited partnership due to the passive activity loss limitations previously discussed. Limited partners are not allowed to actively participate in the management of the limited partnership; therefore, the ability for limited partners to deduct rental losses (either as an active participant or as a real estate professional) is eliminated in a limited partnership.

A Comparison of the Various Business Entities

If You Want to:	You Should Consider Using:	You Should Not Use:
Have liability protection	C or S corporation, LLC, limited partnership	Sole proprietorship or general partnership
Hire your children	Sole proprietorship, LLC	C or S corporation, possibly partnership (if the side partners are not a husband and wife)
Limit/control Social Security and Medicare taxes (self-employment taxes)	S or C corporation, possibly limited partnership	Sole proprietorship, LLC, or general partnership
Deduct business losses on personal tax return	S corporation, LLC, sole proprietorship, partnership (limited or general)	C corporation
Limit recordkeeping/filing and startup filing requirements	Sole proprietorship, general partnership	S and C corporations, LLC, and limited partnership
Maximize retirement benefits	Any entity	N/A
Maximize group life insurance deductions	C corporation	S corporation, LLC, sole proprietorship, and partnership (general or limited)
Maximize fringe benefits	C corporation	S corporation, partnership (general or limited), LLC, and sole proprietorship
Lower income tax on net income under $50,000	C corporation	S corporation, LLC, sole proprietorship, and partnership (general or limited)
Maximize disability insurance benefits	C corporation	Partnership (general or limited), sole proprietorship, S corporation, and LLC
Eliminate double taxation	S corporation, LLC, sole proprietorship, partnership (general or limited)	C corporation

If You Want to:	You Should Consider Using:	You Should Not Use:
Raise additional money via loans or new investors	C corporation, limited partnership	General partnership, sole proprietorship, LLC, and S corporation
Lower IRS audit risk	S or C corporation, partnership (general or limited)	Sole proprietorship and LLC (that is disregarded for tax purposes and files a Schedule C or E)
Maximize accumulation of earnings/income in business	Partnership (general or limited), LLC, sole proprietorship, S corporation	C corporation

Business Tax Returns and Due Dates for the Various Entities

	Income Tax	
Sole proprietorship	Schedules C or E, Form 1040	April 15
S corporation	1120S	March 15
C corporation	1120	March 15 (or 2½ months after close of fiscal year)
Partnership (general or limited)	1065	April 15
LLC	Schedules C or E, Form 1040 (if disregarded) or 1065	April 15

	Employment/Self-Employment Taxes	
Entity	Form	Due Date
Sole proprietorship	1040-ES	April 15, June 15, September 15, and January 15
S corporation	941	941: April 30, July 31, October 31, and January 31
	940	940: January 31
C corporation	941	941: April 30, July 31, October 31, and January 31
	940	940: January 31
Partnership	1040-ES	April 15, June 15, September 15, and January 15
LLC	1040-ES	April 15, June 15, September 15, and January 15

Conclusion

All real estate investors and dealers should strongly consider setting up one or more business entities to conduct their real estate activities. Given the litigious nature of today's society, the ownership of real estate effectively puts a target on the back of the titleholder. If the owner is a business entity, it can limit the overall risk of loss. For instance, if you own your rental property in your personal name and are sued, you potentially could lose all your personal assets (home, savings, car, investments) if you lose a lawsuit. By separating your personal assets from your real estate activities by the use of one or more of the entities discussed in this chapter, you are not putting all your eggs in one basket.

In addition to the asset protection issues, the use of business entities may also provide some attractive tax planning options. You may be able to lower your overall income tax bills and reduce the amount of self-employment taxes that also may be owed. The tax savings alone may more than pay for the extra costs associated with the business entity (including startup costs and the extra tax return preparation fees).

Conclusion

We hope that this text has been helpful in assisting you with the tax considerations and calculations involved in your real estate endeavors. However, your tax situation is unique, and you should make sure that you discuss any and all tax strategies with your personal tax professional before implementing any of them.

For many Americans today, investing in real estate is the best and most realistic chance for economic success and freedom. This is the case even in declining real estate markets. By understanding how taxes fit into the picture, you should be able to keep more of your own hard-earned money so that you and your family can achieve the financial freedom and independence that you desire. Best of luck with all your real estate ventures today and in the future.

IRS Tax Forms

940 Employer's Annual Federal Unemployment (FUTA) Tax Return

941 Employer's Quarterly Federal Tax Return

966 Corporate Dissolution or Liquidation

1040 U.S. Individual Income Tax Return

1065 U.S. Return of Partnership Income

1120 U.S. Corporation Income Tax Return

1120S U.S. Income Tax Return for an S Corporation

2553 Election by a Small Business Corporation

3115 Application for Change in Accounting Method

4562 Depreciation and Amortization

4797 Sales of Business Property

6252 Installment Sale Income

8606 Nondeductible IRAs

8824 Like-Kind Exchanges

8825 Rental Real Estate Income and Expenses of a Partnership or an S Corporation

8829 Expenses for Business Use of Your Home

Schedules A&B Itemized Deductions

Schedule C Profit or Loss From Business

Schedule D Capital Gains and Losses

Schedule E Supplemental Income and Loss

SS-4 Application for Employer Identification Number

Form **940 for 2008:** Employer's Annual Federal Unemployment (FUTA) Tax Return
Department of the Treasury — Internal Revenue Service

850108

OMB No. 1545-0028

(EIN)
Employer identification number ☐☐ – ☐☐☐☐☐☐☐

Name *(not your trade name)*

Trade name *(if any)*

Address
Number   Street   Suite or room number
City   State   ZIP code

Type of Return
(Check all that apply.)

☐ **a.** Amended
☐ **b.** Successor employer
☐ **c.** No payments to employees in 2008
☐ **d.** Final: Business closed or stopped paying wages

Read the separate instructions before you fill out this form. Please type or print within the boxes.

Part 1: Tell us about your return. If any line does NOT apply, leave it blank.

1 If you were required to pay your state unemployment tax in ...

    1a One state only, write the state abbreviation . . . . **1a** ☐☐
    - OR -
    1b More than one state (You are a multi-state employer) . . . . **1b** ☐ Check here. Fill out Schedule A.
          Skip line 2 for 2008 and go to line 3.
2 If you paid wages in a state that is subject to CREDIT REDUCTION . . . . **2** ☐ Check here. Fill out Schedule A (Form 940), Part 2.

Part 2: Determine your FUTA tax before adjustments for 2008. If any line does NOT apply, leave it blank.

3 Total payments to all employees . . . . **3** ☐ .

4 Payments exempt from FUTA tax . . . . **4** ☐ .

    Check all that apply: **4a** ☐ Fringe benefits   **4c** ☐ Retirement/Pension   **4e** ☐ Other
                4b ☐ Group-term life insurance   **4d** ☐ Dependent care

5 Total of payments made to each employee in excess of $7,000 . . . . **5** ☐ .

6 Subtotal (line 4 + line 5 = line 6) . . . . **6** ☐ .

7 Total taxable FUTA wages (line 3 – line 6 = line 7) . . . . **7** ☐ .

8 FUTA tax before adjustments (line 7 × .008 = line 8) . . . . **8** ☐ .

Part 3: Determine your adjustments. If any line does NOT apply, leave it blank.

9 If ALL of the taxable FUTA wages you paid were excluded from state unemployment tax, multiply line 7 by .054 (line 7 × .054 = line 9). Then go to line 12 . . . . **9** ☐ .
10 If SOME of the taxable FUTA wages you paid were excluded from state unemployment tax, OR you paid ANY state unemployment tax late (after the due date for filing Form 940), fill out the worksheet in the instructions. Enter the amount from line 7 of the worksheet onto line 10 . . **10** ☐ .
           Skip line 11 for 2008 and go to line 12.
11 If credit reduction applies, enter the amount from line 3 of Schedule A (Form 940) . . . . . **11** ☐ .

Part 4: Determine your FUTA tax and balance due or overpayment for 2008. If any line does NOT apply, leave it blank.

12 Total FUTA tax after adjustments (lines 8 + 9 + 10 + 11 = line 12) . . . . **12** ☐ .

13 FUTA tax deposited for the year, including any payment applied from a prior year . . . . **13** ☐ .
14 **Balance due** (If line 12 is more than line 13, enter the difference on line 14.)
    • If line 14 is more than $500, you must deposit your tax.
    • If line 14 is $500 or less, you may pay with this return. For more information on how to pay, see the separate instructions . . . . **14** ☐ .
15 **Overpayment** (If line 13 is more than line 12, enter the difference on line 15 and check a box below.) . . . . **15** ☐ .

                                  Check one: ☐ Apply to next return.
                                          ☐ Send a refund.

▶ You **MUST** fill out both pages of this form and **SIGN** it.

Next ➡

For Privacy Act and Paperwork Reduction Act Notice, see the back of Form 940-V, Payment Voucher.   Cat. No. 11234O   Form **940** (2008)

Form 940 Employer's Annual Federal Unemployment (FUTA) Tax Return

850208

Name *(not your trade name)*	Employer identification number (EIN)

Part 5: Report your FUTA tax liability by quarter only if line 12 is more than $500. If not, go to Part 6.

16 Report the amount of your FUTA tax liability for each quarter; do NOT enter the amount you deposited. If you had no liability for a quarter, leave the line blank.

16a 1st quarter (January 1 – March 31) . . . . 16a [   ] .

16b 2nd quarter (April 1 – June 30) . . . . 16b [   ] .

16c 3rd quarter (July 1 – September 30) . . . . 16c [   ] .

16d 4th quarter (October 1 – December 31) . . . . 16d [   ] .

17 Total tax liability for the year (lines 16a + 16b + 16c + 16d = line 17) **17** [   ] .   Total must equal line 12.

Part 6: May we speak with your third-party designee?

Do you want to allow an employee, a paid tax preparer, or another person to discuss this return with the IRS? See the instructions for details.

☐ **Yes.**   Designee's name and phone number [   ]   ( ) –

Select a 5-digit Personal Identification Number (PIN) to use when talking to IRS [ ] [ ] [ ] [ ] [ ]

☐ **No.**

Part 7: Sign here. You MUST fill out both pages of this form and SIGN it.

Under penalties of perjury, I declare that I have examined this return, including accompanying schedules and statements, and to the best of my knowledge and belief, it is true, correct, and complete, and that no part of any payment made to a state unemployment fund claimed as a credit was, or is to be, deducted from the payments made to employees. Declaration of preparer (other than taxpayer) is based on all information of which preparer has any knowledge.

✖ **Sign your name here** [   ]   Print your name here [   ]

Print your title here [   ]

Date [/   /]   Best daytime phone ( ) –

Paid preparer's use only   Check if you are self-employed . . . ☐

Preparer's name	[ ]	Preparer's SSN/PTIN	[ ]
Preparer's signature	[ ]	Date	[/ /]
Firm's name (or yours if self-employed)	[ ]	EIN	[ ]
Address	[ ]	Phone	( ) –
City	[ ] State [ ]	ZIP code	[ ]

Form 940 (*Continued*)

Form 940-V,
Payment Voucher

What Is Form 940-V?

Form 940-V is a transmittal form for your check or money order. Using Form 940-V allows us to process your payment more accurately and efficiently. If you have any balance due of $500 or less on your 2008 Form 940, fill out Form 940-V and send it with your check or money order.

Note. If your balance is more than $500, see *When Must You Deposit Your FUTA Tax?* in the Instructions for Form 940.

How Do You Fill Out Form 940-V?

Type or print clearly.

Box 1. Enter your employer identification number (EIN). Do not enter your social security number (SSN).

Box 2. Enter the amount of your payment. Be sure to put dollars and cents in the appropriate spaces.

Box 3. Enter your business name and complete address exactly as they appear on your Form 940.

How Should You Prepare Your Payment?

- Make your check or money order payable to the *United States Treasury.* Do not send cash.
- On the memo line of your check or money order, write:
  — your EIN,
  — Form 940, and
  — 2008.
- Carefully detach Form 940-V along the dotted line.
- Do not staple your payment to the voucher.
- Mail your 2008 Form 940, your payment, and Form 940-V in the envelope that came with your 2008 Form 940 instruction booklet. If you do not have that envelope, use the table in the Instructions for Form 940 to find the mailing address.

✂- - - - - ▼ **Detach Here and Mail With Your Payment and Form 940.** ▼ - - - - ✂

Form **940-V**	**Payment Voucher**	OMB No. 1545-0028
Department of the Treasury Internal Revenue Service	▶ Do not staple or attach this voucher to your payment.	2008

1 Enter your employer identification number (EIN).	2 Enter the amount of your payment. ▶	Dollars	Cents
	3 Enter your business name (individual name if sole proprietor).		
	Enter your address.		
	Enter your city, state, and ZIP code.		

Form 940 (*Continued*)

Privacy Act and Paperwork Reduction Act Notice. We ask for the information on this form to carry out the Internal Revenue laws of the United States. We need it to figure and collect the right amount of tax. Chapter 23, Federal Unemployment Tax Act, of Subtitle C, Employment Taxes, of the Internal Revenue Code imposes a tax on employers with respect to employees. This form is used to determine the amount of the tax that you owe. Section 6011 requires you to provide the requested information if you are liable for FUTA tax under section 3301. Section 6109 requires taxpayers and paid preparers to provide their idenification numbers. If you fail to provide this information in a timely manner, you may be subject to penalties and interest.

You are not required to provide the information requested on a form that is subject to the Paperwork Reduction Act unless the form displays a valid OMB control number. Books and records relating to a form or instructions must be retained as long as their contents may become material in the administration of any Internal Revenue law.

Generally, tax returns and return information are confidential, as required by section 6103. However, section 6103 allows or requires the IRS to disclose or give the information shown on your tax return to others

as described in the Code. For example, we may disclose your tax information to the Department of Justice for civil and criminal litigation, and to cities, states, the District of Columbia, and U.S. commonwealths and possessions to administer their tax laws. We may also disclose this information to other countries under a tax treaty, to federal and state agencies to enforce federal non-tax criminal laws, or to federal law enforcement and intelligence agencies to combat terrorism.

The time needed to complete and file this form will vary depending on individual circumstances. The estimated average time is: Recordkeeping, 23 hr., 39 min.; Learning about the law or the form, 1 hr., 23 min.; Preparing and sending the form to the IRS, 2 hr., 17 min.

If you have comments concerning the accuracy of these time estimates or suggestions for making Form 940 simpler, we would be happy to hear from you. You can write to: Internal Revenue Service, Tax Products Coordinating Committee, SE:W:CAR:MP:T:SP, 1111 Constitution Avenue, NW, IR-6526, Washington, DC 20224. **Do not** send Form 940 to this address. Instead, see *Where Do You File?* on page 2 of the Instructions for Form 940.

Form 940 (*Continued*)

Form **941 for 2009:** **Employer's QUARTERLY Federal Tax Return**　　950109

(Rev. January 2009)　　Department of the Treasury — Internal Revenue Service

OMB No. 1545-0029

(EIN)
Employer identification number　☐☐ – ☐☐☐☐☐☐☐

Name *(not your trade name)*

Trade name *(if any)*

Address　Number　　Street　　Suite or room number

City　　State　　ZIP code

Report for this Quarter of 2009
(Check one.)

☐ **1:** January, February, March

☐ **2:** April, May, June

☐ **3:** July, August, September

☐ **4:** October, November, December

Read the separate instructions before you complete Form 941. Type or print within the boxes.

Part 1: Answer these questions for this quarter.

1　Number of employees who received wages, tips, or other compensation for the pay period including: *Mar. 12* (Quarter 1), *June 12* (Quarter 2), *Sept. 12* (Quarter 3), *Dec. 12* (Quarter 4)　**1**

2　Wages, tips, and other compensation . . . .　**2**

3　Income tax withheld from wages, tips, and other compensation . . . .　**3**

4　If no wages, tips, and other compensation are subject to social security or Medicare tax　☐ Check and go to line 6.

5　Taxable social security and Medicare wages and tips:

	Column 1		Column 2
5a Taxable social security wages		× .124 =	
5b Taxable social security tips		× .124 =	
5c Taxable Medicare wages & tips		× .029 =	

5d　Total social security and Medicare taxes (*Column 2,* lines 5a + 5b + 5c = line 5d) . .　**5d**

6　Total taxes before adjustments (lines 3 + 5d = line 6) . . . .　**6**

7　**CURRENT QUARTER'S ADJUSTMENTS,** for example, a fractions of cents adjustment. See the instructions.

7a　Current quarter's fractions of cents . . . .

7b　Current quarter's sick pay . . . .

7c　Current quarter's adjustments for tips and group-term life insurance

7d　**TOTAL ADJUSTMENTS.** Combine all amounts on lines 7a through 7c . . . .　**7d**

8　Total taxes after adjustments. Combine lines 6 and 7d . . . .　**8**

9　Advance earned income credit (EIC) payments made to employees . . . .　**9**

10　Total taxes after adjustment for advance EIC (line 8 – line 9 = line 10) . . . .　**10**

11　Total deposits for this quarter, including overpayment applied from a prior quarter and overpayment applied from Form 941-X or Form 944-X . . . .

12a　COBRA premium assistance payments (see instructions) . . . . .

12b　Number of individuals provided COBRA premium assistance reported on line 12a . . . .

13　Add lines 11 and 12a . . . .　**13**

14　**Balance due.** If line 10 is more than line 13, write the difference here . . . .　**14**
For information on how to pay, see the instructions.

15　**Overpayment.** If line 13 is more than line 10, write the difference here

☐ Apply to next return.
Check one ☐ Send a refund.

▶ You **MUST** complete both pages of Form 941 and **SIGN** it.　　Next ➡

For Privacy Act and Paperwork Reduction Act Notice, see the back of the Payment Voucher.　Cat. No. 17001Z　Form **941** (Rev. 1-2009)

Form 941 Employer's Quarterly Federal Tax Return

950209

Name *(not your trade name)*

Employer identification number (EIN)

Part 2: Tell us about your deposit schedule and tax liability for this quarter.

If you are unsure about whether you are a monthly schedule depositor or a semiweekly schedule depositor, see *Pub. 15 (Circular E)*, section 11.

16 ☐☐ Write the state abbreviation for the state where you made your deposits OR write "MU" if you made your deposits in *multiple* states.

17 Check one: ☐ Line 10 is less than $2,500. Go to Part 3.

☐ You were a monthly schedule depositor for the entire quarter. Enter your tax liability for each month. Then go to Part 3.

Tax liability: Month 1 [   ] .

Month 2 [   ] .

Month 3 [   ] .

Total liability for quarter [   ] . Total must equal line 10.

☐ You were a semiweekly schedule depositor for any part of this quarter. Complete *Schedule B (Form 941): Report of Tax Liability for Semiweekly Schedule Depositors*, and attach it to Form 941.

Part 3: Tell us about your business. If a question does NOT apply to your business, leave it blank.

18 If your business has closed or you stopped paying wages . . . . ☐ Check here, and

enter the final date you paid wages [/   /   ] .

19 If you are a seasonal employer and you do not have to file a return for every quarter of the year . . ☐ Check here.

Part 4: May we speak with your third-party designee?

Do you want to allow an employee, a paid tax preparer, or another person to discuss this return with the IRS? See the instructions for details.

☐ Yes. Designee's name and phone number [   ] ( ) –

Select a 5-digit Personal Identification Number (PIN) to use when talking to the IRS. ☐☐☐☐☐

☐ No.

Part 5: Sign here. You MUST complete both pages of Form 941 and SIGN it.

Under penalties of perjury, I declare that I have examined this return, including accompanying schedules and statements, and to the best of my knowledge and belief, it is true, correct, and complete. Declaration of preparer (other than taxpayer) is based on all information of which preparer has any knowledge.

✗ Sign your name here [   ]

Print your name here [   ]

Print your title here [   ]

Date [/   /   ]

Best daytime phone ( ) –

Paid preparer's use only

Check if you are self-employed . . ☐

Preparer's name [ ]	Preparer's SSN/PTIN [ ]
Preparer's signature [ ]	Date [/ /]
Firm's name (or yours if self-employed) [ ]	EIN [ ]
Address [ ]	Phone ( ) –
City [ ] State [ ]	ZIP code [ ]

Page **2**

Form **941** (Rev. 1-2009)

Form 941 (*Continued*)

Form 941-V, Payment Voucher

Purpose of Form

Complete Form 941-V, Payment Voucher, if you are making a payment with Form 941, Employer's QUARTERLY Federal Tax Return. We will use the completed voucher to credit your payment more promptly and accurately, and to improve our service to you.

If you have your return prepared by a third party and make a payment with that return, please provide this payment voucher to the return preparer.

Making Payments With Form 941

To avoid a penalty, make your payment with Form 941 **only if:**

● Your net taxes for the quarter (line 10 on Form 941) are less than $2,500 and you are paying in full with a timely filed return or

● You are a monthly schedule depositor making a payment in accordance with the Accuracy of Deposits Rule. See section 11 of Pub. 15 (Circular E), Employer's Tax Guide, for details. In this case, the amount of your payment may be $2,500 or more.

Otherwise, you must deposit your payment at an authorized financial institution or by using the Electronic Federal Tax Payment System (EFTPS). See section 11 of Pub. 15 (Circular E) for deposit instructions. Do not use Form 941-V to make federal tax deposits.

Caution. *Use Form 941-V when making any payment with Form 941. However, if you pay an amount with Form 941 that should have been deposited, you may be subject to a penalty. See* Deposit Penalties *in section 11 of Pub. 15 (Circular E).*

Specific Instructions

Box 1—Employer identification number (EIN). If you do not have an EIN, apply for one on Form SS-4, Application for Employer Identification Number, and write "Applied For" and the date you applied in this entry space.

Box 2—Amount paid. Enter the amount paid with Form 941.

Box 3—Tax period. Darken the capsule identifying the quarter for which the payment is made. Darken only one capsule.

Box 4—Name and address. Enter your name and address as shown on Form 941.

● Enclose your check or money order made payable to the "United States Treasury." Be sure to enter your EIN, "Form 941," and the tax period on your check or money order. Do not send cash. Do not staple Form 941-V or your payment to Form 941 (or to each other).

● Detach Form 941-V and send it with your payment and Form 941 to the address in the Instructions for Form 941.

Note. You must also complete the entity information above Part 1 on Form 941.

✂- - - - - ▼ **Detach Here and Mail With Your Payment and Form 941.** ▼ - - - - - ✂

Form **941-V**		**Payment Voucher**	OMB No. 1545-0029
Department of the Treasury Internal Revenue Service		▶ **Do not staple this voucher or your payment to Form 941.**	2009

1 Enter your employer identification number (EIN).	2 **Enter the amount of your payment.** ▶		Dollars	Cents

3 Tax period		4 Enter your business name (individual name if sole proprietor).
⃝ 1st Quarter	⃝ 3rd Quarter	Enter your address.
⃝ 2nd Quarter	⃝ 4th Quarter	Enter your city, state, and ZIP code.

Form 941 (*Continued*)

Privacy Act and Paperwork Reduction Act Notice. We ask for the information on this form to carry out the Internal Revenue laws of the United States. We need it to figure and collect the right amount of tax. Subtitle C, Employment Taxes, of the Internal Revenue Code imposes employment taxes on wages, including income tax withholding. This form is used to determine the amount of the taxes that you owe. Section 6011 requires you to provide the requested information if the tax is applicable to you. Section 6109 requires you to provide your identifying number. If you fail to provide this information in a timely manner, you may be subject to penalties and interest.

You are not required to provide the information requested on a form that is subject to the Paperwork Reduction Act unless the form displays a valid OMB control number. Books and records relating to a form or instructions must be retained as long as their contents may become material in the administration of any Internal Revenue law.

Generally, tax returns and return information are confidential, as required by section 6103. However, section 6103 allows or requires the IRS to disclose or give the information shown on your tax return to others as described in the Code. For example, we may disclose your tax information to the Department of

Justice for civil and criminal litigation, and to cities, states, and the District of Columbia for use in administering their tax laws. We may also disclose this information to other countries under a tax treaty, to federal and state agencies to enforce federal nontax criminal laws, or to federal law enforcement and intelligence agencies to combat terrorism.

The time needed to complete and file Form 941 will vary depending on individual circumstances. The estimated average time is:

Recordkeeping . . . . 12 hr., 39 min.
Learning about the law or the form . . . . . . 40 min.
Preparing the form . . . . 1 hr., 49 min.
Copying, assembling, and sending
the form to the IRS . . . . 16 min.

If you have comments concerning the accuracy of these time estimates or suggestions for making Form 941 simpler, we would be happy to hear from you. You can write to: Internal Revenue Service, Tax Products Coordinating Committee, SE:W:CAR:MP:T:T:SP, 1111 Constitution Ave. NW, IR-6526, Washington, DC 20224. **Do not** send Form 941 to this address. Instead, see *Where Should You File?* on page 4 of the Instructions for Form 941.

Form 941 (*Continued*)

Form **966**
(Rev. December 2007)
Department of the Treasury
Internal Revenue Service

Corporate Dissolution or Liquidation

(Required under section 6043(a) of the Internal Revenue Code)

OMB No. 1545-0041

Please type or print		
Name of corporation		Employer identification number
Number, street, and room or suite no. (If a P.O. box number, see instructions.)		Check type of return
City or town, state, and ZIP code		☐ 1120 ☐ 1120-L ☐ 1120-IC-DISC ☐ 1120S ☐ Other ▶

1 Date incorporated	2 Place incorporated	3 Type of liquidation ☐ Complete ☐ Partial	4 Date resolution or plan of complete or partial liquidation was adopted

5 Service Center where corporation filed its immediately preceding tax return	6 Last month, day, and year of immediately preceding tax year	7a Last month, day, and year of final tax year	7b Was corporation's final tax return filed as part of a consolidated income tax return? If "Yes," complete 7c, 7d, and 7e. ☐ Yes ☐ No

7c Name of common parent		7d Employer identification number of common parent	7e Service Center where consolidated return was filed

		Common	Preferred
8 Total number of shares outstanding at time of adoption of plan of liquidation			
9 Date(s) of any amendments to plan of dissolution			
10 Section of the Code under which the corporation is to be dissolved or liquidated . . .			
11 If this form concerns an amendment or supplement to a resolution or plan, enter the date the previous Form 966 was filed			

Attach a certified copy of the resolution or plan and all amendments or supplements not previously filed.

Under penalties of perjury, I declare that I have examined this form, including accompanying schedules and statements, and to the best of my knowledge and belief, it is true, correct, and complete.

▶ _____   _____   _____
Signature of officer   Title   Date

Instructions

Section references are to the Internal Revenue Code unless otherwise noted.

Who Must File

A corporation (or a farmer's cooperative) must file Form 966 if it adopts a resolution or plan to dissolve the corporation or liquidate any of its stock.

Exempt organizations and qualified subchapter S subsidiaries should not file Form 966. Exempt organizations should see the instructions for Form 990, Return of Organization Exempt from Income Tax or Form 990-PF, Return of Private Foundation or Section 4947(a)(1) Nonexempt Charitable Trust Treated as a Private Foundation. Subchapter S subsidiaries should see Form 8869, Qualified Subchapter S Subsidiary Election.

Caution: *Do not file Form 966 for a deemed liquidation (such as a section 338 election or an election to be treated as a disregarded entity under Regulations section 301.7701-3).*

When To File

File Form 966 within 30 days after the resolution or plan is adopted to dissolve the corporation or liquidate any of its stock. If the resolution or plan is amended or supplemented after Form 966 is filed, file another Form 966 within 30 days after the amendment or supplement is adopted. The additional form will be sufficient if the date the earlier form was filed is entered on line 11 and a certified copy of the amendment or supplement attached. Include all information required by Form 966 that was not given in the earlier form.

Where To File

File Form 966 with the Internal Revenue Service Center at the address where the corporation (or cooperative) files its income tax return.

Distribution of Property

A corporation must recognize gain or loss on the distribution of its assets in the complete liquidation of its stock. For purposes of determining gain or loss, the distributed assets are valued at fair market value. Exceptions to this rule apply to a liquidation of a subsidiary and to a distribution that is made according to a plan of reorganization.

Foreign Corporations

A corporation that files a U.S. tax return must file Form 966 if required under section 6043(a). Foreign corporations that are not required to file Form 1120F or any other U.S. tax return are generally not required to file Form 966.

U.S. shareholders of foreign corporations may be required to report information regarding a corporate dissolution or liquidation. See Form 5471 and its instructions for more information.

For Paperwork Reduction Act Notice, see page 2.   Cat. No. 17053B   Form **966** (Rev. 12-2007)

Form 966 Corporate Dissolution or Liquidation

Address

Include the suite, room, or other unit number after the street address. If mail is not delivered to the street address and the corporation has a P.O. box, enter the box number instead of the street address.

Line 5

If the immediately preceding tax return was filed electronically, enter "efile" on line 5.

Line 7e

If the consolidated return was filed electronically, enter "efile" on line 7e.

Line 10

Identify the code section under which the corporation is to be dissolved or liquidated. For example, enter "section 331" for a complete or partial liquidation of a corporation or enter "section 332" for a complete liquidation of a subsidiary corporation that meets the requirements of section 332(b).

Signature

The return must be signed and dated by the president, vice president, treasurer, assistant treasurer, chief accounting officer, or any other corporate officer (such as tax officer) authorized to sign. A receiver, trustee, or assignee must sign and date any return required to be filed on behalf of a corporation.

Paperwork Reduction Act Notice

We ask for the information on this form to carry out the Internal Revenue laws of the United States. You are required to give us the information. We need it to ensure that you are complying with these laws and to allow us to figure and collect the right amount of tax.

You are not required to provide the information requested by a form or its instructions that is subject to the Paperwork Work Reduction Act unless the form displays a valid OMB control number. Books and records relating to a form or its instructions must be retained as long as their content may become material in the administration of any Internal Revenue law. Generally, tax returns and return information are confidential, as required by section 6103.

The time needed to complete and file this form will vary depending on individual circumstances. The estimated average time is:

Recordkeeping . . . . 5 hr., 1 min.

Learning about the law or the form . . . . 30 min.

Preparing and sending the form to the IRS ˙ ˙ ˙ ˙ 36 min.

If you have comments concerning the accuracy of these time estimates or suggestions for making this form simpler, we would be happy to hear from you. You can write to the Internal Revenue Service, Tax Products Coordinating Committee, SE:W:CAR:MP:T:T:SP, 1111 Constitution Ave. NW, IR-6406, Washington, DC 20224. Do not send the tax form to this office. Instead, see Where To File on page 1.

Form 966 (*Continued*)

Form **1040**

Department of the Treasury—Internal Revenue Service

U.S. Individual Income Tax Return 2008 (99) IRS Use Only—Do not write or staple in this space.

For the year Jan. 1–Dec. 31, 2008, or other tax year beginning , 2008, ending , 20   OMB No. 1545-0074

Label
(See instructions on page 14.)
Use the IRS label.
Otherwise, please print or type.

L A B E L   H E R E

Your first name and initial	Last name
If a joint return, spouse's first name and initial	Last name
Home address (number and street). If you have a P.O. box, see page 14.	Apt. no.
City, town or post office, state, and ZIP code. If you have a foreign address, see page 14.	

Your social security number

Spouse's social security number

▲ You **must** enter your SSN(s) above. ▲

Checking a box below will not change your tax or refund.

Presidential Election Campaign ▶ Check here if you, or your spouse if filing jointly, want $3 to go to this fund (see page 14) ▶ ☐ You ☐ Spouse

Filing Status

Check only one box.

1 ☐ Single
2 ☐ Married filing jointly (even if only one had income)
3 ☐ Married filing separately. Enter spouse's SSN above and full name here. ▶
4 ☐ Head of household (with qualifying person). (See page 15.) If the qualifying person is a child but not your dependent, enter this child's name here. ▶
5 ☐ Qualifying widow(er) with dependent child (see page 16)

Exemptions

If more than four dependents, see page 17.

6a ☐ **Yourself.** If someone can claim you as a dependent, **do not** check box 6a
b ☐ **Spouse**
c Dependents:

(1) First name Last name	(2) Dependent's social security number	(3) Dependent's relationship to you	(4) ✓ if qualifying child for child tax credit (see page 17)
			☐
			☐
			☐
			☐

d Total number of exemptions claimed

Boxes checked on 6a and 6b ____
No. of children on 6c who:
• lived with you ____
• did not live with you due to divorce or separation (see page 18) ____
Dependents on 6c not entered above ____
Add numbers on lines above ▶ ☐

Income

Attach Form(s) W-2 here. Also attach Forms W-2G and 1099-R if tax was withheld.

If you did not get a W-2, see page 21.

Enclose, but do not attach, any payment. Also, please use Form 1040-V.

7	Wages, salaries, tips, etc. Attach Form(s) W-2	7
8a	**Taxable** interest. Attach Schedule B if required	8a
b	**Tax-exempt** interest. Do **not** include on line 8a 8b	
9a	Ordinary dividends. Attach Schedule B if required	9a
b	Qualified dividends (see page 21) 9b	
10	Taxable refunds, credits, or offsets of state and local income taxes (see page 22)	10
11	Alimony received	11
12	Business income or (loss). Attach Schedule C or C-EZ	12
13	Capital gain or (loss). Attach Schedule D if required. If not required, check here ▶ ☐	13
14	Other gains or (losses). Attach Form 4797	14
15a	IRA distributions 15a b Taxable amount (see page 23)	15b
16a	Pensions and annuities 16a b Taxable amount (see page 24)	16b
17	Rental real estate, royalties, partnerships, S corporations, trusts, etc. Attach Schedule E	17
18	Farm income or (loss). Attach Schedule F	18
19	Unemployment compensation	19
20a	Social security benefits 20a b Taxable amount (see page 26)	20b
21	Other income. List type and amount (see page 28)	21
22	Add the amounts in the far right column for lines 7 through 21. This is your **total income** ▶	22

Adjusted Gross Income

23	Educator expenses (see page 28) 23	
24	Certain business expenses of reservists, performing artists, and fee-basis government officials. Attach Form 2106 or 2106-EZ 24	
25	Health savings account deduction. Attach Form 8889 25	
26	Moving expenses. Attach Form 3903 26	
27	One-half of self-employment tax. Attach Schedule SE 27	
28	Self-employed SEP, SIMPLE, and qualified plans 28	
29	Self-employed health insurance deduction (see page 29) 29	
30	Penalty on early withdrawal of savings 30	
31a	Alimony paid b Recipient's SSN ▶ 31a	
32	IRA deduction (see page 30) 32	
33	Student loan interest deduction (see page 33) 33	
34	Tuition and fees deduction. Attach Form 8917 34	
35	Domestic production activities deduction. Attach Form 8903 35	
36	Add lines 23 through 31a and 32 through 35	36
37	Subtract line 36 from line 22. This is your **adjusted gross income** ▶	37

For Disclosure, Privacy Act, and Paperwork Reduction Act Notice, see page 88.   Cat. No. 11320B   Form **1040** (2008)

Form 1040 U.S. Individual Income Tax Return

Form 1040 (2008)   Page **2**

Tax and Credits	**38**	Amount from line 37 (adjusted gross income)	**38**	
	39a	Check ⌠ ☐ **You** were born before January 2, 1944, ☐ Blind. ⌠ Total boxes if: ⌡ ☐ **Spouse** was born before January 2, 1944, ☐ Blind. ⌡ checked ▶ **39a**		
	b	If your spouse itemizes on a separate return or you were a dual-status alien, see page 34 and check here ▶ **39b** ☐		
Standard Deduction for—	**c**	Check if standard deduction includes real estate taxes or disaster loss (see page 34) ▶ **39c** ☐		
	40	**Itemized deductions** (from Schedule A) **or** your **standard deduction** (see left margin) .	**40**	
• People who checked any box on line 39a, 39b, or 39c **or** who can be claimed as a dependent, see page 34.	**41**	Subtract line 40 from line 38	**41**	
	42	If line 38 is over $119,975, or you provided housing to a Midwestern displaced individual, see page 36. Otherwise, multiply $3,500 by the total number of exemptions claimed on line 6d	**42**	
	43	**Taxable income.** Subtract line 42 from line 41. If line 42 is more than line 41, enter -0-	**43**	
	44	**Tax** (see page 36). Check if any tax is from: **a** ☐ Form(s) 8814 **b** ☐ Form 4972 .	**44**	
• All others:	**45**	**Alternative minimum tax** (see page 39). Attach Form 6251	**45**	
Single or Married filing separately, $5,450	**46**	Add lines 44 and 45 . . . . ▶	**46**	
	47	Foreign tax credit. Attach Form 1116 if required	**47**	
	48	Credit for child and dependent care expenses. Attach Form 2441	**48**	
Married filing jointly or Qualifying widow(er), $10,900	**49**	Credit for the elderly or the disabled. Attach Schedule R . .	**49**	
	50	Education credits. Attach Form 8863	**50**	
	51	Retirement savings contributions credit. Attach Form 8880 .	**51**	
	52	Child tax credit (see page 42). Attach Form 8901 if required .	**52**	
Head of household, $8,000	**53**	Credits from Form: **a** ☐ 8396 **b** ☐ 8839 **c** ☐ 5695	**53**	
	54	Other credits from Form: **a** ☐ 3800 **b** ☐ 8801 **c** ☐ ____	**54**	
	55	Add lines 47 through 54. These are your **total credits**	**55**	
	56	Subtract line 55 from line 46. If line 55 is more than line 46, enter -0- . . . ▶	**56**	
Other Taxes	**57**	Self-employment tax. Attach Schedule SE	**57**	
	58	Unreported social security and Medicare tax from Form: **a** ☐ 4137 **b** ☐ 8919 . .	**58**	
	59	Additional tax on IRAs, other qualified retirement plans, etc. Attach Form 5329 if required	**59**	
	60	Additional taxes: **a** ☐ AEIC payments **b** ☐ Household employment taxes. Attach Schedule H	**60**	
	61	Add lines 56 through 60. This is your **total tax** . . . . ▶	**61**	
Payments	**62**	Federal income tax withheld from Forms W-2 and 1099	**62**	
	63	2008 estimated tax payments and amount applied from 2007 return	**63**	
If you have a qualifying child, attach Schedule EIC.	**64a**	**Earned income credit (EIC)**	**64a**	
	b	Nontaxable combat pay election **64b**		
	65	Excess social security and tier 1 RRTA tax withheld (see page 61)	**65**	
	66	Additional child tax credit. Attach Form 8812	**66**	
	67	Amount paid with request for extension to file (see page 61)	**67**	
	68	Credits from Form: **a** ☐ 2439 **b** ☐ 4136 **c** ☐ 8801 **d** ☐ 8885	**68**	
	69	First-time homebuyer credit. Attach Form 5405	**69**	
	70	Recovery rebate credit (see worksheet on pages 62 and 63) .	**70**	
	71	Add lines 62 through 70. These are your **total payments** . . . . . . ▶	**71**	
Refund	**72**	If line 71 is more than line 61, subtract line 61 from line 71. This is the amount you **overpaid**	**72**	
Direct deposit? See page 63 and fill in 73b, 73c, and 73d, or Form 8888.	**73a**	Amount of line 72 you want **refunded to you.** If Form 8888 is attached, check here ▶ ☐	**73a**	
	b	Routing number ▶ **c** Type: ☐ Checking ☐ Savings		
	d	Account number		
	74	Amount of line 72 you want **applied to your 2009 estimated tax** ▶ **74**		
Amount You Owe	**75**	**Amount you owe.** Subtract line 71 from line 61. For details on how to pay, see page 65 ▶	**75**	
	76	Estimated tax penalty (see page 65) **76**		

Third Party Designee	Do you want to allow another person to discuss this return with the IRS (see page 66)? ☐ **Yes.** Complete the following. ☐ **No**
	Designee's name ▶ _____ Phone no. ▶ ( ) _____ Personal identification number (PIN) ▶ ☐☐☐☐☐

Sign Here
Joint return? See page 15.
Keep a copy for your records.

Under penalties of perjury, I declare that I have examined this return and accompanying schedules and statements, and to the best of my knowledge and belief, they are true, correct, and complete. Declaration of preparer (other than taxpayer) is based on all information of which preparer has any knowledge.

Your signature	Date	Your occupation	Daytime phone number
			( )
Spouse's signature. If a joint return, **both** must sign.	Date	Spouse's occupation	

Paid Preparer's Use Only	Preparer's signature ▶		Date	Check if self-employed ☐	Preparer's SSN or PTIN
	Firm's name (or yours if self-employed), address, and ZIP code ▶			EIN	
				Phone no.	( )

Form **1040** (2008)

Form 1040 (*Continued*)

Form **1065**		**U.S. Return of Partnership Income**	OMB No. 1545-0099
Department of the Treasury Internal Revenue Service		For calendar year 2008, or tax year beginning _ _ _ _ _ _ , 2008, ending _ _ _ _ _ _ , 20 _ _ _ . ▶ **See separate instructions.**	20**08**

A Principal business activity	Use the IRS label. Other-wise, print or type.	Name of partnership	D Employer identification number
B Principal product or service		Number, street, and room or suite no. If a P.O. box, see the instructions.	E Date business started
C Business code number		City or town, state, and ZIP code	F Total assets (see the instructions) $

G   Check applicable boxes: **(1)** ☐ Initial return   **(2)** ☐ Final return   **(3)** ☐ Name change   **(4)** ☐ Address change   **(5)** ☐ Amended return
    (6) ☐ Technical termination - also check (1) or (2)
H   Check accounting method: **(1)** ☐ Cash   **(2)** ☐ Accrual   **(3)** ☐ Other (specify) ▶ _
I   Number of Schedules K-1. Attach one for each person who was a partner at any time during the tax year ▶ _
J   Check if Schedule M-3 attached . . . . ☐

Caution. *Include **only** trade or business income and expenses on lines 1a through 22 below. See the instructions for more information.*

Income	**1a** Gross receipts or sales	1a			
	b Less returns and allowances	1b		1c	
	2 Cost of goods sold (Schedule A, line 8)			2	
	3 Gross profit. Subtract line 2 from line 1c			3	
	4 Ordinary income (loss) from other partnerships, estates, and trusts *(attach statement)* . . .			4	
	5 Net farm profit (loss) *(attach Schedule F (Form 1040))*			5	
	6 Net gain (loss) from Form 4797, Part II, line 17 *(attach Form 4797)* . . .			6	
	7 Other income (loss) *(attach statement)*			7	
	8 **Total income (loss).** Combine lines 3 through 7			8	
Deductions (see the instructions for limitations)	**9** Salaries and wages (other than to partners) (less employment credits) . . .			9	
	10 Guaranteed payments to partners			10	
	11 Repairs and maintenance			11	
	12 Bad debts			12	
	13 Rent			13	
	14 Taxes and licenses			14	
	15 Interest			15	
	16a Depreciation *(if required, attach Form 4562)*	16a			
	b Less depreciation reported on Schedule A and elsewhere on return	16b		16c	
	17 Depletion **(Do not deduct oil and gas depletion.)**			17	
	18 Retirement plans, etc.			18	
	19 Employee benefit programs			19	
	20 Other deductions *(attach statement)*			20	
	21 **Total deductions.** Add the amounts shown in the far right column for lines 9 through 20 .			21	
	22 **Ordinary business income (loss).** Subtract line 21 from line 8			22	

Sign Here	Under penalties of perjury, I declare that I have examined this return, including accompanying schedules and statements, and to the best of my knowledge and belief, it is true, correct, and complete. Declaration of preparer (other than general partner or limited liability company member manager) is based on all information of which preparer has any knowledge.		
	▶ _____ Signature of general partner or limited liability company member manager	▶ _____ Date	May the IRS discuss this return with the preparer shown below (see instructions)? ☐ Yes ☐ No

Paid Preparer's Use Only	Preparer's signature		Date	Check if self-employed ▶ ☐	Preparer's SSN or PTIN
	Firm's name (or yours if self-employed), address, and ZIP code	▶		EIN ▶	
				Phone no. ( )	

For Privacy Act and Paperwork Reduction Act Notice, see separate instructions.   Cat. No. 11390Z   Form **1065** (2008)

Form 1065 U.S. Return of Partnership Income

Form 1065 (2008)   Page **2**

Schedule A   **Cost of Goods Sold** (see the instructions)

1	Inventory at beginning of year	1	
2	Purchases less cost of items withdrawn for personal use	2	
3	Cost of labor	3	
4	Additional section 263A costs *(attach statement)*	4	
5	Other costs *(attach statement)*	5	
6	**Total.** Add lines 1 through 5	6	
7	Inventory at end of year	7	
8	**Cost of goods sold.** Subtract line 7 from line 6. Enter here and on page 1, line 2	8	

9a Check all methods used for valuing closing inventory:
- **(i)** ☐ Cost as described in Regulations section 1.471-3
- **(ii)** ☐ Lower of cost or market as described in Regulations section 1.471-4
- **(iii)** ☐ Other (specify method used and attach explanation) ▶ _____

b Check this box if there was a writedown of "subnormal" goods as described in Regulations section 1.471-2(c) . . ▶ ☐

c Check this box if the LIFO inventory method was adopted this tax year for any goods *(if checked, attach Form 970)* ▶ ☐

d Do the rules of section 263A (for property produced or acquired for resale) apply to the partnership? . . ☐ Yes ☐ No

e Was there any change in determining quantities, cost, or valuations between opening and closing inventory? ☐ Yes ☐ No
    If "Yes," attach explanation.

Schedule B   **Other Information**

		Yes	No
1	What type of entity is filing this return? Check the applicable box:		

   a ☐ Domestic general partnership   **b** ☐ Domestic limited partnership
   c ☐ Domestic limited liability company   **d** ☐ Domestic limited liability partnership
   e ☐ Foreign partnership   **f** ☐ Other ▶ _____

2 At any time during the tax year, was any partner in the partnership a disregarded entity, a partnership (including an entity treated as a partnership), a trust, an S corporation, an estate (other than an estate of a deceased partner), or a nominee or similar person?

3 At the end of the tax year:

a Did any foreign or domestic corporation, partnership (including any entity treated as a partnership), or trust own, directly or indirectly, an interest of 50% or more in the profit, loss, or capital of the partnership? For rules of constructive ownership, see instructions. If "Yes," complete (i) through (v) below

(i) Name of Entity	(ii) Employer Identification Number (if any)	(iii) Type of Entity	(iv) Country of Organization	(v) Maximum Percentage Owned in Profit, Loss, or Capital

b Did any individual or estate own, directly or indirectly, an interest of 50% or more in the profit, loss, or capital of the partnership? For rules of constructive ownership, see instructions. If "Yes," complete (i) through (iv) below

(i) Name of Individual or Estate	(ii) Social Security Number or Employer Identification Number (if any)	(iii) Country of Citizenship (see instructions)	(iv) Maximum Percentage Owned in Profit, Loss, or Capital

4 At the end of the tax year, did the partnership:

a Own directly 20% or more, or own, directly or indirectly, 50% or more of the total voting power of all classes of stock entitled to vote of any foreign or domestic corporation? For rules of constructive ownership, see instructions. If "Yes," complete (i) through (iv) below

(i) Name of Corporation	(ii) Employer Identification Number (if any)	(iii) Country of Incorporation	(iv) Percentage Owned in Voting Stock

Form **1065** (2008)

Form 1065 (*Continued*)

Form 1065 (2008)   Page **3**

					Yes	No

b Own directly an interest of 20% or more, or own, directly or indirectly, an interest of 50% or more in the profit, loss, or capital in any foreign or domestic partnership (including an entity treated as a partnership) or in the beneficial interest of a trust? For rules of constructive ownership, see instructions. If "Yes," complete (i) through (v) below .

(i) Name of Entity	(ii) Employer Identification Number (if any)	(iii) Type of Entity	(iv) Country of Organization	(v) Maximum Percentage Owned in Profit, Loss, or Capital

5 Did the partnership file Form 8893, Election of Partnership Level Tax Treatment, or an election statement under section 6231(a)(1)(B)(ii) for partnership-level tax treatment, that is in effect for this tax year? See Form 8893 for more details . . . .

6 Does the partnership satisfy **all four** of the following conditions?
a The partnership's total receipts for the tax year were less than $250,000.
b The partnership's total assets at the end of the tax year were less than $1 million.
c Schedules K-1 are filed with the return and furnished to the partners on or before the due date (including extensions) for the partnership return.
d The partnership is not filing and is not required to file Schedule M-3 . . . .
If "Yes," the partnership is not required to complete Schedules L, M-1, and M-2; Item F on page 1 of Form 1065; or Item L on Schedule K-1.

7 Is this partnership a publicly traded partnership as defined in section 469(k)(2)? . . . .

8 During the tax year, did the partnership have any debt that was cancelled, was forgiven, or had the terms modified so as to reduce the principal amount of the debt? . . . .

9 Has this partnership filed, or is it required to file, Form 8918, Material Advisor Disclosure Statement, to provide information on any reportable transaction? . . . .

10 At any time during calendar year 2008, did the partnership have an interest in or a signature or other authority over a financial account in a foreign country (such as a bank account, securities account, or other financial account)? See the instructions for exceptions and filing requirements for Form TD F 90-22.1, Report of Foreign Bank and Financial Accounts. If "Yes," enter the name of the foreign country. ▶ _

11 At any time during the tax year, did the partnership receive a distribution from, or was it the grantor of, or transferor to, a foreign trust? If "Yes," the partnership may have to file Form 3520, Annual Return To Report Transactions With Foreign Trusts and Receipt of Certain Foreign Gifts. See instructions . . . .

12a Is the partnership making, or had it previously made (and not revoked), a section 754 election? . . . . .
See instructions for details regarding a section 754 election.

b Did the partnership make for this tax year an optional basis adjustment under section 743(b) or 734(b)? If "Yes," attach a statement showing the computation and allocation of the basis adjustment. See instructions

c Is the partnership required to adjust the basis of partnership assets under section 743(b) or 734(b) because of a substantial built-in loss (as defined under section 743(d)) or substantial basis reduction (as defined under section 734(d))? If "Yes," attach a statement showing the computation and allocation of the basis adjustment. See instructions

13 Check this box if, during the current or prior tax year, the partnership distributed any property received in a like-kind exchange or contributed such property to another entity (including a disregarded entity) . . ▶ ☐

14 At any time during the tax year, did the partnership distribute to any partner a tenancy-in-common or other undivided interest in partnership property? . . . .

15 If the partnership is required to file Form 8858, Information Return of U.S. Persons With Respect To Foreign Disregarded Entities, enter the number of Forms 8858 attached. See instructions ▶ _ _ _ _ _ _ _ _ _ _ _ _ _ _ _ _ _

16 Does the partnership have any foreign partners? If "Yes," enter the number of Forms 8805, Foreign Partner's Information Statement of Section 1446 Withholding Tax, filed for this partnership. ▶ _ _ _ _ _ _ _ _ _ _ _ _ _ _ _ _ _

17 Enter the number of Forms 8865, Return of U.S. Persons With Respect to Certain Foreign Partnerships, attached to this return. ▶ _ _ _ _ _ _ _ _ _ _ _ _ _ _ _ _ _

Designation of Tax Matters Partner (see instructions)
Enter below the general partner designated as the tax matters partner (TMP) for the tax year of this return:

Name of designated TMP ▶		Identifying number of TMP ▶	
Address of designated TMP ▶			

Form **1065** (2008)

Form 1065 (*Continued*)

Form 1065 (2008)   Page **4**

Schedule K   Partners' Distributive Share Items

			Total amount

Income (Loss)

1	Ordinary business income (loss) (page 1, line 22)	1	
2	Net rental real estate income (loss) *(attach Form 8825)*	2	
3a	Other gross rental income (loss) · · · · · 3a		
b	Expenses from other rental activities *(attach statement)* · · · 3b		
c	Other net rental income (loss). Subtract line 3b from line 3a	3c	
4	Guaranteed payments	4	
5	Interest income	5	
6	Dividends: **a** Ordinary dividends	6a	
	b Qualified dividends · · · · 6b		
7	Royalties	7	
8	Net short-term capital gain (loss) *(attach Schedule D (Form 1065))*	8	
9a	Net long-term capital gain (loss) *(attach Schedule D (Form 1065))*	9a	
b	Collectibles (28%) gain (loss) · · · · · 9b		
c	Unrecaptured section 1250 gain *(attach statement)* · · · 9c		
10	Net section 1231 gain (loss) *(attach Form 4797)*	10	
11	Other income (loss) *(see instructions)* Type ▶_____	11	

Deductions

12	Section 179 deduction *(attach Form 4562)*	12	
13a	Contributions	13a	
b	Investment interest expense	13b	
c	Section 59(e)(2) expenditures: **(1)** Type ▶_____ **(2)** Amount ▶	13c(2)	
d	Other deductions *(see instructions)* Type ▶_____	13d	

Self-Employment

14a	Net earnings (loss) from self-employment	14a	
b	Gross farming or fishing income	14b	
c	Gross nonfarm income	14c	

Credits

15a	Low-income housing credit (section 42(j)(5))	15a	
b	Low-income housing credit (other)	15b	
c	Qualified rehabilitation expenditures (rental real estate) *(attach Form 3468)*	15c	
d	Other rental real estate credits *(see instructions)* Type ▶_____	15d	
e	Other rental credits *(see instructions)* Type ▶_____	15e	
f	Other credits *(see instructions)* Type ▶_____	15f	

Foreign Transactions

16a	Name of country or U.S. possession ▶_____		
b	Gross income from all sources	16b	
c	Gross income sourced at partner level	16c	
	Foreign gross income sourced at partnership level		
d	Passive category ▶_____ **e** General category ▶_____ **f** Other ▶	16f	
	Deductions allocated and apportioned at partner level		
g	Interest expense ▶_____ **h** Other · · · · · ▶	16h	
	Deductions allocated and apportioned at partnership level to foreign source income		
i	Passive category ▶_____ **j** General category ▶_____ **k** Other ▶	16k	
l	Total foreign taxes (check one): ▶ Paid ☐ Accrued ☐	16l	
m	Reduction in taxes available for credit *(attach statement)*	16m	
n	Other foreign tax information *(attach statement)*		

Alternative Minimum Tax (AMT) Items

17a	Post-1986 depreciation adjustment	17a	
b	Adjusted gain or loss	17b	
c	Depletion (other than oil and gas)	17c	
d	Oil, gas, and geothermal properties—gross income	17d	
e	Oil, gas, and geothermal properties—deductions	17e	
f	Other AMT items *(attach statement)*	17f	

Other Information

18a	Tax-exempt interest income	18a	
b	Other tax-exempt income	18b	
c	Nondeductible expenses	18c	
19a	Distributions of cash and marketable securities	19a	
b	Distributions of other property	19b	
20a	Investment income	20a	
b	Investment expenses	20b	
c	Other items and amounts *(attach statement)*		

Form **1065** (2008)

Form 1065 (*Continued*)

Form 1065 (2008)   Page **5**

Analysis of Net Income (Loss)

1	Net income (loss). Combine Schedule K, lines 1 through 11. From the result, subtract the sum of Schedule K, lines 12 through 13d, and 16l	**1**	

2	Analysis by partner type:	**(i)** Corporate	**(ii)** Individual (active)	**(iii)** Individual (passive)	**(iv)** Partnership	**(v)** Exempt organization	**(vi)** Nominee/Other
	a General partners						
	b Limited partners						

Schedule L — Balance Sheets per Books

		Beginning of tax year		End of tax year	
	Assets	**(a)**	**(b)**	**(c)**	**(d)**
1	Cash				
2a	Trade notes and accounts receivable				
b	Less allowance for bad debts				
3	Inventories				
4	U.S. government obligations				
5	Tax-exempt securities				
6	Other current assets (attach statement) . . .				
7	Mortgage and real estate loans				
8	Other investments (attach statement)				
9a	Buildings and other depreciable assets . . .				
b	Less accumulated depreciation				
10a	Depletable assets				
b	Less accumulated depletion				
11	Land (net of any amortization)				
12a	Intangible assets (amortizable only) . . .				
b	Less accumulated amortization				
13	Other assets (attach statement)				
14	Total assets				
	Liabilities and Capital				
15	Accounts payable				
16	Mortgages, notes, bonds payable in less than 1 year.				
17	Other current liabilities (attach statement) . . .				
18	All nonrecourse loans				
19	Mortgages, notes, bonds payable in 1 year or more .				
20	Other liabilities (attach statement)				
21	Partners' capital accounts				
22	Total liabilities and capital				

Schedule M-1 — Reconciliation of Income (Loss) per Books With Income (Loss) per Return
Note. Schedule M-3 may be required instead of Schedule M-1 (see instructions).

1	Net income (loss) per books		6	Income recorded on books this year not included on Schedule K, lines 1 through 11 (itemize):	
2	Income included on Schedule K, lines 1, 2, 3c, 5, 6a, 7, 8, 9a, 10, and 11, not recorded on books this year (itemize): _____		a	Tax-exempt interest $ _____	
3	Guaranteed payments (other than health insurance)		7	Deductions included on Schedule K, lines 1 through 13d, and 16l, not charged against book income this year (itemize):	
4	Expenses recorded on books this year not included on Schedule K, lines 1 through 13d, and 16l (itemize):		a	Depreciation $ _____	
a	Depreciation $ _____			_____	
b	Travel and entertainment $ _____		8	Add lines 6 and 7	
	_____		9	Income (loss) (Analysis of Net Income (Loss), line 1). Subtract line 8 from line 5	
5	Add lines 1 through 4				

Schedule M-2 — Analysis of Partners' Capital Accounts

1	Balance at beginning of year		6	Distributions: a Cash	
2	Capital contributed: a Cash			b Property	
	b Property . . .		7	Other decreases (itemize): _____	
3	Net income (loss) per books			_____	
4	Other increases (itemize): _____		8	Add lines 6 and 7	
	_____		9	Balance at end of year. Subtract line 8 from line 5	
5	Add lines 1 through 4				

Form **1065** (2008)

Form 1065 (*Continued*)

Form **1120**		**U.S. Corporation Income Tax Return**		OMB No. 1545-0123
Department of the Treasury Internal Revenue Service		For calendar year 2008 or tax year beginning _____ , 2008, ending _____ , 20 ____ ▶ **See separate instructions.**		**20**08

A Check if:		Name		**B** Employer identification number
1a Consolidated return (attach Form 851) . . ☐	**Use IRS label. Otherwise, print or type.**			
b Life/nonlife consolidated return . . . . . . ☐		Number, street, and room or suite no. If a P.O. box, see instructions.		**C** Date incorporated
2 Personal holding co. (attach Sch. PH) . . . ☐		City or town, state, and ZIP code		**D** Total assets (see instructions)
3 Personal service corp. (see instructions) . . ☐				$
4 Schedule M-3 attached ☐	**E** Check if: **(1)** ☐ Initial return **(2)** ☐ Final return **(3)** ☐ Name change **(4)** ☐ Address change			

Income	**1a**	Gross receipts or sales	**b** Less returns and allowances	**c** Bal ▶	**1c**	
	2	Cost of goods sold (Schedule A, line 8)			**2**	
	3	Gross profit. Subtract line 2 from line 1c			**3**	
	4	Dividends (Schedule C, line 19)			**4**	
	5	Interest			**5**	
	6	Gross rents			**6**	
	7	Gross royalties			**7**	
	8	Capital gain net income (attach Schedule D (Form 1120))			**8**	
	9	Net gain or (loss) from Form 4797, Part II, line 17 (attach Form 4797)			**9**	
	10	Other income (see instructions—attach schedule)			**10**	
	11	**Total income.** Add lines 3 through 10 . . . . ▶			**11**	
Deductions (See instructions for limitations on deductions.)	**12**	Compensation of officers (Schedule E, line 4) . . . . ▶			**12**	
	13	Salaries and wages (less employment credits)			**13**	
	14	Repairs and maintenance			**14**	
	15	Bad debts			**15**	
	16	Rents			**16**	
	17	Taxes and licenses			**17**	
	18	Interest			**18**	
	19	Charitable contributions			**19**	
	20	Depreciation from Form 4562 not claimed on Schedule A or elsewhere on return (attach Form 4562)			**20**	
	21	Depletion			**21**	
	22	Advertising			**22**	
	23	Pension, profit-sharing, etc., plans			**23**	
	24	Employee benefit programs			**24**	
	25	Domestic production activities deduction (attach Form 8903)			**25**	
	26	Other deductions (attach schedule)			**26**	
	27	**Total deductions.** Add lines 12 through 26 . . . . ▶			**27**	
	28	Taxable income before net operating loss deduction and special deductions. Subtract line 27 from line 11 . .			**28**	
	29	**Less: a** Net operating loss deduction (see instructions)	**29a**			
		b Special deductions (Schedule C, line 20)	**29b**		**29c**	
Tax, Refundable Credits, and Payments	**30**	**Taxable income.** Subtract line 29c from line 28 (see instructions)			**30**	
	31	**Total tax** (Schedule J, line 10)			**31**	
	32a	2007 overpayment credited to 2008 . .	**32a**			
	b	2008 estimated tax payments	**32b**			
	c	2008 refund applied for on Form 4466	**32c**	( )	**d** Bal ▶	**32d**	
	e	Tax deposited with Form 7004			**32e**	
	f	Credits: **(1)** Form 2439 _____ **(2)** Form 4136 _____			**32f**	
	g	Refundable credits from Form 3800, line 19c, and Form 8827, line 8c . . .	**32g**		**32h**	
	33	Estimated tax penalty (see instructions). Check if Form 2220 is attached . . . . . ▶ ☐			**33**	
	34	**Amount owed.** If line 32h is smaller than the total of lines 31 and 33, enter amount owed			**34**	
	35	**Overpayment.** If line 32h is larger than the total of lines 31 and 33, enter amount overpaid			**35**	
	36	Enter amount from line 35 you want: **Credited to 2009 estimated tax** ▶ _____ **Refunded** ▶			**36**	

Sign Here	Under penalties of perjury, I declare that I have examined this return, including accompanying schedules and statements, and to the best of my knowledge and belief, it is true, correct, and complete. Declaration of preparer (other than taxpayer) is based on all information of which preparer has any knowledge.		May the IRS discuss this return with the preparer shown below (see instructions)? ☐ **Yes** ☐ **No**
	▶ _____ Signature of officer _____ Date	_____ Title	

Paid Preparer's Use Only	Preparer's signature	▶		Date		Check if self- employed ☐	Preparer's SSN or PTIN
	Firm's name (or yours if self-employed), address, and ZIP code	▶				EIN	
						Phone no.	

For Privacy Act and Paperwork Reduction Act Notice, see separate instructions.   Cat. No. 11450Q   Form **1120** (2008)

Form 1120 U.S. Corporation Income Tax Return

Form 1120 (2008)   Page **2**

Schedule A   Cost of Goods Sold (see instructions)

1	Inventory at beginning of year	1
2	Purchases	2
3	Cost of labor	3
4	Additional section 263A costs (attach schedule)	4
5	Other costs (attach schedule)	5
6	**Total.** Add lines 1 through 5	6
7	Inventory at end of year	7
8	**Cost of goods sold.** Subtract line 7 from line 6. Enter here and on page 1, line 2	8

9a Check all methods used for valuing closing inventory:
  (i) ☐ Cost
  (ii) ☐ Lower of cost or market
  (iii) ☐ Other (Specify method used and attach explanation.) ▶ _____

  b Check if there was a writedown of subnormal goods . . . . ▶ ☐
  c Check if the LIFO inventory method was adopted this tax year for any goods (if checked, attach Form 970) . . . . . . ▶ ☐
  d If the LIFO inventory method was used for this tax year, enter percentage (or amounts) of closing inventory computed under LIFO | 9d |
  e If property is produced or acquired for resale, do the rules of section 263A apply to the corporation? . . . . ☐ Yes   ☐ No
  f Was there any change in determining quantities, cost, or valuations between opening and closing inventory? If "Yes," attach explanation . . . . ☐ Yes   ☐ No

Schedule C   Dividends and Special Deductions (see instructions)

		(a) Dividends received	(b) %	(c) Special deductions (a) × (b)
1	Dividends from less-than-20%-owned domestic corporations (other than debt-financed stock)		70	
2	Dividends from 20%-or-more-owned domestic corporations (other than debt-financed stock)		80	
3	Dividends on debt-financed stock of domestic and foreign corporations		see instructions	
4	Dividends on certain preferred stock of less-than-20%-owned public utilities		42	
5	Dividends on certain preferred stock of 20%-or-more-owned public utilities		48	
6	Dividends from less-than-20%-owned foreign corporations and certain FSCs		70	
7	Dividends from 20%-or-more-owned foreign corporations and certain FSCs		80	
8	Dividends from wholly owned foreign subsidiaries		100	
9	**Total.** Add lines 1 through 8. See instructions for limitation			
10	Dividends from domestic corporations received by a small business investment company operating under the Small Business Investment Act of 1958		100	
11	Dividends from affiliated group members		100	
12	Dividends from certain FSCs		100	
13	Dividends from foreign corporations not included on lines 3, 6, 7, 8, 11, or 12			
14	Income from controlled foreign corporations under subpart F (attach Form(s) 5471)			
15	Foreign dividend gross-up			
16	IC-DISC and former DISC dividends not included on lines 1, 2, or 3			
17	Other dividends			
18	Deduction for dividends paid on certain preferred stock of public utilities ▶			
19	**Total dividends.** Add lines 1 through 17. Enter here and on page 1, line 4 . . . ▶			
20	**Total special deductions.** Add lines 9, 10, 11, 12, and 18. Enter here and on page 1, line 29b . . . . . ▶			

Schedule E   Compensation of Officers (see instructions for page 1, line 12)

Note: *Complete Schedule E only if total receipts (line 1a plus lines 4 through 10 on page 1) are $500,000 or more.*

	(a) Name of officer	(b) Social security number	(c) Percent of time devoted to business	Percent of corporation stock owned		(f) Amount of compensation
				(d) Common	(e) Preferred	
1			%	%	%	
			%	%	%	
			%	%	%	
			%	%	%	
			%	%	%	

2	Total compensation of officers	
3	Compensation of officers claimed on Schedule A and elsewhere on return	
4	Subtract line 3 from line 2. Enter the result here and on page 1, line 12	

Form **1120** (2008)

Form 1120 (*Continued*)

Form 1120 (2008)   Page **3**

Schedule J	Tax Computation (see instructions)

1   Check if the corporation is a member of a controlled group (attach Schedule O (Form 1120)) . . . . ▶ ☐

2   Income tax. Check if a qualified personal service corporation (see instructions) . . . . ▶ ☐   **2**

3   Alternative minimum tax (attach Form 4626) **3**

4   Add lines 2 and 3 . . . . **4**

5a   Foreign tax credit (attach Form 1118) **5a**

  b   Credit from Form 8834 . . . .   **5b**

  c   General business credit (attach Form 3800) **5c**

  d   Credit for prior year minimum tax (attach Form 8827) **5d**

  e   Bond credits from Form 8912 . . . .   **5e**

6   **Total credits.** Add lines 5a through 5e **6**

7   Subtract line 6 from line 4 . . . . **7**

8   Personal holding company tax (attach Schedule PH (Form 1120)) **8**

9   Other taxes. Check if from: ☐ Form 4255   ☐ Form 8611   ☐ Form 8697

                           ☐ Form 8866   ☐ Form 8902   ☐ Other (attach schedule) **9**

10   **Total tax.** Add lines 7 through 9. Enter here and on page 1, line 31 . . . . **10**

Schedule K	Other Information (see instructions)		Yes	No

1   Check accounting method: **a** ☐ Cash   **b** ☐ Accrual   **c** ☐ Other (specify) ▶ _____

2   See the instructions and enter the:

  a   Business activity code no. ▶ _____

  b   Business activity ▶ _____

  c   Product or service ▶ _____

3   Is the corporation a subsidiary in an affiliated group or a parent-subsidiary controlled group? _____

     If "Yes," enter name and EIN of the parent corporation ▶ _____

     _____

4   At the end of the tax year:

  a   Did any foreign or domestic corporation, partnership (including any entity treated as a partnership), or trust own directly 20% or more, or own, directly or indirectly, 50% or more of the total voting power of all classes of the corporation's stock entitled to vote? For rules of constructive ownership, see instructions. If "Yes," complete (i) through (v).

(i) Name of Entity	(ii) Employer Identification Number (if any)	(iii) Type of Entity	(iv) Country of Organization	(v) Percentage Owned in Voting Stock

  b   Did any individual or estate own directly 20% or more, or own, directly or indirectly, 50% or more of the total voting power of all classes of the corporation's stock entitled to vote? For rules of constructive ownership, see instructions. If "Yes," complete (i) through (iv).

(i) Name of Individual or Estate	(ii) Identifying Number (if any)	(iii) Country of Citizenship (see instructions)	(iv) Percentage Owned in Voting Stock

Form **1120** (2008)

Form 1120 (*Continued*)

Form 1120 (2008)   Page **4**

Schedule K	Continued

5 At the end of the tax year, did the corporation:

	Yes	No

a Own directly 20% or more, or own, directly or indirectly, 50% or more of the total voting power of all classes of stock entitled to vote of any foreign or domestic corporation not included on **Form 851,** Affiliations Schedule? For rules of constructive ownership, see instructions. If "Yes," complete (i) through (iv).

(i) Name of Corporation	(ii) Employer Identification Number (if any)	(iii) Country of Incorporation	(iv) Percentage Owned in Voting Stock

b Own directly an interest of 20% or more, or own, directly or indirectly, an interest of 50% or more in any foreign or domestic partnership (including an entity treated as a partnership) or in the beneficial interest of a trust? For rules of constructive ownership, see instructions. If "Yes," complete (i) through (iv).

(i) Name of Entity	(ii) Employer Identification Number (if any)	(iii) Country of Organization	(iv) Maximum Percentage Owned in Profit, Loss, or Capital

6 During this tax year, did the corporation pay dividends (other than stock dividends and distributions in exchange for stock) in excess of the corporation's current and accumulated earnings and profits? (See sections 301 and 316.) . . . .
If "Yes," file **Form 5452,** Corporate Report of Nondividend Distributions.

If this is a consolidated return, answer here for the parent corporation and on Form 851 for each subsidiary.

7 At any time during the tax year, did one foreign person own, directly or indirectly, at least 25% of **(a)** the total voting power of all classes of the corporation's stock entitled to vote or **(b)** the total value of all classes of the corporation's stock? . . . . .
For rules of attribution, see section 318. If "Yes," enter:

(i) Percentage owned ▶ _____ and **(ii)** Owner's country ▶ _____

(c) The corporation may have to file **Form 5472,** Information Return of a 25% Foreign-Owned U.S. Corporation or a Foreign Corporation Engaged in a U.S. Trade or Business. Enter the number of Forms 5472 attached ▶ _____

8 Check this box if the corporation issued publicly offered debt instruments with original issue discount . . . . . . ▶ ☐
If checked, the corporation may have to file **Form 8281,** Information Return for Publicly Offered Original Issue Discount Instruments.

9 Enter the amount of tax-exempt interest received or accrued during the tax year ▶ $ _____

10 Enter the number of shareholders at the end of the tax year (if 100 or fewer) ▶ _____

11 If the corporation has an NOL for the tax year and is electing to forego the carryback period, check here . . . . . . ▶ ☐
If the corporation is filing a consolidated return, the statement required by Regulations section 1.1502-21(b)(3) must be attached or the election will not be valid.

12 Enter the available NOL carryover from prior tax years (do not reduce it by any deduction on line 29a.) ▶ $ _____

13 Are the corporation's total receipts (line 1a plus lines 4 through 10 on page 1) for the tax year **and** its total assets at the end of the tax year less than $250,000? . . . .
If "Yes," the corporation is not required to complete Schedules L, M-1, and M-2 on page 5. Instead, enter the total amount of cash distributions and the book value of property distributions (other than cash) made during the tax year. ▶ $

Form **1120** (2008)

Form 1120 (*Continued*)

Form 1120 (2008)   Page **5**

Schedule L	Balance Sheets per Books	Beginning of tax year		End of tax year	
	Assets	**(a)**	**(b)**	**(c)**	**(d)**
1	Cash				
2a	Trade notes and accounts receivable				
b	Less allowance for bad debts	( )		( )	
3	Inventories				
4	U.S. government obligations				
5	Tax-exempt securities (see instructions)				
6	Other current assets (attach schedule)				
7	Loans to shareholders				
8	Mortgage and real estate loans				
9	Other investments (attach schedule)				
10a	Buildings and other depreciable assets				
b	Less accumulated depreciation	( )		( )	
11a	Depletable assets				
b	Less accumulated depletion	( )		( )	
12	Land (net of any amortization)				
13a	Intangible assets (amortizable only)				
b	Less accumulated amortization	( )		( )	
14	Other assets (attach schedule)				
15	Total assets				
	Liabilities and Shareholders' Equity				
16	Accounts payable				
17	Mortgages, notes, bonds payable in less than 1 year				
18	Other current liabilities (attach schedule)				
19	Loans from shareholders				
20	Mortgages, notes, bonds payable in 1 year or more				
21	Other liabilities (attach schedule)				
22	Capital stock: a Preferred stock				
	b Common stock				
23	Additional paid-in capital				
24	Retained earnings—Appropriated (attach schedule)				
25	Retained earnings—Unappropriated				
26	Adjustments to shareholders' equity (attach schedule)				
27	Less cost of treasury stock		( )		( )
28	Total liabilities and shareholders' equity				

Schedule M-1	Reconciliation of Income (Loss) per Books With Income per Return

Note: Schedule M-3 required instead of Schedule M-1 if total assets are $10 million or more—see instructions

1	Net income (loss) per books		7	Income recorded on books this year not
2	Federal income tax per books			included on this return (itemize):
3	Excess of capital losses over capital gains			Tax-exempt interest $ _____
4	Income subject to tax not recorded on books this			_____
	year (itemize): _____			_____
	_____		8	Deductions on this return not charged
5	Expenses recorded on books this year not			against book income this year (itemize):
	deducted on this return (Itemize):		a	Depreciation . . . $ _____
a	Depreciation . . . . $ _____		b	Charitable contributions $ _____
b	Charitable contributions $ _____			_____
c	Travel and entertainment $ _____			_____
			9	Add lines 7 and 8
6	Add lines 1 through 5		10	Income (page 1, line 28)—line 6 less line 9

Schedule M-2	Analysis of Unappropriated Retained Earnings per Books (Line 25, Schedule L)

1	Balance at beginning of year		5	Distributions: a Cash	
2	Net income (loss) per books			b Stock	
3	Other increases (itemize): _____			c Property	
	_____		6	Other decreases (itemize): _____	
	_____		7	Add lines 5 and 6	
4	Add lines 1, 2, and 3		8	Balance at end of year (line 4 less line 7)	

Form **1120** (2008)

Form 1120 (*Continued*)

Form **1120S**	**U.S. Income Tax Return for an S Corporation**	OMB No. 1545-0130
Department of the Treasury Internal Revenue Service	▶ Do not file this form unless the corporation has filed or is attaching Form 2553 to elect to be an S corporation. ▶ See separate instructions.	20**08**

For calendar year 2008 or tax year beginning _____ , 2008, ending _____ , 20 ____

A Selection effective date	Use IRS label. Other- wise, print or type.	Name	**D** Employer identification number
B Business activity code number *(see instructions)*		Number, street, and room or suite no. If a P.O. box, see instructions.	**E** Date incorporated
C Check if Sch. M-3 attached ☐		City or town, state, and ZIP code	**F** Total assets *(see instructions)* $

G Is the corporation electing to be an S corporation beginning with this tax year? ☐ Yes ☐ No   If "Yes," attach Form 2553 if not already filed

H Check if: **(1)** ☐ Final return   **(2)** ☐ Name change   **(3)** ☐ Address change

(4) ☐ Amended return   **(5)** ☐ S election termination or revocation

I Enter the number of shareholders who were shareholders during any part of the tax year ▶

Caution. *Include only trade or business income and expenses on lines 1a through 21. See the instructions for more information.*

Income

1a	Gross receipts or sales _____	**b** Less returns and allowances _____	**c** Bal ▶	**1c**
2	Cost of goods sold (Schedule A, line 8)	**2**
3	Gross profit. Subtract line 2 from line 1c	**3**
4	Net gain (loss) from Form 4797, Part II, line 17 *(attach Form 4797)* . . .	**4**
5	Other income (loss) *(see instructions—attach statement)*	**5**
6	**Total income (loss).** Add lines 3 through 5 . . . . ▶	**6**

Deductions *(see instructions for limitations)*

7	Compensation of officers	**7**
8	Salaries and wages (less employment credits)	**8**
9	Repairs and maintenance	**9**
10	Bad debts	**10**
11	Rents	**11**
12	Taxes and licenses	**12**
13	Interest	**13**
14	Depreciation not claimed on Schedule A or elsewhere on return *(attach Form 4562)*	**14**
15	Depletion **(Do not deduct oil and gas depletion.)**	**15**
16	Advertising	**16**
17	Pension, profit-sharing, etc., plans	**17**
18	Employee benefit programs	**18**
19	Other deductions *(attach statement)*	**19**
20	**Total deductions.** Add lines 7 through 19 . . . . ▶	**20**
21	**Ordinary business income (loss).** Subtract line 20 from line 6	**21**

Tax and Payments

22a	Excess net passive income or LIFO recapture tax *(see instructions)*	**22a**	
b	Tax from Schedule D (Form 1120S)	**22b**	
c	Add lines 22a and 22b *(see instructions for additional taxes)* . .		**22c**
23a	2008 estimated tax payments and 2007 overpayment credited to 2008	**23a**	
b	Tax deposited with Form 7004	**23b**	
c	Credit for federal tax paid on fuels *(attach Form 4136)*	**23c**	
d	Add lines 23a through 23c		**23d**
24	Estimated tax penalty *(see instructions)*. Check if Form 2220 is attached . . . . . ▶ ☐		**24**
25	**Amount owed.** If line 23d is smaller than the total of lines 22c and 24, enter amount owed . .	**25**
26	**Overpayment.** If line 23d is larger than the total of lines 22c and 24, enter amount overpaid .	**26**
27	Enter amount from line 26 **Credited to 2009 estimated tax** ▶ _____ **Refunded** ▶	**27**

Sign Here ▶

Under penalties of perjury, I declare that I have examined this return, including accompanying schedules and statements, and to the best of my knowledge and belief, it is true, correct, and complete. Declaration of preparer (other than taxpayer) is based on all information of which preparer has any knowledge.

Signature of officer	Date	▶	Title

May the IRS discuss this return with the preparer shown below (see instructions)? ☐ **Yes** ☐ **No**

Paid Preparer's Use Only

Preparer's signature ▶		Date	Check if self-employed ☐	Preparer's SSN or PTIN
Firm's name (or yours if self-employed), address, and ZIP code ▶			EIN	
			Phone no. ( )	

For Privacy Act and Paperwork Reduction Act Notice, see separate instructions.   Cat. No. 11510H   Form **1120S** (2008)

Form 1120S U.S. Income Tax Return for an S Corporation

Form 1120S (2008) Page **2**

Schedule A	Cost of Goods Sold (see instructions)		
1	Inventory at beginning of year	1	
2	Purchases	2	
3	Cost of labor	3	
4	Additional section 263A costs *(attach statement)*	4	
5	Other costs *(attach statement)*	5	
6	**Total.** Add lines 1 through 5	6	
7	Inventory at end of year	7	
8	**Cost of goods sold.** Subtract line 7 from line 6. Enter here and on page 1, line 2	8	

9a Check all methods used for valuing closing inventory: *(i)* ☐ Cost as described in Regulations section 1.471-3

   (ii) ☐ Lower of cost or market as described in Regulations section 1.471-4

   (iii) ☐ Other (Specify method used and attach explanation.) ▶ _

 b Check if there was a writedown of subnormal goods as described in Regulations section 1.471-2(c) . . . . . ▶ ☐

 c Check if the LIFO inventory method was adopted this tax year for any goods (if checked, attach Form 970) . . . . ▶ ☐

 d If the LIFO inventory method was used for this tax year, enter percentage (or amounts) of closing
    inventory computed under LIFO | 9d | |

 e If property is produced or acquired for resale, do the rules of section 263A apply to the corporation? . . . . ☐ Yes ☐ No

 f Was there any change in determining quantities, cost, or valuations between opening and closing inventory? . . . ☐ Yes ☐ No
    If "Yes," attach explanation.

Schedule B	Other Information (see instructions)	Yes	No
1	Check accounting method: **a** ☐ Cash **b** ☐ Accrual **c** ☐ Other (specify) ▶ _ _ _ _ _ _ _ _ _ _ _ _ _		
2	See the instructions and enter the:		
	a Business activity ▶ _ _ _ _ _ _ _ _ _ _ _ _ _ _ _ _ _ _ **b** Product or service ▶ _ _ _ _ _ _ _ _ _ _ _ _ _ _ _		
3	At the end of the tax year, did the corporation own, directly or indirectly, 50% or more of the voting stock of a domestic corporation? (For rules of attribution, see section 267(c).) If "Yes," attach a statement showing: **(a)** name and employer identification number (EIN), **(b)** percentage owned, and **(c)** if 100% owned, was a QSub election made?		
4	Has this corporation filed, or is it required to file, a return under section 6111 to provide information on any reportable transaction?		
5	Check this box if the corporation issued publicly offered debt instruments with original issue discount . . ▶ ☐		
	If checked, the corporation may have to file **Form 8281,** Information Return for Publicly Offered Original Issue Discount Instruments.		
6	If the corporation: **(a)** was a C corporation before it elected to be an S corporation **or** the corporation acquired an asset with a basis determined by reference to its basis (or the basis of any other property) in the hands of a C corporation **and (b)** has net unrealized built-in gain (defined in section 1374(d)(1)) in excess of the net recognized built-in gain from prior years, enter the net unrealized built-in gain reduced by net recognized built-in gain from prior years . . . . ▶ $		
7	Enter the accumulated earnings and profits of the corporation at the end of the tax year. . . . . $		
8	Are the corporation's total receipts *(see instructions)* for the tax year **and** its total assets at the end of the tax year less than $250,000? If "Yes," the corporation is not required to complete Schedules L and M-1		

Schedule K	Shareholders' Pro Rata Share Items		Total amount
Income (Loss)	1 Ordinary business income (loss) (page 1, line 21)	1	
	2 Net rental real estate income (loss) *(attach Form 8825)*	2	
	3a Other gross rental income (loss)	3a		
	b Expenses from other rental activities *(attach statement)*.	3b		
	c Other net rental income (loss). Subtract line 3b from line 3a	3c	
	4 Interest income	4	
	5 Dividends: **a** Ordinary dividends	5a	
	b Qualified dividends	5b		
	6 Royalties	6	
	7 Net short-term capital gain (loss) *(attach Schedule D (Form 1120S))*.	7	
	8a Net long-term capital gain (loss) *(attach Schedule D (Form 1120S))*	8a	
	b Collectibles (28%) gain (loss)	8b		
	c Unrecaptured section 1250 gain *(attach statement)* . . .	8c		
	9 Net section 1231 gain (loss) *(attach Form 4797)*	9	
	10 Other income (loss) *(see instructions)* . . . . Type ▶	10	

Form **1120S** (2008)

Form 1120S (*Continued*)

Form 1120S (2008)   Page 3

	Shareholders' Pro Rata Share Items (continued)		Total amount
Deductions	**11** Section 179 deduction (attach Form 4562)	11	
	12a Contributions	12a	
	b Investment interest expense	12b	
	c Section 59(e)(2) expenditures **(1)** Type ▶_____ **(2)** Amount ▶	12c(2)	
	d Other deductions (see instructions) . . . . Type ▶	12d	
Credits	**13a** Low-income housing credit (section 42(j)(5))	13a	
	b Low-income housing credit (other)	13b	
	c Qualified rehabilitation expenditures (rental real estate) (attach Form 3468)	13c	
	d Other rental real estate credits (see instructions)Type ▶ _____	13d	
	e Other rental credits (see instructions) . . . Type ▶ _____	13e	
	f Alcohol and cellulosic biofuel fuels credit (attach Form 6478)	13f	
	g Other credits (see instructions) . . . . . .Type ▶	13g	
Foreign Transactions	**14a** Name of country or U.S. possession ▶_____		
	b Gross income from all sources	14b	
	c Gross income sourced at shareholder level	14c	
	Foreign gross income sourced at corporate level		
	d Passive category	14d	
	e General category	14e	
	f Other (attach statement)	14f	
	Deductions allocated and apportioned at shareholder level		
	g Interest expense	14g	
	h Other	14h	
	Deductions allocated and apportioned at corporate level to foreign source income		
	i Passive category	14i	
	j General category	14j	
	k Other (attach statement)	14k	
	Other information		
	l Total foreign taxes (check one): ▶ ☐ Paid ☐ Accrued	14l	
	m Reduction in taxes available for credit (attach statement)	14m	
	n Other foreign tax information (attach statement)		
Alternative Minimum Tax (AMT) Items	**15a** Post-1986 depreciation adjustment	15a	
	b Adjusted gain or loss	15b	
	c Depletion (other than oil and gas)	15c	
	d Oil, gas, and geothermal properties—gross income	15d	
	e Oil, gas, and geothermal properties—deductions	15e	
	f Other AMT items (attach statement)	15f	
Items Affecting Shareholder Basis	**16a** Tax-exempt interest income	16a	
	b Other tax-exempt income	16b	
	c Nondeductible expenses	16c	
	d Property distributions	16d	
	e Repayment of loans from shareholders	16e	
Other Information	**17a** Investment income	17a	
	b Investment expenses	17b	
	c Dividend distributions paid from accumulated earnings and profits	17c	
	d Other items and amounts (attach statement)		
Reconciliation	**18** **Income/loss reconciliation.** Combine the amounts on lines 1 through 10 in the far right column. From the result, subtract the sum of the amounts on lines 11 through 12d and 14l	18	

Form **1120S** (2008)

Form 1120S (*Continued*)

Form 1120S (2008)

Schedule L — Balance Sheets per Books

Assets	Beginning of tax year		End of tax year	
	(a)	(b)	(c)	(d)
1 Cash				
2a Trade notes and accounts receivable				
b Less allowance for bad debts	( )		( )	
3 Inventories				
4 U.S. government obligations				
5 Tax-exempt securities (see instructions)				
6 Other current assets (attach statement)				
7 Loans to shareholders				
8 Mortgage and real estate loans				
9 Other investments (attach statement)				
10a Buildings and other depreciable assets				
b Less accumulated depreciation	( )		( )	
11a Depletable assets				
b Less accumulated depletion	( )		( )	
12 Land (net of any amortization)				
13a Intangible assets (amortizable only)				
b Less accumulated amortization	( )		( )	
14 Other assets (attach statement)				
15 Total assets				
Liabilities and Shareholders' Equity				
16 Accounts payable				
17 Mortgages, notes, bonds payable in less than 1 year				
18 Other current liabilities (attach statement)				
19 Loans from shareholders				
20 Mortgages, notes, bonds payable in 1 year or more				
21 Other liabilities (attach statement)				
22 Capital stock				
23 Additional paid-in capital				
24 Retained earnings				
25 Adjustments to shareholders' equity (attach statement)				
26 Less cost of treasury stock		( )		( )
27 Total liabilities and shareholders' equity				

Schedule M-1 — Reconciliation of Income (Loss) per Books With Income (Loss) per Return

Note: Schedule M-3 required instead of Schedule M-1 if total assets are $10 million or more—see instructions

1	Net income (loss) per books		5	Income recorded on books this year not included on Schedule K, lines 1 through 10 (itemize):	
2	Income included on Schedule K, lines 1, 2, 3c, 4, 5a, 6, 7, 8a, 9, and 10, not recorded on books this year (itemize): _____		a	Tax-exempt interest $ _____	
3	Expenses recorded on books this year not included on Schedule K, lines 1 through 12 and 14l (itemize):		6	Deductions included on Schedule K, lines 1 through 12 and 14l, not charged against book income this year (itemize):	
a	Depreciation $ _____		a	Depreciation $ _____	
b	Travel and entertainment $ _____			_____	
	_____		7	Add lines 5 and 6	
4	Add lines 1 through 3		8	Income (loss) (Schedule K, line 18). Line 4 less line 7	

Schedule M-2 — Analysis of Accumulated Adjustments Account, Other Adjustments Account, and Shareholders' Undistributed Taxable Income Previously Taxed (see instructions)

		(a) Accumulated adjustments account	(b) Other adjustments account	(c) Shareholders' undistributed taxable income previously taxed
1	Balance at beginning of tax year			
2	Ordinary income from page 1, line 21			
3	Other additions			
4	Loss from page 1, line 21	( )		
5	Other reductions	( )	( )	
6	Combine lines 1 through 5			
7	Distributions other than dividend distributions			
8	Balance at end of tax year. Subtract line 7 from line 6			

Form **1120S** (2008)

Form 1120S (*Continued*)

Form **2553**		**Election by a Small Business Corporation**		
(Rev. December 2007)		(Under section 1362 of the Internal Revenue Code)		OMB No. 1545-0146
Department of the Treasury Internal Revenue Service		▶ See Parts II and III on page 3 and the separate instructions. ▶ The corporation can fax this form to the IRS (see separate instructions).		

Note. This election to be an S corporation can be accepted only if all the tests are met under **Who May Elect** on page 1 of the instructions; all shareholders have signed the consent statement; an officer has signed below; and the exact name and address of the corporation and other required form information are provided.

Part I	**Election Information**		
Type or Print	Name (see instructions)	**A**	Employer identification number
	Number, street, and room or suite no. (If a P.O. box, see instructions.)	**B**	Date incorporated
	City or town, state, and ZIP code	**C**	State of incorporation

D Check the applicable box(es) if the corporation, after applying for the EIN shown in **A** above, changed its ☐ name or ☐ address

E Election is to be effective for tax year beginning (month, day, year) (see instructions) . . . . . ▶ ___ / ___ / ___

Caution. A corporation (entity) making the election for its first tax year in existence will usually enter the beginning date of a short tax year that begins on a date other than January 1.

F Selected tax year:

(1) ☐ Calendar year

(2) ☐ Fiscal year ending (month and day) ▶ _____

(3) ☐ 52-53-week year ending with reference to the month of December

(4) ☐ 52-53-week year ending with reference to the month of ▶ _____

If box (2) or (4) is checked, complete Part II

G If more than 100 shareholders are listed for item J (see page 2), check this box if treating members of a family as one shareholder results in no more than 100 shareholders (see test 2 under **Who May Elect** in the instructions) ▶ ☐

H Name and title of officer or legal representative who the IRS may call for more information	**I** Telephone number of officer or legal representative ( )

If this S corporation election is being filed with Form 1120S, I declare that I had reasonable cause for not filing Form 2553 timely, and if this election is made by an entity eligible to elect to be treated as a corporation, I declare that I also had reasonable cause for not filing an entity classification election timely. See below for my explanation of the reasons the election or elections were not made on time (see instructions).

Sign Here ▶ Under penalties of perjury, I declare that I have examined this election, including accompanying schedules and statements, and to the best of my knowledge and belief, it is true, correct, and complete.

Signature of officer	Title	Date

For Paperwork Reduction Act Notice, see separate instructions.   Cat. No. 18629R   Form **2553** (Rev. 12-2007)

Form 2553 Election by a Small Business Corporation

Form 2553 (Rev. 12-2007) Page **2**

Part I **Election Information** (continued)

J Name and address of each shareholder or former shareholder required to consent to the election. (See the instructions for column K.)	**K** Shareholders' Consent Statement. Under penalties of perjury, we declare that we consent to the election of the above-named corporation to be an S corporation under section 1362(a) and that we have examined this consent statement, including accompanying schedules and statements, and to the best of our knowledge and belief, it is true, correct, and complete. We understand our consent is binding and may not be withdrawn after the corporation has made a valid election. (Sign and date below.)		**L** Stock owned or percentage of ownership (see instructions)		**M** Social security number or employer identification number (see instructions)	**N** Shareholder's tax year ends (month and day)
	Signature	Date	Number of shares or percentage of ownership	Date(s) acquired		

Form 2553 (Rev. 12-2007)

Form 2553 (*Continued*)

Form 2553 (Rev. 12-2007)

Part II   Selection of Fiscal Tax Year (see instructions)

Note. All corporations using this part must complete item O and item P, Q, or R.

O   Check the applicable box to indicate whether the corporation is:

1. ☐ A new corporation **adopting** the tax year entered in item F, Part I.
2. ☐ An existing corporation **retaining** the tax year entered in item F, Part I.
3. ☐ An existing corporation **changing** to the tax year entered in item F, Part I.

P   Complete item P if the corporation is using the automatic approval provisions of Rev. Proc. 2006-46, 2006-45 I.R.B. 859, to request **(1)** a natural business year (as defined in section 5.07 of Rev. Proc. 2006-46) or **(2)** a year that satisfies the ownership tax year test (as defined in section 5.08 of Rev. Proc. 2006-46). Check the applicable box below to indicate the representation statement the corporation is making.

1. Natural Business Year ▶ ☐ I represent that the corporation is adopting, retaining, or changing to a tax year that qualifies as its natural business year (as defined in section 5.07 of Rev. Proc. 2006-46) and has attached a statement showing separately for each month the gross receipts for the most recent 47 months (see instructions). I also represent that the corporation is not precluded by section 4.02 of Rev. Proc. 2006-46 from obtaining automatic approval of such adoption, retention, or change in tax year.

2. Ownership Tax Year ▶ ☐ I represent that shareholders (as described in section 5.08 of Rev. Proc. 2006-46) holding more than half of the shares of the stock (as of the first day of the tax year to which the request relates) of the corporation have the same tax year or are concurrently changing to the tax year that the corporation adopts, retains, or changes to per item F, Part I, and that such tax year satisfies the requirement of section 4.01(3) of Rev. Proc. 2006-46. I also represent that the corporation is not precluded by section 4.02 of Rev. Proc. 2006-46 from obtaining automatic approval of such adoption, retention, or change in tax year.

Note. If you do not use item P and the corporation wants a fiscal tax year, complete either item Q or R below. Item Q is used to request a fiscal tax year based on a business purpose and to make a back-up section 444 election. Item R is used to make a regular section 444 election.

Q   Business Purpose—To request a fiscal tax year based on a business purpose, check box Q1. See instructions for details including payment of a user fee. You may also check box Q2 and/or box Q3.

1. Check here ▶ ☐ if the fiscal year entered in item F, Part I, is requested under the prior approval provisions of Rev. Proc. 2002-39, 2002-22 I.R.B. 1046. Attach to Form 2553 a statement describing the relevant facts and circumstances and, if applicable, the gross receipts from sales and services necessary to establish a business purpose. See the instructions for details regarding the gross receipts from sales and services. If the IRS proposes to disapprove the requested fiscal year, do you want a conference with the IRS National Office?

☐ Yes   ☐ No

2. Check here ▶ ☐ to show that the corporation intends to make a back-up section 444 election in the event the corporation's business purpose request is not approved by the IRS. (See instructions for more information.)

3. Check here ▶ ☐ to show that the corporation agrees to adopt or change to a tax year ending December 31 if necessary for the IRS to accept this election for S corporation status in the event (1) the corporation's business purpose request is not approved and the corporation makes a back-up section 444 election, but is ultimately not qualified to make a section 444 election, or (2) the corporation's business purpose request is not approved and the corporation did not make a back-up section 444 election.

R   Section 444 Election—To make a section 444 election, check box R1. You may also check box R2.

1. Check here ▶ ☐ to show that the corporation will make, if qualified, a section 444 election to have the fiscal tax year shown in item F, Part I. To make the election, you must complete **Form 8716,** Election To Have a Tax Year Other Than a Required Tax Year, and either attach it to Form 2553 or file it separately.

2. Check here ▶ ☐ to show that the corporation agrees to adopt or change to a tax year ending December 31 if necessary for the IRS to accept this election for S corporation status in the event the corporation is ultimately not qualified to make a section 444 election.

Part III   Qualified Subchapter S Trust (QSST) Election Under Section 1361(d)(2)*

Income beneficiary's name and address	Social security number
Trust's name and address	Employer identification number

Date on which stock of the corporation was transferred to the trust (month, day, year) . . . . ▶   /   /

In order for the trust named above to be a QSST and thus a qualifying shareholder of the S corporation for which this Form 2553 is filed, I hereby make the election under section 1361(d)(2). Under penalties of perjury, I certify that the trust meets the definitional requirements of section 1361(d)(3) and that all other information provided in Part III is true, correct, and complete.

_____   _____
Signature of income beneficiary or signature and title of legal representative or other qualified person making the election   Date

*Use Part III to make the QSST election only if stock of the corporation has been transferred to the trust on or before the date on which the corporation makes its election to be an S corporation. The QSST election must be made and filed separately if stock of the corporation is transferred to the trust **after** the date on which the corporation makes the S election.

Form **2553** (Rev. 12-2007)

Form 2553 (*Continued*)

Form **3115**
(Rev. December 2003)
Department of the Treasury
Internal Revenue Service

Application for Change in Accounting Method

OMB No. 1545-0152

Name of filer (name of parent corporation if a consolidated group) (see instructions)	Identification number (see instructions)
	Principal business activity code number (see instructions)
Number, street, and room or suite no. If a P.O. box, see the instructions.	Tax year of change begins (MM/DD/YYYY)
	Tax year of change ends (MM/DD/YYYY)
City or town, state, and ZIP code	Name of contact person (see instructions)
Name of applicant(s) (if different than filer) and identification number(s) (see instructions)	Contact person's telephone number ( )

If the applicant is a member of a consolidated group, check this box . . . . ▶ ☐

If **Form 2848**, Power of Attorney and Declaration of Representative, is attached, check this box . . . . ▶ ☐

Check the box to indicate the applicant.

☐ Individual
☐ Corporation
☐ Controlled foreign corporation (Sec. 957)
☐ 10/50 corporation (Sec. 904(d)(2)(E))
☐ Qualified personal service corporation (Sec. 448(d)(2))
☐ Exempt organization. Enter Code section ▶

☐ Cooperative (Sec. 1381)
☐ Partnership
☐ S corporation
☐ Insurance co. (Sec. 816(a))
☐ Insurance co. (Sec. 831)
☐ Other (specify) ▶ _ _ _ _ _ _

Check the appropriate box to indicate the type of accounting method change being requested. (see instructions)

☐ Depreciation or Amortization
☐ Financial Products and/or Financial Activities of Financial Institutions
☐ Other (specify) ▶ _ _ _ _ _ _ _ _ _ _ _ _ _ _ _ _

Caution: *The applicant must provide the requested information to be eligible for approval of the requested accounting method change. The applicant may be required to provide information specific to the accounting method change such as an attached statement. The applicant must provide all information relevant to the requested accounting method change, even if not specifically requested by the Form 3115.*

Part I	**Information For Automatic Change Request**	Yes	No

1   Enter the requested designated accounting method change number from the **List of Automatic Accounting Method Changes** (see instructions). Enter only one method change number, except as provided for in the instructions. If the requested change is not included in that list, check "Other," and provide a description.

▶ (a) Change No. _____ (b) Other ☐ Description ▶ _____

2   Is the accounting method change being requested one for which the scope limitations of section 4.02 of Rev. Proc. 2002-9 (or its successor) **do not** apply? . . . .

If "Yes," go to Part II.

3   Is the tax year of change the final tax year of a trade or business for which the taxpayer would be required to take the entire amount of the section 481(a) adjustment into account in computing taxable income? . . .

If "Yes," the applicant is not eligible to make the change under automatic change request procedures.

Note: *Complete Part II below and then Part IV, and also Schedules A through E of this form (if applicable).*

Part II	**Information For All Requests**	Yes	No

4a   Does the applicant (or any present or former consolidated group in which the applicant was a member during the applicable tax year(s)) have any Federal income tax return(s) under examination (see instructions)? . . .

If you answered "No," go to line 5.

b   Is the method of accounting the applicant is requesting to change an issue (with respect to either the applicant or any present or former consolidated group in which the applicant was a member during the applicable tax year(s)) either (i) under consideration or (ii) placed in suspense (see instructions)? . . . .

Signature *(see instructions)*

Under penalties of perjury, I declare that I have examined this application, including accompanying schedules and statements, and to the best of my knowledge and belief, the application contains all the relevant facts relating to the application, and it is true, correct, and complete. Declaration of preparer (other than applicant) is based on all information of which preparer has any knowledge.

Filer	Preparer (other than filer/applicant)
_____ Signature and date	_____ Signature of individual preparing the application and date
_____ Name and title (print or type)	_____ Name of individual preparing the application (print or type)
	_____ Name of firm preparing the application

For Privacy Act and Paperwork Reduction Act Notice, see the instructions.   Cat. No. 19280E   Form **3115** (Rev. 12-2003)

Form 3115 Application for Change in Accounting Method

Form 3115 (Rev. 12-2003)   Page **2**

Part II	Information For All Requests (continued)	Yes	No

4c Is the method of accounting the applicant is requesting to change an issue pending (with respect to either the applicant or any present or former consolidated group in which the applicant was a member during the applicable tax year(s)) for any tax year under examination (see instructions)?

d Is the request to change the method of accounting being filed under the procedures requiring that the operating division director consent to the filing of the request (see instructions)?

If "Yes," attach the consent statement from the director.

e Is the request to change the method of accounting being filed under the 90-day or 120-day window period?

If "Yes," check the box for the applicable window period and attach the required statement (see instructions).

☐ 90 day 120 day   ☐

f If you answered "Yes" to line 4a, enter the name and telephone number of the examining agent and the tax year(s) under examination.

Name ▶ _____ Telephone number ▶ _____ Tax year(s) ▶ _____

g Has a copy of this Form 3115 been provided to the examining agent identified on line 4f?

5a Does the applicant (or any present or former consolidated group in which the applicant was a member during the applicable tax year(s)) have any Federal income tax return(s) before Appeals and/or a Federal court?

If "Yes," enter the name of the (check the box)   ☐ Appeals officer and/or   ☐ counsel for the government, and the tax year(s) before Appeals and/or a Federal court.

Name ▶ _____ Telephone number ▶ _____ Tax year(s) ▶ _____

b Has a copy of this Form 3115 been provided to the Appeals officer and/or counsel for the government identified on line 5a?

c Is the method of accounting the applicant is requesting to change an issue under consideration by Appeals and/or a Federal court (for either the applicant or any present or former consolidated group in which the applicant was a member for the tax year(s) the applicant was a member)?

If "Yes," attach an explanation.

6 If the applicant answered "Yes" to line 4a and/or 5a with respect to any present or former consolidated group, provide each parent corporation's **(a)** name, **(b)** identification number, **(c)** address, and **(d)** tax year(s) during which the applicant was a member that is under examination, before an Appeals office, and/or before a Federal court.

7 If the applicant is an entity (including a limited liability company) treated as a partnership or S corporation for Federal income tax purposes, is it requesting a change from a method of accounting that is an issue under consideration in an examination, before Appeals, or before a Federal court, with respect to a Federal income tax return of a partner, member, or shareholder of that entity?

If "Yes," the applicant is **not** eligible to make the change.

8 Is the applicant making a change to which audit protection does not apply (see instructions)?

9a Has the applicant, its predecessor, or a related party requested or made (under either an automatic change procedure or a procedure requiring advance consent) a change in accounting method within the past 5 years (including the year of the requested change)?

b If "Yes," attach a description of each change and the year of change for each separate trade or business and whether consent was obtained.

c If any application was withdrawn, not perfected, or denied, or if a Consent Agreement was sent to the taxpayer but was not signed and returned to the IRS, or if the change was not made or not made in the requested year of change, include an explanation.

10a Does the applicant, its predecessor, or a related party currently have pending any request (including any concurrently filed request) for a private letter ruling, change in accounting method, or technical advice?

b If "Yes," for each request attach a statement providing the name(s) of the taxpayer, identification number(s), the type of request (private letter ruling, change in accounting method, or technical advice), and the specific issue(s) in the request(s).

11 Is the applicant requesting to change its **overall** method of accounting?

If "Yes," check the appropriate boxes below to indicate the applicant's present and proposed methods of accounting. Also, complete Schedule A on page 4 of the form.

Present method: ☐ Cash   ☐ Accrual   ☐ Hybrid (attach description)

Proposed method: ☐ Cash   ☐ Accrual   ☐ Hybrid (attach description)

12 If the applicant is **not** changing its overall method of accounting, attach a detailed and complete description for each of the following:

a The item(s) being changed.

b The applicant's present method for the item(s) being changed.

c The applicant's proposed method for the item(s) being changed.

d The applicant's present overall method of accounting (cash, accrual, or hybrid).

Form **3115** (Rev. 12-2003)

Form 3115 (*Continued*)

Form 3115 (Rev. 12-2003)   Page **3**

Part II	Information For All Requests (continued)	Yes	No

13 Attach a detailed and complete description of the applicant's trade(s) or business(es), and the principal business activity code for each. If the applicant has more than one trade or business as defined in Regulations section 1.446-1(d), describe: whether each trade or business is accounted for separately; the goods and services provided by each trade or business and any other types of activities engaged in that generate gross income; the overall method of accounting for each trade or business; and which trade or business is requesting to change its accounting method as part of this application or a separate application.

14 Will the proposed method of accounting be used for the applicant's books and records and financial statements? For insurance companies, see the instructions . . . .
If "No," attach an explanation.

15a Has the applicant engaged, or will it engage, in a transaction to which section 381(a) applies (e.g., a reorganization, merger, or liquidation) during the proposed tax year of change determined without regard to any potential closing of the year under section 381(b)(1)? . . . .

  b If "Yes," for the items of income and expense that are the subject of this application, attach a statement identifying the methods of accounting used by the parties to the section 381(a) transaction immediately before the date of distribution or transfer and the method(s) that would be required by section 381(c)(4) or (c)(5) absent consent to the change(s) requested in this application.

16 Does the applicant request a **conference of right** with the IRS National Office if the IRS proposes an adverse response?. . . . .

17 If the applicant is changing to or from the cash method or changing its method of accounting under sections 263A, 448, 460, or 471, enter the gross receipts of the 3 tax years preceding the year of change.

1st preceding year ended: mo. yr.	2nd preceding year ended: mo. yr.	3rd preceding year ended: mo. yr.
$	$	$

Part III	Information For Advance Consent Request	Yes	No

18 Is the applicant's requested change described in any revenue procedure, revenue ruling, notice, regulation, or other published guidance as an automatic change request? . . . .
If "Yes," attachan explanation describing why the applicant is submitting its request under advance consent request procedures.

19 Attach a full explanation of the legal basis supporting the proposed method for the item being changed. Include a detailed and complete description of the facts that explains how the law specifically applies to the applicant's situation and that demonstrates that the applicant is authorized to use the proposed method. Include all authority (statutes, regulations, published rulings, court cases, etc.) supporting the proposed method. The applicant should include a discussion of any authorities that may be contrary to its use of the proposed method.

20 Attach a copy of all documents related to the proposed change (see instructions).

21 Attach a statement of the applicant's reasons for the proposed change.

22 If the applicant is a member of a consolidated group for the year of change, do all other members of the consolidated group use the proposed method of accounting for the item being changed? . . . . .
If "No," attach an explanation.

23a Enter the amount of **user fee** attached to this application (see instructions). ▶ $ _____

  b If the applicant qualifies for a reduced user fee, attach the necessary information or certification required by Rev. Proc. 2003-1 (or its successor) (see instructions).

Part IV	Section 481(a) Adjustment	Yes	No

24 Do the procedures for the accounting method change being requested require the use of the cut-off method? If "Yes," do not complete lines 25, 26, and 27 below.

25 Enter the section 481(a) adjustment. Indicate whether the adjustment is an increase (+) or a decrease (-) in income. ▶ $ _____ Attach a summary of the computation and an explanation of the methodology used to determine the section 481(a) adjustment. If it is based on more than one component, show the computation for each component. If more than one applicant is applying for the method change on the same application, attach a list of the name, identification number, principal business activity code (see instructions), and the amount of the section 481(a) adjustment attributable to each applicant.

26 If the section 481(a) adjustment is an increase to income of less than $25,000, does the applicant elect to take the entire amount of the adjustment into account in the year of change? . . . .

27 Is any part of the section 481(a) adjustment attributable to transactions between members of an affiliated group, a consolidated group, a controlled group, or other related parties? . . . .
If "Yes," attach an explanation.

Form **3115** (Rev. 12-2003)

Form 3115 (*Continued*)

Form 3115 (Rev. 12-2003)   Page **4**

Schedule A—Change in Overall Method of Accounting (If Schedule A applies, Part I below must be completed.)

Part I   Change in Overall Method (see instructions)

1   Enter the following amounts as of the close of the tax year preceding the year of change. If none, state "None." Also, attach a statement providing a breakdown of the amounts entered on lines 1a through 1g.

		Amount
a	Income accrued but not received	$
b	Income received or reported before it was earned. Attach a description of the income and the legal basis for the proposed method	
c	Expenses accrued but not paid	
d	Prepaid expenses previously deducted	
e	Supplies on hand previously deducted and/or not previously reported	
f	Inventory on hand previously deducted and/or not previously reported. Complete Schedule D, Part II .	
g	Other amounts (specify) ▶ _____	
h	**Net section 481(a) adjustment** (Combine lines 1a–1g.)	$

2   Is the applicant also requesting the recurring item exception under section 461(h)(3)? . . . .   ☐ **Yes**   ☐ **No**

3   Attach copies of the profit and loss statement (Schedule F (Form 1040) for farmers) and the balance sheet, if applicable, as of the close of the tax year preceding the year of change. On a separate sheet, state the accounting method used when preparing the balance sheet. If books of account are not kept, attach a copy of the business schedules submitted with the Federal income tax return or other return (e.g., tax-exempt organization returns) for that period. If the amounts in Part I, lines 1a through 1g, do not agree with those shown on both the profit and loss statement and the balance sheet, explain the differences on a separate sheet.

Part II   Change to the Cash Method For Advance Consent Request (see instructions)

Applicants requesting a change to the cash method must attach the following information:

1   A description of inventory items (items whose production, purchase, or sale is an income-producing factor) and materials and supplies used in carrying out the business.

2   An explanation as to whether the applicant is required to use the accrual method under any section of the Code or regulations.

Schedule B—Change in Reporting Advance Payments (see instructions)

1   If the applicant is requesting to defer advance payment for services under Rev. Proc. 71-21, 1971-2 C.B. 549, attach the following information:

a   Sample copies of all service agreements used by the applicant that are subject to the requested change in accounting method. Indicate the particular parts of the service agreement that require the taxpayer to perform services.

b   If any parts or materials are provided, explain whether the obligation to provide parts or materials is incidental (of minor or secondary importance) to an agreement providing for the performance of personal services.

c   If the change relates to contingent service contracts, explain how the contracts relate to merchandise that is sold, leased, installed, or constructed by the applicant and whether the applicant offers to sell, lease, install, or construct without the service agreement.

d   A description of the method the applicant will use to determine the amount of income earned each year on service contracts and why that method clearly reflects income earned and related expenses in each year.

e   An explanation of how the method the applicant will use to determine the amount of gross receipts each year will be no less than the amount included in gross receipts for purposes of its books and records. See section 3.11 of Rev. Proc. 71-21.

2   If the applicant is requesting a deferral of advance payments for goods under Regulations section 1.451-5, attach the following information:

a   Sample copies of all agreements for goods or items requiring advance payments used by the applicant that are subject to the requested change in accounting method. Indicate the particular parts of the agreement that require the applicant to provide goods or items.

b   A statement providing that the entire advance payment is for goods or items. If not entirely for goods or items, a statement that an amount equal to 95% of the total contract price is properly allocable to the obligation to provide activities described in Regulations section 1.451-5(a)(1)(i) or (ii) (including services as an integral part of those activities).

c   An explanation of how the method the applicant will use to determine the amount of gross receipts each year will be no less than the amount included in gross receipts for purposes of its books and records. See Regulations section 1.451-5(b)(1).

Form **3115** (Rev. 12-2003)

Form 3115 (*Continued*)

Schedule C—Changes Within the LIFO Inventory Method (see instructions)

Part I   General LIFO Information

Complete this section if the requested change involves changes within the LIFO inventory method. Also, attach a copy of all **Forms 970,** Application To Use LIFO Inventory Method, filed to adopt or expand the use of the LIFO method.

1   Attach a description of the applicant's present and proposed LIFO methods and submethods for each of the following items:

a   Valuing inventory (e.g., unit method or dollar-value method).

b   Pooling (e.g., by line or type or class of goods, natural business unit, multiple pools, raw material content, simplified dollar-value method, inventory price index computation (IPIC) pools, etc.).

c   Pricing dollar-value pools (e.g., double-extension, index, link-chain, link-chain index, IPIC method, etc.).

d   Determining the current year cost of goods in the ending inventory (e.g., most recent purchases, earliest acquisitions during the year, average cost of purchases during the year, etc.).

2   If any present method or submethod used by the applicant is not the same as indicated on Form(s) 970 filed to adopt or expand the use of the method, attach an explanation.

3   If the proposed change is not requested for all the LIFO inventory, specify the inventory to which the change is and is not applicable.

4   If the proposed change is not requested for all of the LIFO pools, specify the LIFO pool(s) to which the change is applicable.

5   Attach a statement addressing whether the applicant values any of its LIFO inventory on a method other than cost. For example, if the applicant values some of its LIFO inventory at retail and the remainder at cost, the applicant should identify which inventory items are valued under each method.

6   If changing to the IPIC method, attach a completed Form 970 and a statement indicating the indexes, tables, and categories the applicant proposes to use.

Part II   Change in Pooling Inventories

1   If the applicant is proposing to change its pooling method or the number of pools, attach a description of the contents of, and state the base year for, each dollar-value pool the applicant presently uses and proposes to use.

2   If the applicant is proposing to use natural business unit (NBU) pools or requesting to change the number of NBU pools, attach the following information (to the extent not already provided) in sufficient detail to show that each proposed NBU was determined under Regulations section 1.472-8(b)(1) and (2):

a   A description of the types of products produced by the applicant. If possible, attach a brochure.

b   A description of the types of processes and raw materials used to produce the products in each proposed pool.

c   If all of the products to be included in the proposed NBU pool(s) are not produced at one facility, the applicant should explain the reasons for the separate facilities, indicate the location of each facility, and provide a description of the products each facility produces.

d   A description of the natural business divisions adopted by the taxpayer. State whether separate cost centers are maintained and if separate profit and loss statements are prepared.

e   A statement addressing whether the applicant has inventories of items purchased and held for resale that are not further processed by the applicant, including whether such items, if any, will be included in any proposed NBU pool.

f   A statement addressing whether all items including raw materials, goods-in-process, and finished goods entering into the entire inventory investment for each proposed NBU pool are presently valued under the LIFO method. Describe any items that are not presently valued under the LIFO method that are to be included in each proposed pool.

g   A statement addressing whether, within the proposed NBU pool(s), there are items both sold to unrelated parties and transferred to a different unit of the applicant to be used as a component part of another product prior to final processing.

3   If the applicant is engaged in manufacturing and is proposing to use the multiple pooling method or raw material content pools, attach information to show that each proposed pool will consist of a group of items that are substantially similar. See Regulations section 1.472-8(b)(3).

4   If the applicant is engaged in the wholesaling or retailing of goods and is requesting to change the number of pools used, attach information to show that each of the proposed pools is based on customary business classifications of the applicant's trade or business. See Regulations section 1.472-8(c).

Form 3115 (*Continued*)

Form 3115 (Rev. 12-2003) Page **6**

Schedule D—Change in the Treatment of Long-Term Contracts Under Section 460, Inventories, or Other Section 263A Assets (see instructions)

Part I   Change in Reporting Income From Long-Term Contracts (Also complete Part III on pages 7 and 8.)

1   To the extent not already provided, attach a description of the applicant's present and proposed methods for reporting income and expenses from long-term contracts. If the applicant is a construction contractor, include a detailed description of its construction activities.

2a Are the applicant's contracts long-term contracts as defined in section 460(f)(1) (see instructions)? . . . ☐ **Yes**   ☐ **No**

b If "Yes," do all the contracts qualify for the exception under section 460(e) (see instructions)? . . . . . ☐ **Yes**   ☐ **No**
If line 2b is "No," attach an explanation.

c If line 2b is "Yes," is the applicant requesting to use the percentage-of-completion method using cost-to-cost under Regulations section 1.460-4(b)? . . . . ☐ **Yes**   ☐ **No**

d If line 2c is "No," is the applicant requesting to use the exempt-contract percentage-of-completion method under Regulations section 1.460-4(c)(2)? . . . . ☐ **Yes**   ☐ **No**
If line 2d is "Yes," explain what cost comparison the applicant will use to determine a contract's completion factor.
If line 2d is "No," explain what method the applicant is using and the authority for its use.

3a Does the applicant have long-term manufacturing contracts as defined in section 460(f)(2)? . . . . . ☐ **Yes**   ☐ **No**

b If "Yes," explain the applicant's present and proposed method(s) of accounting for long-term manufacturing contracts.

c Describe the applicant's manufacturing activities, including any required installation of manufactured goods.

4   To determine a contract's completion factor using the percentage-of-completion method:

a Will the applicant use the cost-to-cost method in Regulations section 1.460-4(b)? . . . . ☐ **Yes**   ☐ **No**

b If line 4a is "No," is the applicant electing the simplified cost-to-cost method (see section 460(b)(3) and Regulations section 1.460-5(c))? . . . . ☐ **Yes**   ☐ **No**

5   Attach a statement indicating whether any of the applicant's contracts are either cost-plus long-term contracts or Federal long-term contracts.

Part II   Change in Valuing Inventories Including Cost Allocation Changes (Also complete Part III on pages 7 and 8.)

1   Attach a description of the inventory goods being changed.

2   Attach a description of the inventory goods (if any) NOT being changed.

3   If the applicant is subject to section 263A, is its present inventory valuation method in compliance with section 263A (see instructions)? . . . . ☐ **Yes**   ☐ **No**

	Inventory Being Changed		Inventory Not Being Changed
4a Check the appropriate boxes below.	Present method	Proposed method	Present method
Identification methods:			
Specific identification			
FIFO			
LIFO			
Other (attach explanation)			
Valuation methods:			
Cost			
Cost or market, whichever is lower			
Retail cost			
Retail, lower of cost or market			
Other (attach explanation)			
b Enter the value at the end of the tax year preceding the year of change . . .			////////

5   If the applicant is changing from the LIFO inventory method to a non-LIFO method, attach the following information (see instructions).

a Copies of Form(s) 970 filed to adopt or expand the use of the method.

b **Only for applicants requesting advance consent.** A statement describing whether the applicant is changing to the method required by Regulations section 1.472-6(a) or (b), or whether the applicant is proposing a different method.

c **Only for applicants requesting an automatic change.** Attach the statement required by section 10.01(4) of the Appendix of Rev. Proc. 2002-9 (or its successor).

Form **3115** (Rev. 12-2003)

Form 3115 (*Continued*)

Form 3115 (Rev. 12-2003)   Page **7**

Part III **Method of Cost Allocation** (Complete this part if the requested change involves either property subject
to section 263A or long-term contracts as described in section 460 (see instructions).)

Section A—Allocation and Capitalization Methods

Attach a description (including sample computations) of the present and proposed method(s) the applicant uses to capitalize direct
and indirect costs properly allocable to real or tangible personal property produced and property acquired for resale, or to allocate and,
where appropriate, capitalize direct and indirect costs properly allocable to long-term contracts. Include a description of the method(s)
used for allocating indirect costs to intermediate cost objectives such as departments or activities prior to the allocation of such costs
to long-term contracts, real or tangible personal property produced, and property acquired for resale. The description must include the
following:

1   The method of allocating direct and indirect costs (i.e., specific identification, burden rate, standard cost, or other reasonable
allocation method).

2   The method of allocating mixed service costs (i.e., direct reallocation, step-allocation, simplified service cost using the labor-
based allocation ratio, simplified service cost using the production cost allocation ratio, or other reasonable allocation method).

3   The method of capitalizing additional section 263A costs (i.e., simplified production with or without the historic absorption ratio
election, simplified resale with or without the historic absorption ratio election including permissible variations, the U.S. ratio, or
other reasonable allocation method).

Section B—Direct and Indirect Costs Required To Be Allocated (Check the appropriate boxes in Section B showing the costs
that are or will be fully included, to the extent required, in the cost of real or tangible personal property produced or property
acquired for resale under section 263A or allocated to long-term contracts under section 460. Mark "N/A" in a box if those costs are
not incurred by the applicant. If a box is not checked, it is assumed that those costs are not fully included to the extent required.
Attach an explanation for boxes that are not checked.)

		Present method	Proposed method
1	Direct material		
2	Direct labor		
3	Indirect labor		
4	Officers' compensation (not including selling activities)		
5	Pension and other related costs		
6	Employee benefits		
7	Indirect materials and supplies		
8	Purchasing costs		
9	Handling, processing, assembly, and repackaging costs		
10	Offsite storage and warehousing costs		
11	Depreciation, amortization, and cost recovery allowance for equipment and facilities placed in
service and not temporarily idle		
12	Depletion		
13	Rent		
14	Taxes other than state, local, and foreign income taxes		
15	Insurance		
16	Utilities		
17	Maintenance and repairs that relate to a production, resale, or long-term contract activity . .		
18	Engineering and design costs (not including section 174 research and experimental
expenses).		
19	Rework labor, scrap, and spoilage		
20	Tools and equipment		
21	Quality control and inspection		
22	Bidding expenses incurred in the solicitation of contracts awarded to the applicant		
23	Licensing and franchise costs		
24	Capitalizable service costs (including mixed service costs)		
25	Administrative costs (not including any costs of selling or any return on capital)		
26	Research and experimental expenses attributable to long-term contracts		
27	Interest		
28	Other costs (Attach a list of these costs.)		

Form **3115** (Rev. 12-2003)

Form 3115 (*Continued*)

Form 3115 (Rev. 12-2003)   Page **8**

Part III   Method of Cost Allocation (see instructions) (continued)

Section C—Other Costs Not Required To Be Allocated (Complete Section C only if the applicant is requesting to change its method for these costs.)

		Present method	Proposed method
1	Marketing, selling, advertising, and distribution expenses		
2	Research and experimental expenses not included on line 26 above		
3	Bidding expenses not included on line 22 above		
4	General and administrative costs not included in Section B above		
5	Income taxes		
6	Cost of strikes		
7	Warranty and product liability costs		
8	Section 179 costs		
9	On-site storage		
10	Depreciation, amortization, and cost recovery allowance not included on line 11 above		
11	Other costs (Attach a list of these costs.)		

Schedule E—Change in Depreciation or Amortization (see instructions)

Applicants requesting approval to change their method of accounting for depreciation or amortization complete this section. Applicants must provide this information for each item or class of property for which a change is requested.

Note: *See the **List of Automatic Accounting Method Changes** in the instructions for information regarding automatic changes under sections 56, 167, 168, 197, 1400I, 1400L, or former section 168. Do not file Form 3115 with respect to certain late elections and election revocations (see instructions).*

1   Is depreciation for the property determined under Regulations section 1.167(a)-11 (CLADR)? . . . . ☐ **Yes** ☐ **No**
    If "Yes," the only changes permitted are under Regulations section 1.167(a)-11(c)(1)(iii).

2   Is any of the depreciation or amortization required to be capitalized under any Code section (e.g., section
    263A)? . . . . ☐ **Yes** ☐ **No**
    If "Yes," enter the applicable section ▶ _____

3   Has a depreciation or amortization election been made for the property (e.g., the election under section
    168(f)(1))? . . . . ☐ **Yes** ☐ **No**
    If "Yes," state the election made ▶ _____

4a To the extent not already provided, attach a statement describing the property being changed. Include in the description the type of property, the year the property was placed in service, and the property's use in the applicant's trade or business or income-producing activity.

  b If the property is residential rental property, did the applicant live in the property before renting it? . . ☐ **Yes** ☐ **No**
  c Is the property public utility property? . . . . ☐ **Yes** ☐ **No**

5   To the extent not already provided in the applicant's description of its present method, explain how the property is treated under the applicant's present method (e.g., depreciable property, inventory property, supplies under Regulations section 1.162-3, nondepreciable section 263(a) property, property deductible as a current expense, etc.).

6   If the property is not currently treated as depreciable or amortizable property, provide the facts supporting the proposed change to depreciate or amortize the property.

7   If the property is currently treated and/or will be treated as depreciable or amortizable property, provide the following information under both the present (if applicable) and proposed methods:

  a The Code section under which the property is or will be depreciated or amortized (e.g., section 168(g)).

  b The applicable asset class from Rev. Proc. 87-56, 1987-2 C.B. 674, for each asset depreciated under section 168 (MACRS) or under section 1400L; the applicable asset class from Rev. Proc. 83-35, 1983-1 C.B. 745, for each asset depreciated under former section 168 (ACRS); an explanation why no asset class is identified for each asset for which an asset class has not been identified by the applicant.

  c The facts to support the asset class for the proposed method.

  d The depreciation or amortization method of the property, including the applicable Code section (e.g., 200% declining balance method under section 168(b)(1)).

  e The useful life, recovery period, or amortization period of the property.

  f The applicable convention of the property.

Form **3115** (Rev. 12-2003)

Form 3115 (*Continued*)

Form **4562**	**Depreciation and Amortization**	OMB No. 1545-0172
Department of the Treasury Internal Revenue Service (99)	(Including Information on Listed Property) ▶ See separate instructions. ▶ Attach to your tax return.	**2008** Attachment Sequence No. **67**
Name(s) shown on return	Business or activity to which this form relates	Identifying number

Part I   Election To Expense Certain Property Under Section 179

Note: *If you have any listed property, complete Part V before you complete Part I.*

1	Maximum amount. See the instructions for a higher limit for certain businesses	**1**	$250,000
2	Total cost of section 179 property placed in service (see instructions)	**2**	
3	Threshold cost of section 179 property before reduction in limitation (see instructions)	**3**	$800,000
4	Reduction in limitation. Subtract line 3 from line 2. If zero or less, enter -0-	**4**	
5	Dollar limitation for tax year. Subtract line 4 from line 1. If zero or less, enter -0-. If married filing separately, see instructions	**5**	

(a) Description of property	**(b)** Cost (business use only)	**(c)** Elected cost
6		

7	Listed property. Enter the amount from line 29	**7**	
8	Total elected cost of section 179 property. Add amounts in column (c), lines 6 and 7	**8**	
9	Tentative deduction. Enter the **smaller** of line 5 or line 8.	**9**	
10	Carryover of disallowed deduction from line 13 of your 2007 Form 4562	**10**	
11	Business income limitation. Enter the smaller of business income (not less than zero) or line 5 (see instructions)	**11**	
12	Section 179 expense deduction. Add lines 9 and 10, but do not enter more than line 11 . . .	**12**	
13	Carryover of disallowed deduction to 2009. Add lines 9 and 10, less line 12 ▶	**13**	

Note: *Do not use Part II or Part III below for listed property. Instead, use Part V.*

Part II   Special Depreciation Allowance and Other Depreciation (Do not include listed property.) (See instructions.)

14	Special depreciation allowance for qualified property (other than listed property) placed in service during the tax year (see instructions)	**14**	
15	Property subject to section 168(f)(1) election	**15**	
16	Other depreciation (including ACRS)	**16**	

Part III   MACRS Depreciation (Do not include listed property.) (See instructions.)

Section A

17	MACRS deductions for assets placed in service in tax years beginning before 2008	**17**	
18	If you are electing to group any assets placed in service during the tax year into one or more general asset accounts, check here . . . . ▶ ☐		

Section B—Assets Placed in Service During 2008 Tax Year Using the General Depreciation System

(a) Classification of property	**(b)** Month and year placed in service	**(c)** Basis for depreciation (business/investment use only—see instructions)	**(d)** Recovery period	**(e)** Convention	**(f)** Method	**(g)** Depreciation deduction
19a 3-year property						
b 5-year property						
c 7-year property						
d 10-year property						
e 15-year property						
f 20-year property						
g 25-year property			25 yrs.		S/L	
h Residential rental property			27.5 yrs.	MM	S/L	
			27.5 yrs.	MM	S/L	
i Nonresidential real property			39 yrs.	MM	S/L	
				MM	S/L	

Section C—Assets Placed in Service During 2008 Tax Year Using the Alternative Depreciation System

20a Class life					S/L	
b 12-year			12 yrs.		S/L	
c 40-year			40 yrs.	MM	S/L	

Part IV   Summary (See instructions.)

21	Listed property. Enter amount from line 28	**21**	
22	**Total.** Add amounts from line 12, lines 14 through 17, lines 19 and 20 in column (g), and line 21. Enter here and on the appropriate lines of your return. Partnerships and S corporations—see instr.	**22**	
23	For assets shown above and placed in service during the current year, enter the portion of the basis attributable to section 263A costs . .	**23**	

For Paperwork Reduction Act Notice, see separate instructions.   Cat. No. 12906N   Form **4562** (2008)

Form 4562 Depreciation and Amortization

Form 4562 (2008)   Page **2**

Part V   **Listed Property** (Include automobiles, certain other vehicles, cellular telephones, certain computers, and property used for entertainment, recreation, or amusement.)

Note: *For any vehicle for which you are using the standard mileage rate or deducting lease expense, complete **only** 24a, 24b, columns (a) through (c) of Section A, all of Section B, and Section C if applicable.*

Section A—Depreciation and Other Information (Caution: *See the instructions for limits for passenger automobiles.***)**

24a Do you have evidence to support the business/investment use claimed? ☐ **Yes** ☐ **No**   **24b** If "Yes," is the evidence written? ☐ **Yes** ☐ **No**

(a) Type of property (list vehicles first)	(b) Date placed in service	(c) Business/investment use percentage	(d) Cost or other basis	(e) Basis for depreciation (business/investment use only)	(f) Recovery period	(g) Method/Convention	(h) Depreciation deduction	(i) Elected section 179 cost
25 Special depreciation allowance for qualified listed property placed in service during the tax year and used more than 50% in a qualified business use (see instructions)					**25**			
26 Property used more than 50% in a qualified business use:								
		%						
		%						
		%						
27 Property used 50% or less in a qualified business use:								
		%				S/L –		
		%				S/L –		
		%				S/L –		
28 Add amounts in column (h), lines 25 through 27. Enter here and on line 21, page 1 . . .						**28**		
29 Add amounts in column (i), line 26. Enter here and on line 7, page 1							**29**	

Section B—Information on Use of Vehicles

Complete this section for vehicles used by a sole proprietor, partner, or other "more than 5% owner," or related person.
If you provided vehicles to your employees, first answer the questions in Section C to see if you meet an exception to completing this section for those vehicles.

		(a) Vehicle 1		(b) Vehicle 2		(c) Vehicle 3		(d) Vehicle 4		(e) Vehicle 5		(f) Vehicle 6	
30	Total business/investment miles driven during the year (**do not** include commuting miles)												
31	Total commuting miles driven during the year												
32	Total other personal (noncommuting) miles driven												
33	Total miles driven during the year. Add lines 30 through 32												
34	Was the vehicle available for personal use during off-duty hours?	Yes	No	Yes	No	Yes	No	Yes	No	Yes	No	Yes	No
35	Was the vehicle used primarily by a more than 5% owner or related person?												
36	Is another vehicle available for personal use?												

Section C—Questions for Employers Who Provide Vehicles for Use by Their Employees

Answer these questions to determine if you meet an exception to completing Section B for vehicles used by employees who **are not** more than 5% owners or related persons (see instructions).

		Yes	No
37	Do you maintain a written policy statement that prohibits all personal use of vehicles, including commuting, by your employees?		
38	Do you maintain a written policy statement that prohibits personal use of vehicles, except commuting, by your employees? See the instructions for vehicles used by corporate officers, directors, or 1% or more owners		
39	Do you treat all use of vehicles by employees as personal use?		
40	Do you provide more than five vehicles to your employees, obtain information from your employees about the use of the vehicles, and retain the information received?		
41	Do you meet the requirements concerning qualified automobile demonstration use? (See instructions.)		

Note: *If your answer to 37, 38, 39, 40, or 41 is "Yes," do not complete Section B for the covered vehicles.*

Part VI   **Amortization**

(a) Description of costs	(b) Date amortization begins	(c) Amortizable amount	(d) Code section	(e) Amortization period or percentage	(f) Amortization for this year
42 Amortization of costs that begins during your 2008 tax year (see instructions):					
43 Amortization of costs that began before your 2008 tax year **43**					
44 **Total.** Add amounts in column (f). See the instructions for where to report **44**					

Form **4562** (2008)

Form 4562 (*Continued*)

Form **4797**		**Sales of Business Property**				OMB No. 1545-0184
		(Also Involuntary Conversions and Recapture Amounts Under Sections 179 and 280F(b)(2))				**2008**
Department of the Treasury Internal Revenue Service (99)		▶ Attach to your tax return. ▶ See separate instructions.				Attachment Sequence No. **27**
Name(s) shown on return					Identifying number	

1 Enter the gross proceeds from sales or exchanges reported to you for 2008 on Form(s) 1099-B or 1099-S (or substitute statement) that you are including on line 2, 10, or 20 (see instructions) **1**

Part I   Sales or Exchanges of Property Used in a Trade or Business and Involuntary Conversions From Other Than Casualty or Theft—Most Property Held More Than 1 Year (see instructions)

2	(a) Description of property	(b) Date acquired (mo., day, yr.)	(c) Date sold (mo., day, yr.)	(d) Gross sales price	(e) Depreciation allowed or allowable since acquisition	(f) Cost or other basis, plus improvements and expense of sale	(g) Gain or (loss) Subtract (f) from the sum of (d) and (e)

3 Gain, if any, from Form 4684, line 45 . . . . **3**

4 Section 1231 gain from installment sales from Form 6252, line 26 or 37 . . . . **4**

5 Section 1231 gain or (loss) from like-kind exchanges from Form 8824 . . . . **5**

6 Gain, if any, from line 32, from other than casualty or theft **6**

7 Combine lines 2 through 6. Enter the gain or (loss) here and on the appropriate line as follows: **7**

Partnerships (except electing large partnerships) and S corporations. Report the gain or (loss) following the instructions for Form 1065, Schedule K, line 10, or Form 1120S, Schedule K, line 9. Skip lines 8, 9, 11, and 12 below.

Individuals, partners, S corporation shareholders, and all others. If line 7 is zero or a loss, enter the amount from line 7 on line 11 below and skip lines 8 and 9. If line 7 is a gain and you did not have any prior year section 1231 losses, or they were recaptured in an earlier year, enter the gain from line 7 as a long-term capital gain on the Schedule D filed with your return and skip lines 8, 9, 11, and 12 below.

8 Nonrecaptured net section 1231 losses from prior years (see instructions) **8**

9 Subtract line 8 from line 7. If zero or less, enter -0-. If line 9 is zero, enter the gain from line 7 on line 12 below. If line 9 is more than zero, enter the amount from line 8 on line 12 below and enter the gain from line 9 as a long-term capital gain on the Schedule D filed with your return (see instructions) **9**

Part II   Ordinary Gains and Losses (see instructions)

10 Ordinary gains and losses not included on lines 11 through 16 (include property held 1 year or less):

11 Loss, if any, from line 7 . . . . **11** (   )

12 Gain, if any, from line 7 or amount from line 8, if applicable **12**

13 Gain, if any, from line 31 . . . . **13**

14 Net gain or (loss) from Form 4684, lines 37 and 44a **14**

15 Ordinary gain from installment sales from Form 6252, line 25 or 36 . . . . **15**

16 Ordinary gain or (loss) from like-kind exchanges from Form 8824. . . . . **16**

17 Combine lines 10 through 16 . . . . **17**

18 For all except individual returns, enter the amount from line 17 on the appropriate line of your return and skip lines a and b below. For individual returns, complete lines a and b below:

a If the loss on line 11 includes a loss from Form 4684, line 41, column (b)(ii), enter that part of the loss here. Enter the part of the loss from income-producing property on Schedule A (Form 1040), line 28, and the part of the loss from property used as an employee on Schedule A (Form 1040), line 23. Identify as from "Form 4797, line 18a." See instructions . . **18a**

b Redetermine the gain or (loss) on line 17 excluding the loss, if any, on line 18a. Enter here and on Form 1040, line 14 **18b**

For Paperwork Reduction Act Notice, see separate instructions.   Cat. No. 13086I   Form **4797** (2008)

Form 4797 Sales of Business Property

Form 4797 (2008)   Page **2**

Part III Gain From Disposition of Property Under Sections 1245, 1250, 1252, 1254, and 1255
(see instructions)

19	(a) Description of section 1245, 1250, 1252, 1254, or 1255 property:			(b) Date acquired (mo., day, yr.)	(c) Date sold (mo., day, yr.)
A					
B					
C					
D					

	These columns relate to the properties on lines 19A through 19D. ▶		Property A	Property B	Property C	Property D
20	Gross sales price (**Note:** *See line 1 before completing.*).	20				
21	Cost or other basis plus expense of sale	21				
22	Depreciation (or depletion) allowed or allowable . . .	22				
23	Adjusted basis. Subtract line 22 from line 21	23				
24	Total gain. Subtract line 23 from line 20	24				
25	**If section 1245 property:**					
a	Depreciation allowed or allowable from line 22 . . .	25a				
b	Enter the **smaller** of line 24 or 25a	25b				
26	**If section 1250 property:** If straight line depreciation was used, enter -0- on line 26g, except for a corporation subject to section 291.					
a	Additional depreciation after 1975 (see instructions).	26a				
b	Applicable percentage multiplied by the **smaller** of line 24 or line 26a (see instructions)	26b				
c	Subtract line 26a from line 24. If residential rental property **or** line 24 is not more than line 26a, skip lines 26d and 26e	26c				
d	Additional depreciation after 1969 and before 1976 . .	26d				
e	Enter the **smaller** of line 26c or 26d	26e				
f	Section 291 amount (corporations only)	26f				
g	Add lines 26b, 26e, and 26f	26g				
27	**If section 1252 property:** Skip this section if you did not dispose of farmland or if this form is being completed for a partnership (other than an electing large partnership).					
a	Soil, water, and land clearing expenses	27a				
b	Line 27a multiplied by applicable percentage (see instructions)	27b				
c	Enter the **smaller** of line 24 or 27b	27c				
28	**If section 1254 property:**					
a	Intangible drilling and development costs, expenditures for development of mines and other natural deposits, and mining exploration costs (see instructions) . . .	28a				
b	Enter the **smaller** of line 24 or 28a	28b				
29	**If section 1255 property:**					
a	Applicable percentage of payments excluded from income under section 126 (see instructions)	29a				
b	Enter the **smaller** of line 24 or 29a (see instructions) .	29b				

Summary of Part III Gains. Complete property columns A through D through line 29b before going to line 30.

30	Total gains for all properties. Add property columns A through D, line 24	30	
31	Add property columns A through D, lines 25b, 26g, 27c, 28b, and 29b. Enter here and on line 13	31	
32	Subtract line 31 from line 30. Enter the portion from casualty or theft on Form 4684, line 39. Enter the portion from other than casualty or theft on Form 4797, line 6	32	

Part IV Recapture Amounts Under Sections 179 and 280F(b)(2) When Business Use Drops to 50% or Less
(see instructions)

			(a) Section 179	(b) Section 280F(b)(2)
33	Section 179 expense deduction or depreciation allowable in prior years	33		
34	Recomputed depreciation (see instructions)	34		
35	Recapture amount. Subtract line 34 from line 33. See the instructions for where to report . .	35		

Form **4797** (2008)

Form 4797 (*Continued*)

Form **6252**

Department of the Treasury
Internal Revenue Service

Installment Sale Income

▶ Attach to your tax return.
▶ Use a separate form for each sale or other disposition of
property on the installment method.

OMB No. 1545-0228

2008

Attachment
Sequence No. **79**

Name(s) shown on return

Identifying number

1	Description of property ▶
2a	Date acquired (month, day, year) ▶ [/ /] **b** Date sold (month, day, year) ▶ [/ /]
3	Was the property sold to a related party (see instructions) after May 14, 1980? If "No," skip line 4. . . . . ☐ Yes ☐ No
4	Was the property you sold to a related party a marketable security? If "Yes," complete Part III. If "No," complete Part III for the year of sale and the 2 years after the year of sale . . . . ☐ Yes ☐ No

Part I   Gross Profit and Contract Price. Complete this part for the year of sale only.

5	Selling price including mortgages and other debts. **Do not** include interest whether stated or unstated		**5**	
6	Mortgages, debts, and other liabilities the buyer assumed or took the property subject to (see instructions)	**6**		
7	Subtract line 6 from line 5	**7**		
8	Cost or other basis of property sold	**8**		
9	Depreciation allowed or allowable	**9**		
10	Adjusted basis. Subtract line 9 from line 8	**10**		
11	Commissions and other expenses of sale	**11**		
12	Income recapture from Form 4797, Part III (see instructions) . .	**12**		
13	Add lines 10, 11, and 12		**13**	
14	Subtract line 13 from line 5. If zero or less, **do not** complete the rest of this form (see instructions)		**14**	
15	If the property described on line 1 above was your main home, enter the amount of your excluded gain (see instructions). Otherwise, enter -0-		**15**	
16	**Gross profit.** Subtract line 15 from line 14		**16**	
17	Subtract line 13 from line 6. If zero or less, enter -0-		**17**	
18	**Contract price.** Add line 7 and line 17		**18**	

Part II   Installment Sale Income. Complete this part for the year of sale **and** any year you receive a payment or have certain debts you must treat as a payment on installment obligations.

19	Gross profit percentage (expressed as a decimal amount). Divide line 16 by line 18. For years after the year of sale, see instructions		**19**	
20	If this is the year of sale, enter the amount from line 17. Otherwise, enter -0-		**20**	
21	Payments received during year (see instructions). **Do not** include interest, whether stated or unstated		**21**	
22	Add lines 20 and 21		**22**	
23	Payments received in prior years (see instructions). **Do not** include interest, whether stated or unstated	**23**		
24	**Installment sale income.** Multiply line 22 by line 19		**24**	
25	Enter the part of line 24 that is ordinary income under the recapture rules (see instructions) . .		**25**	
26	Subtract line 25 from line 24. Enter here and on Schedule D or Form 4797 (see instructions)		**26**	

Part III   Related Party Installment Sale Income. Do not complete if you received the final payment this tax year.

27	Name, address, and taxpayer identifying number of related party

28	Did the related party resell or dispose of the property ("second disposition") during this tax year? . . . . ☐ Yes ☐ No
29	**If the answer to question 28 is "Yes," complete lines 30 through 37 below unless one of the following conditions is met. Check the box that applies.**
a	☐ The second disposition was more than 2 years after the first disposition (other than dispositions of marketable securities). If this box is checked, enter the date of disposition (month, day, year) ▶ [/ /]
b	☐ The first disposition was a sale or exchange of stock to the issuing corporation.
c	☐ The second disposition was an involuntary conversion and the threat of conversion occurred after the first disposition.
d	☐ The second disposition occurred after the death of the original seller or buyer.
e	☐ It can be established to the satisfaction of the Internal Revenue Service that tax avoidance was not a principal purpose for either of the dispositions. If this box is checked, attach an explanation (see instructions).

30	Selling price of property sold by related party (see instructions)	**30**	
31	Enter contract price from line 18 for year of first sale	**31**	
32	Enter the **smaller** of line 30 or line 31	**32**	
33	Total payments received by the end of your 2008 tax year (see instructions)	**33**	
34	Subtract line 33 from line 32. If zero or less, enter -0-	**34**	
35	Multiply line 34 by the gross profit percentage on line 19 for year of first sale	**35**	
36	Enter the part of line 35 that is ordinary income under the recapture rules (see instructions) . .	**36**	
37	Subtract line 36 from line 35. Enter here and on Schedule D or Form 4797 (see instructions)	**37**	

For Paperwork Reduction Act Notice, see page 4.   Cat. No. 13601R   Form **6252** (2008)

Form 6252 Installment Sale Income

General Instructions

Section references are to the Internal Revenue Code unless otherwise noted.

Purpose of Form

Generally, use Form 6252 to report income from casual sales during this tax year of real or personal property (other than inventory) if you will receive any payments in a tax year after the year of sale. For years after the year of an installment sale, see *Which Parts To Complete* below.

Do not file Form 6252 for sales that do not result in a gain, even if you will receive a payment in a tax year after the year of sale. Instead, report the entire sale on Form 4797, Sales of Business Property, or the Schedule D for your tax return, whichever applies.

Do not file Form 6252 to report sales during the tax year of stock or securities traded on an established securities market. Instead, treat all payments as received during this tax year.

Do not file Form 6252 if you elect not to report the sale on the installment method. To elect out, report the full amount of the gain on a timely filed return (including extensions) on Form 4797 or the Schedule D for your tax return, whichever applies. If you filed your original return on time without making the election, you can make the election on an amended return filed no later than 6 months after the due date of your tax return, excluding extensions. Write "Filed pursuant to section 301.9100-2" at the top of the amended return.

Which Parts To Complete

Year of Sale

Complete lines 1 through 4, Part I, and Part II. If you sold property to a related party during the year, also complete Part III.

Later Years

Complete lines 1 through 4 and Part II for any year in which you receive a payment from an installment sale.

If you sold a marketable security to a related party after May 14, 1980, and before January 1, 1987, complete Form 6252 for each year of the installment agreement, even if you did not receive a payment. Complete lines 1 through 4. Complete Part II for any year in which you receive a payment from the sale. Complete Part III unless you received the final payment during the tax year.

After December 31, 1986, the installment method is not available for the sale of marketable securities.

If you sold property other than a marketable security to a related party after May 14, 1980, complete Form 6252 for the year of sale and for 2 years after the year of sale, even if you did not receive a payment. Complete lines 1 through 4. Complete Part II for any year during this 2-year period in which you receive a payment from the sale. Complete Part III for the 2 years after the year of sale unless you received the final payment during the tax year.

Special Rules

Interest

If any part of an installment payment you received is for interest or original issue discount, report that income on the appropriate form or schedule. Do not report interest received, carrying charges received, or unstated interest on Form 6252. See Pub. 537, Installment Sales, for details on unstated interest.

Installment Sales to Related Party

A special rule applies to a first disposition (sale or exchange) of property under the installment method to a related party who then makes a second disposition (sale, exchange, gift, or cancellation of installment note) before making all payments on the first disposition. For this purpose, a related party includes your spouse, child, grandchild, parent, brother, sister, or a related corporation, S corporation, partnership, estate, or trust. See section 453(f)(1) for more details.

Under this rule, treat part or all of the amount the related party realized (or the fair market value (FMV) if the disposed property is not sold or exchanged) from the second disposition as if you received it from the first disposition at the time of the second disposition. Figure the gain, if any, on lines 30 through 37. This rule does not apply if any of the conditions listed on line 29 are met.

Sale of Depreciable Property to Related Person

Generally, if you sell depreciable property to a related person (as defined in section 453(g)(3)), you cannot report the sale using the installment method. For this purpose, depreciable property is any property that can be depreciated by a person or entity to whom you transfer it. However, you can use the installment method if you can show to the satisfaction of the IRS that avoidance of federal income taxes was not one of the principal purposes of the sale (for example, no significant tax deferral benefits will result from the sale). If the installment method does not apply, report the sale on Schedule D or Form 4797,

whichever applies. Treat all payments you will receive as if they were received in the year of sale. Use FMV for any payment that is contingent as to amount. If the FMV cannot be readily determined, basis is recovered ratably.

Pledge Rule

For certain dispositions under the installment method, if an installment obligation is pledged as security on a debt, the net proceeds of the secured debt are treated as payment on the installment obligation. However, the amount treated as payment cannot be more than the excess of the total installment contract price over any payments received under the contract before the secured debt was obtained.

An installment obligation is pledged as security on a debt to the extent that payment of principal and interest on the debt is directly secured by an interest in the installment obligation. For sales after December 16, 1999, payment on a debt is treated as directly secured by an interest in an installment obligation to the extent an arrangement allows you to satisfy all or part of the debt with the installment obligation.

The pledge rule applies to any installment sale after 1988 with a sales price of over $150,000 except:

- Personal use property disposed of by an individual,
- Farm property, and
- Timeshares and residential lots.

However, the pledge rule does not apply to pledges made after December 17, 1987, if the debt is incurred to refinance the principal amount of a debt that was outstanding on December 17, 1987, and was secured by nondealer real property installment obligations on that date and at all times after that date until the refinancing. This exception does not apply to the extent that the principal amount of the debt resulting from the refinancing exceeds the principal amount of the refinanced debt immediately before the refinancing. Also, the pledge rule does not affect refinancing due to the calling of a debt by the creditor if the debt is then refinanced by a person other than this creditor or someone related to the creditor.

Interest on Deferred Tax

Generally, you must pay interest on the deferred tax related to any obligation that arises during a tax year from the disposition of property under the installment method if:

- The property had a sales price over $150,000, and

Form 6252 *(Continued)*

• The aggregate balance of all nondealer installment obligations arising during, and outstanding at the close of, the tax year is more than $5 million.

You must pay interest in subsequent years if installment obligations that originally required interest to be paid are still outstanding at the close of a tax year.

The interest rules do not apply to dispositions of:

• Farm property,

• Personal use property by an individual,

• Real property before 1988, or

• Personal property before 1989.

See IRC 453(l) for more information on the sale of timeshares and residential lots under the installment method.

How to report the interest. The interest is not figured on Form 6252. See Pub. 537, Installment Sales, for details on how to report the interest.

Additional Information

See Pub. 537 for additional information, including details about reductions in selling price, the single sale of several assets, like-kind exchanges, dispositions of installment obligations, and repossessions.

Specific Instructions

Part I—Gross Profit and Contract Price

Line 5

Enter the total of any money, face amount of the installment obligation, and the FMV of other property that you received or will receive in exchange for the property sold. Include on line 5 any existing mortgage or other debt the buyer assumed or took the property subject to. Do not include stated interest, unstated interest, any amount recomputed or recharacterized as interest, or original issue discount.

If there is no stated maximum selling price, such as in a contingent payment sale, attach a schedule showing the computation of gain. Enter the taxable part of the payment on line 24 and also on line 35 if Part III applies. See Temporary Regulations section 15A.453-1.

Line 6

Enter only mortgages or other debts the buyer assumed from the seller or took the property subject to. Do not include new mortgages the buyer gets from a bank, the seller, or other sources.

Line 8

Enter the original cost and other expenses you incurred in buying the property. Add the cost of improvements, etc., and subtract any diesel-powered highway vehicle, enhanced oil recovery,

disabled access, new markets, or employer-provided child care credit or casualty losses previously allowed. For details, see Pub. 551, Basis of Assets.

Line 9

Enter all depreciation or amortization you deducted or were allowed to deduct from the date of purchase until the date of sale. Add any section 179 expense deduction; the commercial revitalization deduction; the basis reduction to investment credit property; the deduction for qualified clean-fuel vehicle property or refueling property; deductions claimed under section 190, 193, or 1253(d)(2) or (3) (as in effect before the enactment of P.L. 103-66); and the basis reduction for the qualified electric vehicle credit. Subtract any recapture of basis reduction to investment credit property; any section 179 or 280F recapture amount included in gross income in a prior tax year; any qualified clean-fuel vehicle property or refueling property deduction you were required to recapture because the property ceased to be eligible for the deduction; any recapture of the employer-provided child care facilities and services credit; and any basis increase for qualified electric vehicle recapture.

Line 11

Enter sales commissions, advertising expenses, attorney and legal fees, etc., incurred to sell the property.

Line 12

Any ordinary income recapture under section 1245 or 1250 (including sections 179 and 291) is fully taxable in the year of sale even if no payments were received. To figure the recapture amount, complete Form 4797, Part III. The ordinary income recapture is the amount on line 31 of Form 4797. Enter it on line 12 of Form 6252 and also on line 13 of Form 4797. Do not enter any gain for this property on line 32 of Form 4797. If you used Form 4797 only to figure the recapture amount on line 12 of Form 6252, enter "N/A" on line 32 of Form 4797. Partnerships and S corporations and their partners and shareholders, see the Instructions for Form 4797.

Line 14

Do not file Form 6252 if line 14 is zero or less. Instead, report the entire sale on Form 4797 or the Schedule D for your tax return.

Line 15

If the property described on line 1 was your main home, you may be able to exclude part or all of your gain. See Pub. 523, Selling Your Home, for details.

Part II—Installment Sale Income

Line 19

Enter the gross profit percentage (expressed as a decimal amount) determined for the year of sale even if you did not file Form 6252 for that year.

Line 21

Enter all money and the FMV of any property you received in 2008. Include as payments any amount withheld to pay off a mortgage or other debt or to pay broker and legal fees. Generally, do not include as a payment the buyer's note, a mortgage, or other debt assumed by the buyer. However, a note or other debt that is payable on demand or readily tradable in an established securities market is considered a payment. For sales occurring before October 22, 2004, a note or other debt is considered a payment only if it was issued by a corporation or governmental entity. If you did not receive any payments in 2008, enter zero. If in prior years an amount was entered on the equivalent of line 32 of the 2008 form, do not include it on this line. Instead, enter it on line 23. See *Pledge Rule* on page 2 for details about proceeds of debt secured by installment obligations that must be treated as payments on installment obligations.

Line 23

Enter all money and the FMV of property you received before 2008 from the sale. Include allocable installment income and any other deemed payments from prior years.

Deemed payments include amounts deemed received because of:

• A second disposition by a related party, or

• The pledge rule of section 453A(d).

Line 25

Enter here and on Form 4797, line 15, any ordinary income recapture on section 1252, 1254, or 1255 property for the year of sale or all remaining recapture from a prior year sale. Do not enter ordinary income from a section 179 expense deduction. If this is the year of sale, complete Form 4797, Part III. The amount from line 27c, 28b, or 29b of Form 4797 is the ordinary income recapture. Do not enter any gain for this property on line 31 or 32 of Form 4797. If you used Form 4797 only to figure the recapture on line 25 or 36 of Form 6252, enter "N/A" on lines 31 and 32 of Form 4797.

Also report on this line any ordinary income recapture remaining from prior years on section 1245 or 1250 property sold before June 7, 1984.

Form 6252 (*Continued*)

Do not enter on line 25 more than the amount shown on line 24. Any excess must be reported in future years on Form 6252 up to the taxable part of the installment sale until all of the recapture has been reported.

Line 26

For trade or business property held more than 1 year, enter this amount on Form 4797, line 4. If the property was held 1 year or less or you have an ordinary gain from the sale of a noncapital asset (even if the holding period is more than 1 year), enter this amount on Form 4797, line 10, and write "From Form 6252." If the property was section 1250 property (generally, real property that you depreciated) held more than 1 year, figure the total amount of unrecaptured section 1250 gain included on line 26 using the *Unrecaptured Section 1250 Gain Worksheet* in the Instructions for Schedule D (Form 1040).

For capital assets, enter this amount on Schedule D as a short- or long-term gain on the lines identified as from Form 6252.

Part III—Related Party Installment Sale Income

Line 29

If one of the conditions is met, check the appropriate box and skip lines 30 through 37. If you checked box 29e, attach an explanation. Generally, the nontax avoidance exception will apply to the second disposition if:

• The disposition was involuntary (for example, a creditor of the related party foreclosed on the property or the related party declared bankruptcy), or

• The disposition was an installment sale under which the terms of payment were substantially equal to or longer than those for the first sale. However, the resale terms must not permit significant deferral of recognition of gain from the first sale (for example, amounts from the resale are being collected sooner).

Line 30

If the related party sold all or part of the property from the original sale in 2008, enter the amount realized from the part resold. If part was sold in an earlier year and part was sold this year, enter the cumulative amount realized from the resale.

Amount realized. The amount realized from a sale or exchange is the total of all money received plus the FMV of all property or services received. The amount realized also includes any liabilities that were assumed by the buyer and any liabilities to which the property transferred is subject, such as real estate taxes or a mortgage. For details, see Pub. 544.

Line 33

If you completed Part II, enter the sum of lines 22 and 23. Otherwise, enter all money and the FMV of property you received before 2008 from the sale. Include allocable installment income and any other deemed payments from prior years. Do not include interest, whether stated or unstated.

Line 36

See the instructions for line 25. Do not enter on line 36 more than the amount shown on line 35. Any excess must be reported in future years on Form 6252 up to the taxable part of the installment sale until all of the recapture has been reported.

Line 37

See the instructions for line 26.

Paperwork Reduction Act Notice. We ask for the information on this form to carry out the Internal Revenue laws of the United States. You are required to give us the information. We need it to ensure that you are complying with these laws and to allow us to figure and collect the right amount of tax.

You are not required to provide the information requested on a form that is subject to the Paperwork Reduction Act unless the form displays a valid OMB control number. Books or records relating to a form or its instructions must be retained as long as their contents may become material in the administration of any Internal Revenue law. Generally, tax returns and return information are confidential, as required by section 6103.

The time needed to complete and file this form will vary depending on individual circumstances. The estimated burden for individual taxpayers filing this form is approved under OMB control number 1545-0074 and is included in the estimates shown in the instructions for their individual income tax return. The estimated burden for all other taxpayers who file this form is shown below.

Recordkeeping . . . . 1 hr., 18 min.

Learning about the law or the form . . . . 24 min.

Preparing the form . . . . 1 hr.

Copying, assembling, and sending the form to the IRS . . . . 20 min.

If you have comments concerning the accuracy of these time estimates or suggestions for making this form simpler, we would be happy to hear from you. See the instructions for the tax return with which this form is filed.

Form 6252 (*Continued*)

Form **8606**	**Nondeductible IRAs**	OMB No. 1545-0074
	▶ See separate instructions.	**2008**
Department of the Treasury Internal Revenue Service (99)	▶ **Attach to Form 1040, Form 1040A, or Form 1040NR.**	Attachment Sequence No. **48**

Name. If married, file a separate form for each spouse required to file Form 8606. See page 5 of the instructions.	Your social security number

Fill in Your Address Only If You Are Filing This Form by Itself and Not With Your Tax Return ▶	Home address (number and street, or P.O. box if mail is not delivered to your home)	Apt. no.
	City, town or post office, state, and ZIP code	

Part I **Nondeductible Contributions to Traditional IRAs and Distributions From Traditional, SEP, and SIMPLE IRAs**

Complete this part only if one or more of the following apply.
▶ You made nondeductible contributions to a traditional IRA for 2008.
▶ You took distributions from a traditional, SEP, or SIMPLE IRA in 2008 **and** you made nondeductible contributions to a traditional IRA in 2008 or an earlier year. For this purpose, a distribution does not include a rollover (other than a repayment of a qualified disaster recovery assistance distribution), qualified charitable distribution, one-time distribution to fund an HSA, conversion, recharacterization, or return of certain contributions.
▶ You converted part, but not all, of your traditional, SEP, and SIMPLE IRAs to Roth IRAs in 2008 (excluding any portion you recharacterized) **and** you made nondeductible contributions to a traditional IRA in 2008 or an earlier year.

1	Enter your nondeductible contributions to traditional IRAs for 2008, including those made for 2008 from January 1, 2009, through April 15, 2009 (see page 5 of the instructions)	**1**	
2	Enter your total basis in traditional IRAs (see page 6 of the instructions)	**2**	
3	Add lines 1 and 2	**3**	

In 2008, did you take a distribution from traditional, SEP, or SIMPLE IRAs, or make a Roth IRA conversion?	— No ▶	Enter the amount from line 3 on line 14. Do not complete the rest of Part I.
	— Yes ▶	Go to line 4.

4	Enter those contributions included on line 1 that were made from January 1, 2009, through April 15, 2009	**4**	
5	Subtract line 4 from line 3	**5**	
6	Enter the value of **all** your traditional, SEP, and SIMPLE IRAs as of December 31, 2008, plus any outstanding rollovers. Subtract any repayments of qualified disaster recovery assistance distributions. If the result is zero or less, enter -0- (see page 6 of the instructions) .	**6**	
7	Enter your distributions from traditional, SEP, and SIMPLE IRAs in 2008. **Do not** include rollovers (other than repayments of qualified disaster recovery assistance distributions), qualified charitable distributions, a one-time distribution to fund an HSA, conversions to a Roth IRA, certain returned contributions, or recharacterizations of traditional IRA contributions (see page 6 of the instructions) . . .	**7**	
8	Enter the net amount you converted from traditional, SEP, and SIMPLE IRAs to Roth IRAs in 2008. **Do not** include amounts converted that you later recharacterized (see page 7 of the instructions). Also enter this amount on line 16	**8**	
9	Add lines 6, 7, and 8	**9**	
10	Divide line 5 by line 9. Enter the result as a decimal rounded to at least 3 places. If the result is 1.000 or more, enter "1.000" . . .	**10**	× .
11	Multiply line 8 by line 10. This is the nontaxable portion of the amount you converted to Roth IRAs. Also enter this amount on line 17 . . .	**11**	
12	Multiply line 7 by line 10. This is the nontaxable portion of your distributions that you did not convert to a Roth IRA	**12**	
13	Add lines 11 and 12. This is the nontaxable portion of all your distributions	**13**	
14	Subtract line 13 from line 3. This is **your total basis in traditional IRAs for 2008 and earlier years** .	**14**	
15a	Subtract line 12 from line 7	**15a**	
b	Amount on line 15a attributable to qualified disaster recovery assistance distributions (see page 7 of the instructions). Also enter this amount on Form 8930, line 13	**15b**	
c	**Taxable amount.** Subtract line 15b from line 15a. If more than zero, also include this amount on Form 1040, line 15b; Form 1040A, line 11b; or Form 1040NR, line 16b . . . . **Note:** You may be subject to an additional 10% tax on the amount on line 15c if you were under age 59 ½ at the time of the distribution (see page 7 of the instructions).	**15c**	

For Privacy Act and Paperwork Reduction Act Notice, see page 9 of the instructions.   Cat. No. 63966F   Form **8606** (2008)

Form 8606 Nondeductible IRAs

Form 8606 (2008)   Page **2**

| Part II | 2008 Conversions From Traditional, SEP, or SIMPLE IRAs to Roth IRAs |

Complete this part if you converted part or all of your traditional, SEP, and SIMPLE IRAs to a Roth IRA in 2008 (excluding any portion you recharacterized).

Caution: *If your modified adjusted gross income is over $100,000 **or** you are married filing separately and you lived with your spouse at any time in 2008, you **cannot** convert any amount from traditional, SEP, or SIMPLE IRAs to Roth IRAs for 2008. If you erroneously made a conversion, you must recharacterize (correct) it (see page 7 of the instructions).*

16	If you completed Part I, enter the amount from line 8. Otherwise, enter the net amount you converted from traditional, SEP, and SIMPLE IRAs to Roth IRAs in 2008. **Do not** include amounts you later recharacterized back to traditional, SEP, or SIMPLE IRAs in 2008 or 2009 (see page 7 of the instructions)	16
17	If you completed Part I, enter the amount from line 11. Otherwise, enter your basis in the amount on line 16 (see page 7 of the instructions)	17
18	**Taxable amount.** Subtract line 17 from line 16. Also include this amount on Form 1040, line 15b; Form 1040A, line 11b; or Form 1040NR, line 16b	18

| Part III | Distributions From Roth IRAs |

Complete this part only if you took a distribution from a Roth IRA in 2008. For this purpose, a distribution does not include a rollover (other than a repayment of a qualified disaster recovery assistance distribution), qualified charitable distribution, one-time distribution to fund an HSA, recharacterization, or return of certain contributions (see page 7 of the instructions).

19	Enter your total nonqualified distributions from Roth IRAs in 2008 including any qualified first-time homebuyer distributions (see page 7 of the instructions)	19
20	Qualified first-time homebuyer expenses (see page 7 of the instructions). **Do not** enter more than $10,000	20
21	Subtract line 20 from line 19. If zero or less, enter -0- and skip lines 22 through 25	21
22	Enter your basis in Roth IRA contributions (see page 8 of the instructions)	22
23	Subtract line 22 from line 21. If zero or less, enter -0- and skip lines 24 and 25. If more than zero, you may be subject to an additional tax (see page 8 of the instructions)	23
24	Enter your basis in conversions from traditional, SEP, and SIMPLE IRAs and rollovers from qualified retirement plans to a Roth IRA (see page 8 of the instructions)	24
25a	Subtract line 24 from line 23. If zero or less, enter -0- and skip lines 25b and 25c	25a
b	Amount on line 25a attributable to qualified disaster recovery assistance distributions (see page 8 of the instructions). Also enter this amount on Form 8930, line 14	25b
c	**Taxable amount.** Subtract line 25b from line 25a. If more than zero, also include this amount on Form 1040, line 15b; Form 1040A, line 11b; or Form 1040NR, line 16b	25c

Under penalties of perjury, I declare that I have examined this form, including accompanying attachments, and to the best of my knowledge and belief, it is true, correct, and complete. Declaration of preparer (other than taxpayer) is based on all information of which preparer has any knowledge.

Sign Here Only If You Are Filing This Form by Itself and Not With Your Tax Return

▶ _____   ▶ _____
Your signature   Date

Paid Preparer's Use Only	Preparer's signature ▶		Date		Check if self-employed ☐	Preparer's SSN or PTIN
	Firm's name (or yours if self-employed), address, and ZIP code ▶				EIN	
					Phone no. ( )	

Form **8606** (2008)

Form 8606 (*Continued*)

Form **8824**

Department of the Treasury
Internal Revenue Service

Like-Kind Exchanges

(and section 1043 conflict-of-interest sales)

▶ Attach to your tax return.

OMB No. 1545-1190

2008

Attachment
Sequence No. **109**

Name(s) shown on tax return

Identifying number

Part I	**Information on the Like-Kind Exchange**

Note: *If the property described on line 1 or line 2 is real or personal property located outside the United States, indicate the country.*

1 Description of like-kind property given up:

2 Description of like-kind property received:

3 Date like-kind property given up was originally acquired (month, day, year) . . . . | **3** | MM/DD/YYYY |

4 Date you actually transferred your property to other party (month, day, year) . . . . . . | **4** | MM/DD/YYYY |

5 Date like-kind property you receive d was identified by written no tice to another party (month, day, year). See instructions for 45-day written notice requirement . . . . | **5** | MM/DD/YYYY |

6 Date you actually received the like-kind property from other party (month, day, year). See instructions | **6** | MM/DD/YYYY |

7 Was the exchange of the property given up or received made with a related party, either directly or indirectly (such as through an intermediary)? See instructions. If "Yes," complete   Part II. If "No," go to Part III   . . . . ☐ Yes ☐ No

Part II	**Related Party Exchange Information**

8 Name of related party | Relationship to you | Related party's identifying number

Address (no., street, and apt., room, or suite no., city or town, state, and ZIP code)

9 During this tax year (and before the date that is 2 years after the last transfer of property that was part of the exchange), did the related party sell or dispose of any part of the like-kind property received from you (or an intermediary) in the exchange or transfer property into the exchange, directly or indirectly (such as through an intermediary), that became your replacement property?   . . . . ☐ Yes ☐ No

10 During this tax year (and before the date that is 2 years after the last transfer of property that was part of the exchange), did you sell or dispose of any part of the like-kind property you received?   . . . . ☐ Yes ☐ No

*If both lines 9 and 10 are "No" and this is the year of the exchange, go to Part III. If both lines 9 and 10 are "No" and this is **not** the year of the exchange, stop here. If either line 9 or line 10 is "Yes," complete Part III an d report on this year's tax return the deferred gain or (loss) from line 24 **unless** one of the exceptions on line 11 applies.*

11 If one of the exceptions below applies to the disposition, check the applicable box:

a ☐ The disposition was after the death of either of the related parties.

b ☐ The disposition was an involuntary conversion, and the threat of conversion occurred after the exchange.

c ☐ You can establish to the satisfaction of the IRS that neither the exchange nor the disposition had tax avoidance as one of its principal purposes. If this box is checked, attach an explanation (see instructions).

For Paperwork Reduction Act Notice, see page 4 of the instructions.   Cat. No. 12311A   Form **8824** (2008)

Form 8824 Like-Kind Exchanges

Form 8824 (2008)   Page **2**

Name(s) shown on tax return. Do not enter name and social security number if shown on other side.	Your social security number

Part III   Realized Gain or (Loss), Recognized Gain, and Basis of Like-Kind Property Received

Caution: *If you transferred* **and** *received* **(a)** *more than one group of like-kind properties or* **(b)** *cash or other (not like-kind) property, see* **Reporting of multi-asset exchanges** *in the instructions.*

Note: *Complete lines 12 through 14* **only** *if you gave up property that was not like-kind. Otherwise, go to line 15.*

12	Fair market value (FMV) of other property given up	12	
13	Adjusted basis of other property given up	13	
14	Gain or (loss) recognized on other property given up. Subtract line 13 from line 12. Report the gain or (loss) in the same manner as if the exchange had been a sale		14
	Caution: *If the property given up was used previously or partly as a home, see* **Property used as home** *in the instructions.*		
15	Cash received, FMV of other property received, plus net liabilities assumed by other party, reduced (but not below zero) by any exchange expenses you incurred (see instructions) . . .		15
16	FMV of like-kind property you received		16
17	Add lines 15 and 16		17
18	Adjusted basis of like-kind property you gave up, net amounts paid to other party, plus any exchange expenses **not** used on line 15 (see instructions)		18
19	**Realized gain or (loss).** Subtract line 18 from line 17		19
20	Enter the smaller of line 15 or line 19, but not less than zero		20
21	Ordinary income under recapture rules. Enter here and on Form 4797, line 16 (see instructions) . . .		21
22	Subtract line 21 from line 20. If zero or less, enter -0-. If more than zero, enter here and on Schedule D or Form 4797, unless the installment method applies (see instructions)		22
23	**Recognized gain.** Add lines 21 and 22		23
24	Deferred gain or (loss). Subtract line 23 from line 19. If a related party exchange, see instructions . .		24
25	**Basis of like-kind property received.** Subtract line 15 from the sum of lines 18 and 23		25

Part IV   Deferral of Gain From Section 1043 Conflict-of-Interest Sales

Note: *This part is to be used* **only** *by officers or employees of the executive branch of the Federal Government or judicial officers of the Federal Government (including certain spouses, minor or dependent children, and trustees as described in section 1043) for reporting nonrecognition of gain under section 1043 on the sale of property to comply with the conflict-of-interest requirements. This part can be used* **only** *if the cost of the replacement property is more than the basis of the divested property.*

26	Enter the number from the upper right corner of your certificate of divestiture. (**Do not** attach a copy of your certificate. Keep the certificate with your records.) . . . . ▶	_____ – _____	
27	Description of divested property ▶ --		
28	Description of replacement property ▶ --		
29	Date divested property was sold (month, day, year)	29	MM/DD/YYYY
30	Sales price of divested property (see instructions)	30	
31	Basis of divested property	31	
32	**Realized gain.** Subtract line 31 from line 30		32
33	Cost of replacement property purchased within 60 days after date of sale	33	
34	Subtract line 33 from line 30. If zero or less, enter -0-		34
35	Ordinary income under recapture rules. Enter here and on Form 4797, line 10 (see instructions) .		35
36	Subtract line 35 from line 34. If zero or less, enter -0-. If more than zero, enter here and on Schedule D or Form 4797 (see instructions)		36
37	**Deferred gain.** Subtract the sum of lines 35 and 36 from line 32		37
38	**Basis of replacement property.** Subtract line 37 from line 33		38

Form **8824** (2008)

Form 8824 (*Continued*)

Form **8825**	Rental Real Estate Income and Expenses of a	
(Rev. December 2006)	Partnership or an S Corporation	OMB No. 1545-1186
Department of the Treasury Internal Revenue Service	▶ See instructions on back. ▶ Attach to Form 1065, Form 1065-B, or Form 1120S.	

Name	Employer identification number

1 Show the kind and location of each property. See page 2 to list additional properties.

A --

B --

C --

D --

		Properties			
Rental Real Estate Income		**A**	**B**	**C**	**D**
2 Gross rents	2				
Rental Real Estate Expenses					
3 Advertising	3				
4 Auto and travel	4				
5 Cleaning and maintenance	5				
6 Commissions	6				
7 Insurance	7				
8 Legal and other professional fees	8				
9 Interest	9				
10 Repairs	10				
11 Taxes	11				
12 Utilities	12				
13 Wages and salaries	13				
14 Depreciation (see instructions)	14				
15 Other (list) ▶ ------------					
------------------------	15				
------------------------					
16 Total expenses for each property. Add lines 3 through 15	16				

17 Total gross rents. Add gross rents from line 2, columns A through H .... | **17** | |

18 Total expenses. Add total expenses from line 16, columns A through H .... | **18** (|) |

19 Net gain (loss) from Form 4797, Part II, line 17, from the disposition of property from rental real estate activities .... | **19** | |

20a Net income (loss) from rental real estate activities from partnerships, estates, and trusts in which this partnership or S corporation is a partner or beneficiary (from Schedule K-1) ..... | **20a** | |

b Identify below the partnerships, estates, or trusts from which net income (loss) is shown on line 20a. Attach a schedule if more space is needed:

(1) Name ------------------------------ ------------------------------ ------------------------------

(2) Employer identification number ------------------------------ ------------------------------ ------------------------------

21 Net rental real estate income (loss). Combine lines 17 through 20a. Enter the result here and on:
- **Form 1065 or 1120S:** Schedule K, line 2, or
- **Form 1065-B:** Part I, line 4 | **21** | |

For Paperwork Reduction Act Notice, see back of form.   Cat. No. 10136Z   Form **8825** (12-2006)

Form 8825 Rental Real Estate Income and Expenses of a Partnership or an S Corporation

Form 8825 (12-2006)   Page **2**

1   Show the kind and location of each property.

E --

F --

G --

H --

		Properties			
		E	**F**	**G**	**H**
Rental Real Estate Income					
2 Gross rents	**2**				
Rental Real Estate Expenses					
3 Advertising	**3**				
4 Auto and travel.	**4**				
5 Cleaning and maintenance. . .	**5**				
6 Commissions	**6**				
7 Insurance	**7**				
8 Legal and other professional fees .	**8**				
9 Interest	**9**				
10 Repairs	**10**				
11 Taxes	**11**				
12 Utilities	**12**				
13 Wages and salaries	**13**				
14 Depreciation (see instructions)	**14**				
15 Other (list) ▶ -	**15**				
16 Total expenses for each property. Add lines 3 through 15	**16**				

Instructions

Section references are to the Internal Revenue Code.

What's New

The IRS will revise this December 2006 version of Form 8825 only when necessary. Continue to use this version of the form for tax years beginning after 2006 until a new revision is issued.

Purpose of form. Partnerships and S corporations use Form 8825 to report income and deductible expenses from rental real estate activities, including net income (loss) from rental real estate activities that flow through from partnerships, estates, or trusts.

Before completing this form, be sure to read:

• *Passive Activity Limitations* in the instructions for Form 1065 or Form 1120S, or *Passive Loss Limitation Activities* in the instructions for Form 1065-B, especially for the definition of "rental activity."

• *Extraterritorial Income Exclusion* in the instructions for Form 1065, 1065-B, or 1120S.

Specific Instructions. Form 8825 provides space for up to eight properties. If there are more than eight properties, attach additional Forms 8825.

The number of columns to be used for reporting income and expenses on this form may differ from the number of rental real estate activities the partnership or S corporation has for purposes of the passive activity limitations. For example, a partnership owns two apartment buildings, each located in a different city. For purposes of the passive activity limitations, the partnership grouped both buildings into a single activity. Although the partnership has only one rental real estate activity for purposes of the passive activity limitations, it must report the income and deductions for each building in separate columns.

However, if the partnership or S corporation has more than one rental real estate activity for purposes of the passive activity limitations, attach a statement to Schedule K that reports the net income (loss) for each separate activity. Also, attach a statement to each Schedule K-1 that reports each partner's or shareholder's share of the net income (loss) by separate activity (except for limited partners in an electing large partnership). See *Passive Activity Reporting Requirements* in the instructions for Form 1065, Form 1065-B, or Form 1120S for additional information that must be provided for each activity.

Complete lines 1 through 16 for each property. But complete lines 17 through 21 on only one Form 8825. The figures on lines 17 and 18 should be the combined totals for all forms.

Do not report on Form 8825 any:

• Income or deductions from a trade or business activity or a rental activity other than rental real estate. These items are reported elsewhere.

• Portfolio income or deductions.

• Section 179 expense deduction.

• Other items that must be reported separately to the partners or shareholders.

• Commercial revitalization deductions.

Line 1. Show the kind of property rented out (for example, "apartment building"). Give the street address, city or town, and state.

Line 14. The partnership or S corporation may claim a depreciation deduction each year for

rental property (except for land, which is not depreciable). If the partnership or S corporation placed property in service during the current tax year or claimed depreciation on any vehicle or other listed property, complete and attach Form 4562, Depreciation and Amortization. See Form 4562 and its instructions to figure the depreciation deduction.

Paperwork Reduction Act Notice. We ask for the information on this form to carry out the Internal Revenue laws of the United States. You are required to give us the information. We need it to ensure that you are complying with these laws and to allow us to figure and collect the right amount of tax.

You are not required to provide the information requested on a form that is subject to the Paperwork Reduction Act unless the form displays a valid OMB control number. Books or records relating to a form or its instructions must be retained as long as their contents may become material in the administration of any Internal Revenue law. Generally, tax returns and return information are confidential, as required by section 6103.

The time needed to complete and file this form will vary depending on individual circumstances. The estimated average time is: Recordkeeping, 6 hr., 27 min.; Learning about the law or the form, 34 min.; Preparing the form, 1 hr., 37 min.; Copying, assembling, and sending the form to the IRS, 16 min.

If you have comments concerning the accuracy of these time estimates or suggestions for making this form simpler, we would be happy to hear from you. See the instructions for the tax return with which this form is filed.

Form **8825** (12-2006)

Form 8825 (*Continued*)

Form **8829**	**Expenses for Business Use of Your Home**	OMB No. 1545-0074
Department of the Treasury Internal Revenue Service (99)	▶ File only with Schedule C (Form 1040). Use a separate Form 8829 for each home you used for business during the year. ▶ See separate instructions.	**2008** Attachment Sequence No. **66**

Name(s) of proprietor(s)	Your social security number

Part I Part of Your Home Used for Business

1	Area used regularly and exclusively for business, regularly for daycare, or for storage of inventory or product samples (see instructions)	**1**	
2	Total area of home	**2**	
3	Divide line 1 by line 2. Enter the result as a percentage	**3**	%
	For daycare facilities not used exclusively for business, go to line 4. All others go to line 7.		
4	Multiply days used for daycare during year by hours used per day **4** hr.		
5	Total hours available for use during the year (366 days × 24 hours) (see instructions) **5** 8,784 hr.		
6	Divide line 4 by line 5. Enter the result as a decimal amount **6**		
7	Business percentage. For daycare facilities not used exclusively for business, multiply line 6 by line 3 (enter the result as a percentage). All others, enter the amount from line 3 ▶	**7**	%

Part II Figure Your Allowable Deduction

8	Enter the amount from Schedule C, line 29, **plus** any net gain or (loss) derived from the business use of your home and shown on Schedule D or Form 4797. If more than one place of business, see instructions	**8**	

See instructions for columns (a) and (b) before completing lines 9–21.

		(a) Direct expenses	(b) Indirect expenses		
9	Casualty losses (see instructions)	**9**			
10	Deductible mortgage interest (see instructions)	**10**			
11	Real estate taxes (see instructions)	**11**			
12	Add lines 9, 10, and 11	**12**			
13	Multiply line 12, column (b) by line 7	**13**			
14	Add line 12, column (a) and line 13			**14**	
15	Subtract line 14 from line 8. If zero or less, enter -0-			**15**	
16	Excess mortgage interest (see instructions)	**16**			
17	Insurance	**17**			
18	Rent	**18**			
19	Repairs and maintenance	**19**			
20	Utilities	**20**			
21	Other expenses (see instructions)	**21**			
22	Add lines 16 through 21	**22**			
23	Multiply line 22, column (b) by line 7	**23**			
24	Carryover of operating expenses from 2007 Form 8829, line 42	**24**			
25	Add line 22 column (a), line 23, and line 24			**25**	
26	Allowable operating expenses. Enter the **smaller** of line 15 or line 25			**26**	
27	Limit on excess casualty losses and depreciation. Subtract line 26 from line 15			**27**	
28	Excess casualty losses (see instructions)	**28**			
29	Depreciation of your home from line 41 below	**29**			
30	Carryover of excess casualty losses and depreciation from 2007 Form 8829, line 43	**30**			
31	Add lines 28 through 30			**31**	
32	Allowable excess casualty losses and depreciation. Enter the **smaller** of line 27 or line 31			**32**	
33	Add lines 14, 26, and 32			**33**	
34	Casualty loss portion, if any, from lines 14 and 32. Carry amount to **Form 4684,** Section B			**34**	
35	**Allowable expenses for business use of your home.** Subtract line 34 from line 33. Enter here and on Schedule C, line 30. If your home was used for more than one business, see instructions ▶			**35**	

Part III Depreciation of Your Home

36	Enter the **smaller** of your home's adjusted basis or its fair market value (see instructions)	**36**	
37	Value of land included on line 36	**37**	
38	Basis of building. Subtract line 37 from line 36	**38**	
39	Business basis of building. Multiply line 38 by line 7	**39**	
40	Depreciation percentage (see instructions)	**40**	%
41	Depreciation allowable (see instructions). Multiply line 39 by line 40. Enter here and on line 29 above	**41**	

Part IV Carryover of Unallowed Expenses to 2009

42	Operating expenses. Subtract line 26 from line 25. If less than zero, enter -0-	**42**	
43	Excess casualty losses and depreciation. Subtract line 32 from line 31. If less than zero, enter -0-	**43**	

For Paperwork Reduction Act Notice, see page 4 of separate instructions.   Cat. No. 13232M   Form **8829** (2008)

Form 8829 Expenses for Business Use of Your Home

SCHEDULES A&B (Form 1040) Department of the Treasury Internal Revenue Service (99)	**Schedule A—Itemized Deductions** (Schedule B is on back) ▶ **Attach to Form 1040.** ▶ **See Instructions for Schedules A&B (Form 1040).**	OMB No. 1545-0074 20**08** Attachment Sequence No. **07**

Name(s) shown on Form 1040 | Your social security number

Medical and Dental Expenses	**Caution.** Do not include expenses reimbursed or paid by others.			
	1 Medical and dental expenses (see page A-1)	1		
	2 Enter amount from Form 1040, line 38 ⌐ 2 ⌐			
	3 Multiply line 2 by 7.5% (.075)	3		
	4 Subtract line 3 from line 1. If line 3 is more than line 1, enter -0-		4	
Taxes You Paid (See page A-2.)	5 State and local **(check only one box):** a ☐ Income taxes, **or** b ☐ General sales taxes	5		
	6 Real estate taxes (see page A-5)	6		
	7 Personal property taxes	7		
	8 Other taxes. List type and amount ▶	8		
	9 Add lines 5 through 8		9	
Interest You Paid (See page A-5.) **Note.** Personal interest is not deductible.	10 Home mortgage interest and points reported to you on Form 1098	10		
	11 Home mortgage interest not reported to you on Form 1098. If paid to the person from whom you bought the home, see page A-6 and show that person's name, identifying no., and address ▶	11		
	12 Points not reported to you on Form 1098. See page A-6 for special rules	12		
	13 Qualified mortgage insurance premiums (see page A-6)	13		
	14 Investment interest. Attach Form 4952 if required. (See page A-6.)	14		
	15 Add lines 10 through 14		15	
Gifts to Charity If you made a gift and got a benefit for it, see page A-7.	16 Gifts by cash or check. If you made any gift of $250 or more, see page A-7	16		
	17 Other than by cash or check. If any gift of $250 or more, see page A-8. You **must** attach Form 8283 if over $500	17		
	18 Carryover from prior year	18		
	19 Add lines 16 through 18		19	
Casualty and Theft Losses	20 Casualty or theft loss(es). Attach Form 4684. (See page A-8.)		20	
Job Expenses and Certain Miscellaneous Deductions (See page A-9.)	21 Unreimbursed employee expenses—job travel, union dues, job education, etc. Attach Form 2106 or 2106-EZ if required. (See page A-9.) ▶	21		
	22 Tax preparation fees	22		
	23 Other expenses—investment, safe deposit box, etc. List type and amount ▶	23		
	24 Add lines 21 through 23	24		
	25 Enter amount from Form 1040, line 38 ⌐ 25 ⌐			
	26 Multiply line 25 by 2% (.02)	26		
	27 Subtract line 26 from line 24. If line 26 is more than line 24, enter -0-		27	
Other Miscellaneous Deductions	28 Other—from list on page A-10. List type and amount ▶		28	
Total Itemized Deductions	29 Is Form 1040, line 38, over $159,950 (over $79,975 if married filing separately)? ☐ **No.** Your deduction is not limited. Add the amounts in the far right column for lines 4 through 28. Also, enter this amount on Form 1040, line 40. ☐ **Yes.** Your deduction may be limited. See page A-10 for the amount to enter. ⎬ ▶		29	
	30 If you elect to itemize deductions even though they are less than your standard deduction, check here . . . . ▶ ☐			

For Paperwork Reduction Act Notice, see Form 1040 instructions.   Cat. No. 11330X   Schedule A (Form 1040) 2008

Schedules A&B Itemized Deductions

Schedules A&B (Form 1040) 2008   OMB No. 1545-0074   Page **2**

Name(s) shown on Form 1040. Do not enter name and social security number if shown on other side.   **Your social security number**

Schedule B—Interest and Ordinary Dividends

Attachment Sequence No. **08**

Part I
Interest

(See page B-1 and the instructions for Form 1040, line 8a.)

Note. If you received a Form 1099-INT, Form 1099-OID, or substitute statement from a brokerage firm, list the firm's name as the payer and enter the total interest shown on that form.

1   List name of payer. If any interest is from a seller-financed mortgage and the buyer used the property as a personal residence, see page B-1 and list this interest first. Also, show that buyer's social security number and address ▶

	Amount
1	

2   Add the amounts on line 1 . . . .   **2**

3   Excludable interest on series EE and I U.S. savings bonds issued after 1989. Attach Form 8815 . . . .   **3**

4   Subtract line 3 from line 2. Enter the result here and on Form 1040, line 8a ▶   **4**

Note. If line 4 is over $1,500, you must complete Part III.

Part II
Ordinary
Dividends

(See page B-1 and the instructions for Form 1040, line 9a.)

Note. If you received a Form 1099-DIV or substitute statement from a brokerage firm, list the firm's name as the payer and enter the ordinary dividends shown on that form.

5   List name of payer ▶

	Amount
5	

6   Add the amounts on line 5. Enter the total here and on Form 1040, line 9a . ▶   **6**

Note. If line 6 is over $1,500, you must complete Part III.

Part III
Foreign
Accounts
and Trusts

(See page B-2.)

You must complete this part if you **(a)** had over $1,500 of taxable interest or ordinary dividends; or **(b)** had a foreign account; or **(c)** received a distribution from, or were a grantor of, or a transferor to, a foreign trust.

	Yes	No

7a   At any time during 2008, did you have an interest in or a signature or other authority over a financial account in a foreign country, such as a bank account, securities account, or other financial account? See page B-2 for exceptions and filing requirements for Form TD F 90-22.1 . . . .

b   If "Yes," enter the name of the foreign country ▶

8   During 2008, did you receive a distribution from, or were you the grantor of, or transferor to, a foreign trust? If "Yes," you may have to file Form 3520. See page B-2. . . . .

For Paperwork Reduction Act Notice, see Form 1040 instructions.   Schedule B (Form 1040) 2008

Schedules A&B (*Continued*)

SCHEDULE C (Form 1040) Department of the Treasury Internal Revenue Service (99)	**Profit or Loss From Business** (Sole Proprietorship) ▶ Partnerships, joint ventures, etc., generally must file Form 1065 or 1065-B. ▶ Attach to Form 1040, 1040NR, or 1041. ▶ See Instructions for Schedule C (Form 1040).	OMB No. 1545-0074 **2008** Attachment Sequence No. **09**

Name of proprietor		Social security number (SSN)

A Principal business or profession, including product or service (see page C-3 of the instructions)   **B** Enter code from pages C-9, 10, & 11 ▶

C Business name. If no separate business name, leave blank.   **D** Employer ID number (EIN), if any

E Business address (including suite or room no.) ▶ ....
City, town or post office, state, and ZIP code

F Accounting method: **(1)** ☐ Cash   **(2)** ☐ Accrual   **(3)** ☐ Other (specify) ▶ ....

G Did you "materially participate" in the operation of this business during 2008? If "No," see page C-4 for limit on losses   ☐ Yes ☐ No

H If you started or acquired this business during 2008, check here   . . . . ▶ ☐

Part I   Income

1	Gross receipts or sales. **Caution.** See page C-4 and check the box if:		
	• This income was reported to you on Form W-2 and the "Statutory employee" box on that form was checked, or	} . . ▶ ☐	
	• You are a member of a qualified joint venture reporting only rental real estate income not subject to self-employment tax. Also see page C-4 for limit on losses.		**1**
2	Returns and allowances		**2**
3	Subtract line 2 from line 1		**3**
4	Cost of goods sold (from line 42 on page 2)		**4**
5	**Gross profit.** Subtract line 4 from line 3		**5**
6	Other income, including federal and state gasoline or fuel tax credit or refund (see page C-4)		**6**
7	**Gross income.** Add lines 5 and 6 . . . . ▶		**7**

Part II   Expenses. Enter expenses for business use of your home **only** on line 30.

8	Advertising	**8**	18	Office expense	**18**
9	Car and truck expenses (see page C-5)	**9**	19	Pension and profit-sharing plans	**19**
10	Commissions and fees .	**10**	20	Rent or lease (see page C-6):	
11	Contract labor (see page C-5)	**11**	a	Vehicles, machinery, and equipment	**20a**
12	Depletion	**12**	b	Other business property . .	**20b**
13	Depreciation and section 179 expense deduction (not included in Part III) (see page C-5)	**13**	21	Repairs and maintenance . .	**21**
			22	Supplies (not included in Part III) .	**22**
			23	Taxes and licenses . . .	**23**
			24	Travel, meals, and entertainment:	
14	Employee benefit programs (other than on line 19) .	**14**	a	Travel	**24a**
15	Insurance (other than health) .	**15**	b	Deductible meals and entertainment (see page C-7)	**24b**
16	Interest:		25	Utilities	**25**
a	Mortgage (paid to banks, etc.) .	**16a**	26	Wages (less employment credits) .	**26**
b	Other	**16b**	27	Other expenses (from line 48 on page 2)	**27**
17	Legal and professional services	**17**			

28	**Total expenses** before expenses for business use of home. Add lines 8 through 27 . . . . ▶	**28**	
29	Tentative profit or (loss). Subtract line 28 from line 7	**29**	
30	Expenses for business use of your home. Attach **Form 8829**	**30**	
31	**Net profit or (loss).** Subtract line 30 from line 29.		
	• If a profit, enter on both **Form 1040, line 12,** and **Schedule SE, line 2,** or on **Form 1040NR, line 13** (if you checked the box on line 1, see page C-7). Estates and trusts, enter on **Form 1041, line 3.** • If a loss, you **must** go to line 32.	}	**31**
32	If you have a loss, check the box that describes your investment in this activity (see page C-8).		
	• If you checked 32a, enter the loss on both **Form 1040, line 12,** and **Schedule SE, line 2,** or on **Form 1040NR, line 13** (if you checked the box on line 1, see the line 31 instructions on page C-7). Estates and trusts, enter on **Form 1041, line 3.** • If you checked 32b, you **must** attach Form 6198. Your loss may be limited.	}	**32a** ☐ All investment is at risk. **32b** ☐ Some investment is not at risk.

For Paperwork Reduction Act Notice, see page C-9 of the instructions.   Cat. No. 11334P   Schedule C (Form 1040) 2008

Schedule C Profit or Loss From Business

| **Part III** | **Cost of Goods Sold** (see page C-8) |

33 Method(s) used to
value closing inventory: **a** ☐ Cost   **b** ☐ Lower of cost or market   **c** ☐ Other (attach explanation)

34 Was there any change in determining quantities, costs, or valuations between opening and closing inventory?
If "Yes," attach explanation . . . . ☐ Yes   ☐ No

35	Inventory at beginning of year. If different from last year's closing inventory, attach explanation . .	**35**
36	Purchases less cost of items withdrawn for personal use	**36**
37	Cost of labor. Do not include any amounts paid to yourself	**37**
38	Materials and supplies	**38**
39	Other costs	**39**
40	Add lines 35 through 39	**40**
41	Inventory at end of year	**41**
42	**Cost of goods sold.** Subtract line 41 from line 40. Enter the result here and on page 1, line 4 . .	**42**

| **Part IV** | **Information on Your Vehicle.** Complete this part **only** if you are claiming car or truck expenses on line 9 and are not required to file Form 4562 for this business. See the instructions for line 13 on page C-5 to find out if you must file Form 4562. |

43 When did you place your vehicle in service for business purposes? (month, day, year) ▶ . . . . / . . . . . / . . . . . .

44 Of the total number of miles you drove your vehicle during 2008, enter the number of miles you used your vehicle for:

a Business . . . .   **b** Commuting (see instructions) . . . .   **c** Other . . . .

45 Was your vehicle available for personal use during off-duty hours? . . . . ☐ Yes   ☐ No

46 Do you (or your spouse) have another vehicle available for personal use? . . . . ☐ Yes   ☐ No

47a Do you have evidence to support your deduction? . . . . ☐ Yes   ☐ No

b If "Yes," is the evidence written? . . . . ☐ Yes   ☐ No

| **Part V** | **Other Expenses.** List below business expenses not included on lines 8–26 or line 30. |

48	**Total other expenses.** Enter here and on page 1, line 27	**48**

Schedule C (*Continued*)

SCHEDULE D
(Form 1040)

Department of the Treasury
Internal Revenue Service (99)

Capital Gains and Losses

▶ Attach to Form 1040 or Form 1040NR. ▶ See Instructions for Schedule D (Form 1040).

▶ Use Schedule D-1 to list additional transactions for lines 1 and 8.

OMB No. 1545-0074

20**08**

Attachment
Sequence No. **12**

Name(s) shown on return

Your social security number

Part I Short-Term Capital Gains and Losses—Assets Held One Year or Less

(a) Description of property (Example: 100 sh. XYZ Co.)	(b) Date acquired (Mo., day, yr.)	(c) Date sold (Mo., day, yr.)	(d) Sales price (see page D-7 of the instructions)	(e) Cost or other basis (see page D-7 of the instructions)	(f) Gain or (loss) Subtract (e) from (d)
1					

2 Enter your short-term totals, if any, from Schedule D-1, line 2	**2**		
3 **Total short-term sales price amounts.** Add lines 1 and 2 in column (d)	**3**		

4 Short-term gain from Form 6252 and short-term gain or (loss) from Forms 4684, 6781, and 8824	**4**	
5 Net short-term gain or (loss) from partnerships, S corporations, estates, and trusts from Schedule(s) K-1	**5**	
6 Short-term capital loss carryover. Enter the amount, if any, from line 8 of your **Capital Loss Carryover Worksheet** on page D-7 of the instructions	**6** ( )
7 **Net short-term capital gain or (loss).** Combine lines 1 through 6 in column (f)	**7**	

Part II Long-Term Capital Gains and Losses—Assets Held More Than One Year

(a) Description of property (Example: 100 sh. XYZ Co.)	(b) Date acquired (Mo., day, yr.)	(c) Date sold (Mo., day, yr.)	(d) Sales price (see page D-7 of the instructions)	(e) Cost or other basis (see page D-7 of the instructions)	(f) Gain or (loss) Subtract (e) from (d)
8					

9 Enter your long-term totals, if any, from Schedule D-1, line 9	**9**		
10 **Total long-term sales price amounts.** Add lines 8 and 9 in column (d)	**10**		

11 Gain from Form 4797, Part I; long-term gain from Forms 2439 and 6252; and long-term gain or (loss) from Forms 4684, 6781, and 8824	**11**	
12 Net long-term gain or (loss) from partnerships, S corporations, estates, and trusts from Schedule(s) K-1	**12**	
13 Capital gain distributions. See page D-2 of the instructions	**13**	
14 Long-term capital loss carryover. Enter the amount, if any, from line 13 of your **Capital Loss Carryover Worksheet** on page D-7 of the instructions	**14** ( )
15 **Net long-term capital gain or (loss).** Combine lines 8 through 14 in column (f). Then go to Part III on the back	**15**	

For Paperwork Reduction Act Notice, see Form 1040 or Form 1040NR instructions.   Cat. No. 11338H   **Schedule D (Form 1040) 2008**

Schedule D Capital Gains and Losses

Part III   **Summary**

16   Combine lines 7 and 15 and enter the result **16**

     If line 16 is:
- A **gain**, enter the amount from line 16 on Form 1040, line 13, or Form 1040NR, line 14. Then go to line 17 below.
- A **loss**, skip lines 17 through 20 below. Then go to line 21. Also be sure to complete line 22.
- **Zero**, skip lines 17 through 21 below and enter -0- on Form 1040, line 13, or Form 1040NR, line 14. Then go to line 22.

17   Are lines 15 and 16 **both** gains?
     ☐ **Yes.** Go to line 18.
     ☐ **No.** Skip lines 18 through 21, and go to line 22.

18   Enter the amount, if any, from line 7 of the **28% Rate Gain Worksheet** on page D-8 of the instructions . . . . ▶   **18**

19   Enter the amount, if any, from line 18 of the **Unrecaptured Section 1250 Gain Worksheet** on page D-9 of the instructions . . . . ▶   **19**

20   Are lines 18 and 19 **both** zero or blank?
     ☐ **Yes.** Complete Form 1040 through line 43, or Form 1040NR through line 40. Then complete the **Qualified Dividends and Capital Gain Tax Worksheet** on page 38 of the Instructions for Form 1040 (or in the Instructions for Form 1040NR). **Do not** complete lines 21 and 22 below.
     ☐ **No.** Complete Form 1040 through line 43, or Form 1040NR through line 40. Then complete the **Schedule D Tax Worksheet** on page D-10 of the instructions. **Do not** complete lines 21 and 22 below.

21   If line 16 is a loss, enter here and on Form 1040, line 13, or Form 1040NR, line 14, the **smaller** of:

     - The loss on line 16 or   ⎫ . . . .   **21** (   )
     - ($3,000), or if married filing separately, ($1,500) ⎭

     Note. When figuring which amount is smaller, treat both amounts as positive numbers.

22   Do you have qualified dividends on Form 1040, line 9b, or Form 1040NR, line 10b?
     ☐ **Yes.** Complete Form 1040 through line 43, or Form 1040NR through line 40. Then complete the **Qualified Dividends and Capital Gain Tax Worksheet** on page 38 of the Instructions for Form 1040 (or in the Instructions for Form 1040NR).
     ☐ **No.** Complete the rest of Form 1040 or Form 1040NR.

Schedule D (*Continued*)

SCHEDULE E
(Form 1040)

Department of the Treasury
Internal Revenue Service (99)

Supplemental Income and Loss
(From rental real estate, royalties, partnerships,
S corporations, estates, trusts, REMICs, etc.)

▶ Attach to Form 1040, 1040NR, or Form 1041.   ▶ See Instructions for Schedule E (Form 1040).

OMB No. 1545-0074

2008

Attachment
Sequence No. **13**

Name(s) shown on return

Your social security number

Part I   **Income or Loss From Rental Real Estate and Royalties**   **Note.** If you are in the business of renting personal property, use **Schedule C** or **C-EZ** (see page E-3). If you are an individual, report farm rental income or loss from **Form 4835** on page 2, line 40.

1 List the type and address of each **rental real estate property:**	2 For each rental real estate property listed on line 1, did you or your family use it during the tax year for personal purposes for more than the greater of: • 14 days **or** • 10% of the total days rented at fair rental value? (See page E-3)		Yes	No
A		A		
B		B		
C		C		

Income:		Properties			Totals
		A	B	C	(Add columns A, B, and C.)
3 Rents received	3				3
4 Royalties received	4				4
Expenses:					
5 Advertising	5				
6 Auto and travel (see page E-4) .	6				
7 Cleaning and maintenance . . .	7				
8 Commissions	8				
9 Insurance	9				
10 Legal and other professional fees	10				
11 Management fees	11				
12 Mortgage interest paid to banks, etc. (see page E-5)	12				12
13 Other interest	13				
14 Repairs	14				
15 Supplies	15				
16 Taxes	16				
17 Utilities	17				
18 Other (list) ▶	18				
19 Add lines 5 through 18	19				19
20 Depreciation expense or depletion (see page E-5)	20				20
21 Total expenses. Add lines 19 and 20	21				
22 Income or (loss) from rental real estate or royalty properties. Subtract line 21 from line 3 (rents) or line 4 (royalties). If the result is a (loss), see page E-5 to find out if you must file **Form 6198** . . .	22				
23 Deductible rental real estate loss. **Caution.** Your rental real estate loss on line 22 may be limited. See page E-5 to find out if you must file **Form 8582.** Real estate professionals **must** complete line 43 on page 2	23	( )	( )	( )	

24	**Income.** Add positive amounts shown on line 22. **Do not** include any losses	24	
25	**Losses.** Add royalty losses from line 22 and rental real estate losses from line 23. Enter total losses here.	25	( )
26	**Total rental real estate and royalty income or (loss).** Combine lines 24 and 25. Enter the result here. If Parts II, III, IV, and line 40 on page 2 do not apply to you, also enter this amount on Form 1040, line 17, or Form 1040NR, line 18. Otherwise, include this amount in the total on line 41 on page 2 . .	26	

For Paperwork Reduction Act Notice, see page E-8 of the instructions.   Cat. No. 11344L   Schedule E (Form 1040) 2008

Schedule E Supplemental Income and Loss

Schedule E (Form 1040) 2008 | Attachment Sequence No. **13** | Page **2**

Name(s) shown on return. Do not enter name and social security number if shown on other side. | Your social security number

Caution. The IRS compares amounts reported on your tax return with amounts shown on Schedule(s) K-1.

Part II | **Income or Loss From Partnerships and S Corporations** | **Note.** If you report a loss from an at-risk activity for which **any** amount is **not** at risk, you **must** check the box in column **(e)** on line 28 and attach **Form 6198.** See page E-1.

27 Are you reporting any loss not allowed in a prior year due to the at-risk or basis limitations, a prior year unallowed loss from a passive activity (if that loss was not reported on Form 8582), or unreimbursed partnership expenses? ☐ **Yes** ☐ **No**
If you answered "Yes," see page E-7 before completing this section.

28	(a) Name	(b) Enter P for partnership; S for S corporation	(c) Check if foreign partnership	(d) Employer identification number	(e) Check if any amount is not at risk
A			☐		☐
B			☐		☐
C			☐		☐
D			☐		☐

	Passive Income and Loss			Nonpassive Income and Loss		
	(f) Passive loss allowed (attach **Form 8582** if required)	(g) Passive income from **Schedule K–1**	(h) Nonpassive loss from **Schedule K–1**	(i) Section 179 expense deduction from **Form 4562**	(j) Nonpassive income from **Schedule K–1**
A					
B					
C					
D					

29a Totals
  b Totals

30 Add columns (g) and (j) of line 29a . . . . | **30** |
31 Add columns (f), (h), and (i) of line 29b . . . . | **31** ( )
32 **Total partnership and S corporation income or (loss).** Combine lines 30 and 31. Enter the result here and include in the total on line 41 below . . . . | **32** |

Part III | **Income or Loss From Estates and Trusts**

33	(a) Name	(b) Employer identification number
A		
B		

	Passive Income and Loss		Nonpassive Income and Loss	
	(c) Passive deduction or loss allowed (attach **Form 8582** if required)	(d) Passive income from **Schedule K–1**	(e) Deduction or loss from **Schedule K–1**	(f) Other income from **Schedule K–1**
A				
B				

34a Totals
  b Totals

35 Add columns (d) and (f) of line 34a . . . . | **35** |
36 Add columns (c) and (e) of line 34b . . . . | **36** ( )
37 **Total estate and trust income or (loss).** Combine lines 35 and 36. Enter the result here and include in the total on line 41 below . . . . | **37** |

Part IV | **Income or Loss From Real Estate Mortgage Investment Conduits (REMICs)—Residual Holder**

38	(a) Name	(b) Employer identification number	(c) Excess inclusion from **Schedules Q,** line 2c (see page E-7)	(d) Taxable income (net loss) from **Schedules Q,** line 1b	(e) Income from **Schedules Q,** line 3b

39 Combine columns (d) and (e) only. Enter the result here and include in the total on line 41 below | **39** |

Part V | **Summary**

40 Net farm rental income or (loss) from **Form 4835.** Also, complete line 42 below . . . . . . | **40** |
41 **Total income or (loss).** Combine lines 26, 32, 37, 39, and 40. Enter the result here and on Form 1040, line 17, or Form 1040NR, line 18 ▶ | **41** |

42 **Reconciliation of farming and fishing income.** Enter your gross arming and fishing income reported on Form 4835, line 7; Schedule K-1 (Form 1065), box 14, code B; Schedule K-1 (Form 1120S), box 17, code T; and Schedule K-1 (Form 1041), line 14, code F (see page E-8). . . . . . | **42** |

43 **Reconciliation for real estate professionals.** If you were a real estate professional (see page E-2), enter the net income or (loss) you reported anywhere on Form 1040 or Form 1040NR from all rental real estate activities in which you materially participated under the passive activity loss rules. | **43** |

Schedule E (Form 1040) 2008

Schedule E (*Continued*)

Form **SS-4**	**Application for Employer Identification Number**	OMB No. 1545-0003
(Rev. January 2009)	(For use by employers, corporations, partnerships, trusts, estates, churches, government agencies, Indian tribal entities, certain individuals, and others.)	EIN
Department of the Treasury Internal Revenue Service	▶ See separate instructions for each line. ▶ Keep a copy for your records.	

Type or print clearly.

1 Legal name of entity (or individual) for whom the EIN is being requested

2 Trade name of business (if different from name on line 1)	**3** Executor, administrator, trustee, "care of" name
4a Mailing address (room, apt., suite no. and street, or P.O. box)	**5a** Street address (if different) (Do not enter a P.O. box.)
4b City, state, and ZIP code (if foreign, see instructions)	**5b** City, state, and ZIP code (if foreign, see instructions)

6 County and state where principal business is located

7a Name of principal officer, general partner, grantor, owner, or trustor	**7b** SSN, ITIN, or EIN

8a Is this application for a limited liability company (LLC) (or a foreign equivalent)? . . . . ☐ Yes ☐ No   **8b** If 8a is "Yes," enter the number of LLC members . . . . ▶

8c If 8a is "Yes," was the LLC organized in the United States? . . . . ☐ Yes ☐ No

9a Type of entity (check only one box). **Caution.** If 8a is "Yes," see the instructions for the correct box to check.

☐ Sole proprietor (SSN) _____
☐ Partnership
☐ Corporation (enter form number to be filed) ▶ _____
☐ Personal service corporation
☐ Church or church-controlled organization
☐ Other nonprofit organization (specify) ▶ _____
☐ Other (specify) ▶ _____

☐ Estate (SSN of decedent) _____
☐ Plan administrator (TIN) _____
☐ Trust (TIN of grantor) _____
☐ National Guard ☐ State/local government
☐ Farmers' cooperative ☐ Federal government/military
☐ REMIC ☐ Indian tribal governments/enterprises
Group Exemption Number (GEN) if any ▶

9b If a corporation, name the state or foreign country (if applicable) where incorporated | State | Foreign country

10 **Reason for applying** (check only one box)

☐ Started new business (specify type) ▶ _____
☐ Hired employees (Check the box and see line 13.)
☐ Compliance with IRS withholding regulations
☐ Other (specify) ▶

☐ Banking purpose (specify purpose) ▶ _____
☐ Changed type of organization (specify new type) ▶ _____
☐ Purchased going business
☐ Created a trust (specify type) ▶ _____
☐ Created a pension plan (specify type) ▶ _____

11 Date business started or acquired (month, day, year). See instructions.   **12** Closing month of accounting year

14 Do you expect your employment tax liability to be $1,000 or less in a full calendar year? ☐ Yes ☐ No (If you expect to pay $4,000 or less in total wages in a full calendar year, you can mark "Yes.")

13 Highest number of employees expected in the next 12 months (enter -0- if none).

Agricultural	Household	Other

15 First date wages or annuities were paid (month, day, year). **Note.** If applicant is a withholding agent, enter date income will first be paid to nonresident alien (month, day, year) . . . . ▶

16 Check **one** box that best describes the principal activity of your business.

☐ Construction ☐ Rental & leasing ☐ Transportation & warehousing
☐ Real estate ☐ Manufacturing ☐ Finance & insurance
☐ Health care & social assistance ☐ Wholesale-agent/broker
☐ Accommodation & food service ☐ Wholesale-other ☐ Retail
☐ Other (specify)

17 Indicate principal line of merchandise sold, specific construction work done, products produced, or services provided.

18 Has the applicant entity shown on line 1 ever applied for and received an EIN? ☐ Yes ☐ No
If "Yes," write previous EIN here ▶

	Complete this section **only** if you want to authorize the named individual to receive the entity's EIN and answer questions about the completion of this form.	
Third Party Designee	Designee's name	Designee's telephone number (include area code) ( )
	Address and ZIP code	Designee's fax number (include area code) ( )

Under penalties of perjury, I declare that I have examined this application, and to the best of my knowledge and belief, it is true, correct, and complete.   Applicant's telephone number (include area code) ( )

Name and title (type or print clearly) ▶

Applicant's fax number (include area code) ( )

Signature ▶   Date ▶

For Privacy Act and Paperwork Reduction Act Notice, see separate instructions.   Cat. No. 16055N   Form **SS-4** (Rev. 1-2009)

SS-4 Application for Employer Identification Number

Do I Need an EIN?

File Form SS-4 if the applicant entity does not already have an EIN but is required to show an EIN on any return, statement, or other document.[1] See also the separate instructions for each line on Form SS-4.

IF the applicant...	AND...	THEN...
Started a new business	Does not currently have (nor expect to have) employees	Complete lines 1, 2, 4a–8a, 8b–c (if applicable), 9a, 9b (if applicable), and 10–14 and 16–18.
Hired (or will hire) employees, including household employees	Does not already have an EIN	Complete lines 1, 2, 4a–6, 7a–b (if applicable), 8a, 8b–c (if applicable), 9a, 9b (if applicable), 10–18.
Opened a bank account	Needs an EIN for banking purposes only	Complete lines 1–5b, 7a–b (if applicable), 8a, 8b–c (if applicable), 9a, 9b (if applicable), 10, and 18.
Changed type of organization	Either the legal character of the organization or its ownership changed (for example, you incorporate a sole proprietorship or form a partnership) [2]	Complete lines 1–18 (as applicable).
Purchased a going business [3]	Does not already have an EIN	Complete lines 1–18 (as applicable).
Created a trust	The trust is other than a grantor trust or an IRA trust [4]	Complete lines 1–18 (as applicable).
Created a pension plan as a plan administrator [5]	Needs an EIN for reporting purposes	Complete lines 1, 3, 4a–5b, 9a, 10, and 18.
Is a foreign person needing an EIN to comply with IRS withholding regulations	Needs an EIN to complete a Form W-8 (other than Form W-8ECI), avoid withholding on portfolio assets, or claim tax treaty benefits [6]	Complete lines 1–5b, 7a–b (SSN or ITIN optional), 8a, 8b–c (if applicable), 9a, 9b (if applicable), 10, and 18.
Is administering an estate	Needs an EIN to report estate income on Form 1041	Complete lines 1–6, 9a, 10–12, 13–17 (if applicable), and 18.
Is a withholding agent for taxes on non-wage income paid to an alien (i.e., individual, corporation, or partnership, etc.)	Is an agent, broker, fiduciary, manager, tenant, or spouse who is required to file Form 1042, Annual Withholding Tax Return for U.S. Source Income of Foreign Persons	Complete lines 1, 2, 3 (if applicable), 4a–5b, 7a–b (if applicable), 8a, 8b–c (if applicable), 9a, 9b (if applicable), 10, and 18.
Is a state or local agency	Serves as a tax reporting agent for public assistance recipients under Rev. Proc. 80-4, 1980-1 C.B. 581 [7]	Complete lines 1, 2, 4a–5b, 9a, 10, and 18.
Is a single-member LLC	Needs an EIN to file Form 8832, Classification Election, for filing employment tax returns and excise tax returns, or for state reporting purposes [8]	Complete lines 1–18 (as applicable).
Is an S corporation	Needs an EIN to file Form 2553, Election by a Small Business Corporation [9]	Complete lines 1–18 (as applicable).

[1] For example, a sole proprietorship or self-employed farmer who establishes a qualified retirement plan, or is required to file excise, employment, alcohol, tobacco, or firearms returns, must have an EIN. A partnership, corporation, REMIC (real estate mortgage investment conduit), nonprofit organization (church, club, etc.), or farmers' cooperative must use an EIN for any tax-related purpose even if the entity does not have employees.

[2] However, do not apply for a new EIN if the existing entity only (a) changed its business name, (b) elected on Form 8832 to change the way it is taxed (or is covered by the default rules), or (c) terminated its partnership status because at least 50% of the total interests in partnership capital and profits were sold or exchanged within a 12-month period. The EIN of the terminated partnership should continue to be used. See Regulations section 301.6109-1(d)(2)(iii).

[3] Do not use the EIN of the prior business unless you became the "owner" of a corporation by acquiring its stock.

[4] However, grantor trusts that do not file using Optional Method 1 and IRA trusts that are required to file Form 990-T, Exempt Organization Business Income Tax Return, must have an EIN. For more information on grantor trusts, see the Instructions for Form 1041.

[5] A plan administrator is the person or group of persons specified as the administrator by the instrument under which the plan is operated.

[6] Entities applying to be a Qualified Intermediary (QI) need a QI-EIN even if they already have an EIN. See Rev. Proc. 2000-12.

[7] See also *Household employer* on page 4 of the instructions. **Note.** State or local agencies may need an EIN for other reasons, for example, hired employees.

[8] See *Disregarded entities* on page 4 of the instructions for details on completing Form SS-4 for an LLC.

[9] An existing corporation that is electing or revoking S corporation status should use its previously-assigned EIN.

SS-4 (*Continued*)

Checklists and Forms

Rental Expenses Checklist

(as noted in Chapter 2)

- ☐ Legal and professional fees
- ☐ Management Fees
- ☐ Utilities
- ☐ Dues, publications, and subscriptions
- ☐ Startup expenses
- ☐ Homeowners association dues
- ☐ Supplies
- ☐ Depreciation
- ☐ Mortgage interest
- ☐ Mortgage expenses and points
- ☐ Credit card interest
- ☐ Mortgage insurance
- ☐ Real estate taxes

- ☐ Repairs and maintenance
- ☐ Improvements
- ☐ Gifts
- ☐ Commissions
- ☐ Travel expenses
- ☐ Automobile used for rental activities
- ☐ Points paid for mortgage
- ☐ Tax return preparation fees
- ☐ Equipment rental
- ☐ Office rental
- ☐ Insurance
- ☐ Cleaning

Identification Form

(as noted in Chapter 4)

According to Internal Revenue Code Section 1031, the exchanger(s) _____ _____, wishes to perform a like-kind exchange of property. According to the 45-day identification period, as specified under Internal Revenue Code Section 1031, the exchanger identifies the following property:

Property 1 _____

Requirements: According to Internal Revenue Code Section 1031, the property to be identified must be given to the owner of the replacement property or the qualified intermediary, in written form, and hand delivered, faxed or mailed no later than 45 days after the exchanger closes on the relinquished property. No extension for holidays or weekends is allowed. The exchanger must sign the identification. The owner of the replacement property need not sign the identification. A written identification that is mailed must be postmarked by the 45th day.

The following alternative properties are identified:

Property 2 _____

Property 3 _____

Signed:

Exchanger _____ Date: _____

Exchanger _____ Date: _____

Notes

Chapter 1   Understanding Capital Gains

1. IRC Section 1221 (a)(1).
2. IRC Reg. Section 1.1221-1(b).
3. IRC Section 1211(b).
4. IRS Revenue Ruling 70-598.
5. IRC Section 1222.
6. IRC Section 1223 (11)(b).
7. IRC Section 1224 (2).
8. IRC Section 1223 (1).
9. IRC Section 1014.
10. See IRS Publication 523.
11. See IRS Publication 551.
12. IRC Section 1041.
13. IRC Section 1041.
14. IRC Section 1031(d).
15. IRC Section 195(b)(1).
16. *Lichtman v. Commissioner*, TC Memo 1982-300; *England, Jr. v. Commissioner*, 34 TC 617 (1960).

17. IRC Section 1221.

18. See IRS Publication 544.

Chapter 2   Your Personal Residence

1. See IRC Section 163.

2. *Mills v. Commissioner*, TC Memo 1999-60; Income Tax Regulations Section 1.163-1(b).

3. *Paul v. Commissioner*, TC Memo 1997-43, where the Tax Court held that the taxpayers could not deduct all of their mortgage interest when the amount of the loans was $1,330,000.

4. IRS Field Service Advice 200137033.

5. See IRC Section 280A (D)(1).

6. Income Tax Regulations Section 1.163-10T(p)(6).

7. Revenue Ruling 87-22.

8. IRC Section 121 (a)(10).

9. From IRS Publication 523. See also *Taylor v. Commissioner*, TC Summary Opinion 2001-17; *Glapham v. Commissioner*, 63 TC 505 (1975).

10. *Bayley v. Commissioner*, 37 TC 288 (1960).

11. From IRS Publication 523.

12. See Income Tax Regulations Section 1.121-1(b).

13. See Income Tax Regulations Section 1.163-10T(p)(2).

14. See *Thomas v. Commissioner*, 92 TC 206 (1989).

15. See IRS Revenue Ruling 77-298.

16. See IRS Regulations Section 1.121-3(6)

17. See IRS Publication 523.

18. IRC Section 121(d)(6).

19. See Income Tax Regulations Section 1.121-3T(e).

20. See IRS Letter 200403049 (cannot be used as precedent for any other case).

21. See IRS Letter 200504012.

22. See Income Tax Regulations Section 1.121-3.

23. See Income Tax Regulations Section 1.121-3.

24. See Income Tax Regulations Section 1.121-3.

25. *Schlicher v. Commissioner*, TC Memo 1997-163.

26. *Richards v. Commissioner*, TC Memo 1993-422.

27. See IRC Section 1041.

28. IRC Section 121 (d)(7)(B).

Chapter 3   Deductions for Rental Property

1. See IRS Publication 527.

2. *Welch v. Helvering*, 290 U.S. 111 (1933).

3. IRS Revenue Ruling 70-413.

4. See IRC Section 195.

5. IRC Section 195(6) was amended by the American Jobs Creation Act of 2004 (P.L. 108-357).

6. Income Tax Regulations Section 1.162-4.

7. For example, see *Evans v. Commissioner*, 557 F.2d 1095 (5th Cir. 1977), in which the court held that $50,000 of expenses in relation to a dam were deductible as a repair because the expenses returned the dam to substantially the same condition it was in prior to any problems.

8. *Ruttenberg v. Commissioner*, TC Memo 1986-414.

9. *Beck v. Commissioner*, TC Memo 1994-122.

10. *Otis v. Commissioner*, 73 TC 671 (1980).

11. *Subt v. Commissioner*, TC Memo 1991-429.

12. *Vanalco, Inc., v. Commissioner*, TC Memo 1999-265; *Schroeder v. Commissioner*, TC Memo 1996-336.

13. *Northern v. Commissioner*, TC Summary Opinion 2003-113.

14. *Hudlow v. Commissioner*, TC Memo 1971-218.

15. *Vanolco, Inc., v. Commissioner*, TC Memo 1999-265.

16. *Stewart Supply Company, Inc., v. Commissioner*, TC Memo 1963-62.

17. *City National Bank v. Commissioner*, 11 TCM 411 (1952).

18. *Jones v. Commissioner*, 25 TC 1100 (1956).

19. *Toledo Home Federal Savings & Loan Association v. United States*, 203 F. Supp. 491 (N.D. Ohio 1962).

20. IRS Revenue Ruling 84-24.

21. See IRS Letter 199903030 and *R. R. Hensler, Inc., v. Commissioner*, 73 TC 168 (1979).

22. See IRS Publication 587.

23. *Curphey v. Commissioner*, 73 TC 766 (1980).

24. See *Frankel v. Commissioner*, 82 TC 318 (1984); *Green v. Commissioner*, 79 TC 428 (1982).

25. See Income Tax Regulation Section 1.166-1(e).

26. See IRS Publication 535 ("environmental cleanup (remediation) costs are generally capital expenditures"). In addition, the IRS has ruled that

removing asbestos is an improvement that must be depreciated. See Private Letter Ruling 9240004 from June 1992.

27. IRC Section 190.

28. IRC Section 280A.

29. See IRS Revenue Ruling 77-254.

30. Reg. 1.1234-(1) (b).

31. See IRC Section 469(i).

32. See IRC Section 469 c(7).

33. See IRC Section 42 (b).

34. See IRC Section 42 (b).

35. See IRC Section 47 (a).

36. See IRC Section 47 (a).

Chapter 4   Like-Kind Exchanges and Section 1031

1. IRC Section 1031(a)(1).

2. See IRS Publication 544.

3. IRC Section 1031(a)(2).

4. IRC Code Section 1031(a)(3).

5. *Starker v. U.S.*, 602 F.2d 1341 (9th Circuit 1979).

6. IRC Section 1031(a)(3).

7. IRC Section 1031(a)(3).

8. See IRS Publication 544.

9. See IRS Publication 544.

10. IRC Section 1031(a)(3)(B).

11. IRS Reg. Section 1.1031(k)-1(b)(2)(iii).

12. *Christensen v. Commissioner*, TC Memo 1996-254.

13. IRS Revenue Procedure 2000-37.

14. See IRS Publication 544.

15. *Kunkel v. Commissioner*, TC Memo 1995-162.

16. *Knight v. Commissioner*, 16 TC 785 (1998).

17. *Dobrich v. Commissioner*, TC Memo 1997-447.

18. IRS Regulations 1031(k)-1(g)4.

19. See IRS Publication 544.

20. IRC Section 357(d).

21. IRS Private Letter Ruling 8429039.

22. Conference Agreement H.R. 4520 Sec. 840.

23. IRC Section 121.

24. IRS Private Letter Ruling 8103117.

25. IRS Private Letter Ruling 8103117.

26. IRC Section 1031 (a)(1).

27. IRC Section 1031.

28. IRC Section 1031 (a)(2)(d).

29. *Regals Realty Co. v. Commissioner,* 43 BTA 194 (1940) aff'd 127 F2d 931 (2d Cir. 1942); accord, Rev. Rul 75-292, 1975-2 CB 333.

30. *Magneson v. Commissioner,* 753 F2d 1490 (9th Cir. 1985).

31. *Penn v. Robertson*, 115 F.2d 167 (4th Cir. 1940).

32. IRC Section 1031(g); *Shelton v. Commissioner*, 105 TC 114 (1995).

33. IRC Section 453 (e)(2); *Shelton v. Commissioner*, 105 TC 114 (1995).

34. *Shelton v. Commissioner*, 105 TC 114 (1995).

35. See IRS Publication 544.

36. IRC Code Section 1031(f).

37. IRS Private Letter Ruling 8434015.

38. IRS Revenue Ruling 72-456.

Chapter 5   The Dealer Issue

1. *Little v. Commissioner*, TC Memo 1993-7380; *Raymond v. Commissioner*, TC Memo 2001-96; *Neal T. Baker Enterprises, Inc., v. Commissioner*, TC Memo 1998-302.

2. *Medlin v. Commissioner*, TC Memo 2003-224; *Little v. Commissioner*, TC Memo 1993-281.

3. IRC Section 1402 (a)(1); *Blythe v. Commissioner*, TC Memo 1999-11.

4. IRC Section 1031 (a)(2).

5. IRC Section 453 (b)(2).

6. See IRS Publication 946.

7. *Gibson v. Commissioner*, TC Memo 1981-240.

8. *Phelan v. Commissioner*, TC Memo 2004-206.

9. *Little v. Commissioner*, TC Memo 1993-281.

10. *U.S. v. Malat*, 383 US 569 (1966).

11. *U.S. v. Malat*, 383 US 569 (1966).

12. *Monney v. Commissioner*, KTC 1997-62 (9th Cir. 1997).

13. *Wood v. Commissioner*, TC Memo 2004-200.

14. *Wood v. Commissioner*, TC Memo 2004-200.

15. *Adam v. Commissioner*, 60 TC 996 (1973).

16. *Howell v. Commissioner*, 57 TC 546 (1972).

17. *Field v. Commissioner*, TC Memo 2/23/49, 8TCM 170.

18. *Maddux v. Commissioner* 54 TC 1278, 1286 (1970); *Howell v. Commissioner*, 57 TC 546 (1972).

19. *Field v. Commissioner*, 8 TCM 170, (1949).

Chapter 6   Installment Sales

1. See IRS Revenue Ruling 70-430.

2. IRC Section 453(b).

3. *Favilla v. Commissioner*, TC Memo 1986-39. See also *Rushing v. Commissioner*, 52 TX 888 (1969), aff'd 441F.2d593 (Stn 5th Cir. 1971).

Chapter 7   Passive Activity Rules Related to Real Estate

1. See IRS Publication 925.

2. See IRS Publication 925.

3. See IRS Publication 925.

4. See IRS Publication 925.

5. IRS Reg. Section 1.469-9(g)(3).

6. *Bailey v. Commissioner*, TC Memo 2001-296.

7. See IRS Publication 925.

8. See IRS Publication 925.

Chapter 8   Trusts, Trusts, Trusts!

1. IRC Section 664c.

2. IRC Section 662.

Chapter 9   Individual Retirement Accounts

1. See Pub. L. 93-406, 88 Stat.829. This can be found in Title 29 of the United States Code.

2. See IRS Publication 598.

3. According to IRC Section 4975(e)(2), an IRA owner is considered a fiduciary for purposes of filing IRS Form 990-T.

Chapter 10   Depreciation Issues with Real Estate

1. IRC Section 167(j).
2. See *Hospital Corporation of America v. Commissioner*, 109 TC 21 (1997).
3. *Whiteco Industries, Inc., v. Commissioner*, 65 TC 664 (1977).
4. See Income Tax Regulations Section 1.48-1(e)(2).

Chapter 11   Business Entities and Real Estate Investors

1. See IRS Regulation Section 1.79-3 (d)(2).
2. IRC Section 162 (a)(1).
3. This change increased the number of shareholders from 75 to 100 as of January 1, 2005. See IRS Section 1361 (b1)(1)(A).

About the Authors

Scott M. Estill, Esq., is a practicing tax attorney in the Denver, Colorado, area. He is a partner of Estill and Long, LLC, a law firm located in Littleton. He is a graduate of the University of Illinois (1983, B.A., political science) and The John Marshall Law School (1988, with High Honors), where he was a member of the *Law Review*. Following law school, he obtained a judicial clerkship with the Honorable Justice Lawrence Inglis of the Illinois Appellate Court, where he worked during a two-year appointment. He then worked for the IRS as a trial attorney in the Chicago District Counsel office. He left the IRS as a senior trial attorney in 1994 to open his own law practice, where he specializes in advising small businesses and individuals on many tax issues. He is the author of *Tax This! An Insider's Guide to Standing Up to the IRS* (Self Counsel Press, sixth edition, 2009), *The Tax Compliance Guide* (Tax Strategies and Solutions Limited, sixth edition, 2009), and *The Tax Deduction Business Kit* (Tax Strategies and Solutions Limited, 2009) and has been a featured guest on numerous television and radio shows around the country. He lectures extensively on small business tax issues and is considered an expert on the subject. He is married and has two daughters, Sara and Caitlin.

Stephanie F. Long, Esq., is a practicing tax attorney and a managing partner of Estill & Long, LLC, of Littleton, Colorado. She is a graduate of the University of Colorado at Boulder (1998, B.A., philosophy) and The Chicago-Kent College of Law (2001). Following law school, she opened her own law practice in Littleton, Colorado, where she focused on civil tax controversy and tax and business planning. She is the author of *The Go Zone Goldmine* (REITS, Inc., 2008) as well as numerous articles and publications. Her current practice area is limited to tax and business planning for businesses and real estate investors, and resolution of tax controversies. She lectures extensively across the country on real estate investor tax issues as well as tax planning for small businesses. She lives outside of Denver with her husband, and two Boston terriers, Jake and Emma.

Estill & Long, LLC
10354 W. Chatfield Avenue, Suite 201
Littleton, CO 80127
www.reitsinc.com
www.estillandlong.com
(720) 922-1120

Index